ALSO BY GERALD POSNER

Mengele: The Complete Story
Warlords of Crime: Chinese Secret Societies: The New Mafia
The Bio-Assassins
Hitler's Children
Case Closed: Lee Harvey Oswald and the Assassination of JFK
Citizen Perot: His Life and Times
Killing the Dream: James Earl Ray
and the Assassination of Martin Luther King, Jr.
Motown: Music, Money, Sex, and Power

WHY AMERICA SLEPT

WHY AMERICA SLEPT

THE FAILURE TO PREVENT 9/11

GERALD POSNER

RANDOM HOUSE
NEW YORK

RANDOM HOUSE and colophon are registered trademarks
of Random House, Inc.

Library of Congress Cataloging-in-Publication Data

Posner, Gerald
Why America slept: the failure to prevent 9/11 / Gerald Posner.
p.   cm.
Includes bibliographical references and index.
ISBN 0-375-50879-1
1. September 11 Terrorist Attacks, 2001.   2. Terrorism—United States—Prevention.
3. Islamic fundamentalism—United States.   4. National security—United States.   I. Title.
HV6432.7.P685 2003
973.931—dc21   2003047065

Printed in the United States of America on acid-free paper
Random House website address: www.atrandom.com

6897

Book design by Carole Lowenstein

To those few who tried to warn us

CONTENTS

AUTHOR'S NOTE

The September 11, 2001, strikes on the World Trade Center and Pentagon prompted outraged demands—as did the sneak assault on Pearl Harbor almost sixty years earlier—that an independent inquiry investigate the intelligence and government breakdowns that preceded the attack. During the past two years, much information has become public about how law enforcement and intelligence agencies missed signals and government leaders failed to focus on the clear and pending threat from Islamic fundamentalism. An official board of inquiry now under way promises more answers about the failure to connect the dots leading to 9/11.

This book was proposed within a month of the attack on America. The goal was to discover what the CIA, FBI, and others in the government were doing behind the scenes for at least a decade leading up to 9/11. And as for the terrorists themselves, who were they, and who controlled them?

Over time, the project expanded as the reporting led to links between Muslim extremists in Western Europe, Asia, and Africa and terror cells in the United States. It grew to cover the secret facilitators and backdoor operators who transferred the money for the plot against America. The research also led to an inside look at the counterterrorist squads that had fought an underfunded war against fanatical foes.

But in the end, the central question that remained was, what did American intelligence and law enforcement know and what did they ignore? What mistakes were made along the way on the ground by police, FBI, and CIA, and in Washington and state capitals by policy-makers? The hunt for those answers brought to light unexpected discoveries about some American allies, and what they might have known and not told anyone before 9/11.

The result is a far more infuriating book than originally expected. The failure to have prevented 9/11 was a systemic one. Investigators did not get a lucky break early on, and there were many blunders in the immediate run-up to the attack. The seeds of failure, however, were sown repeatedly in almost twenty years of fumbled investigations and misplaced priorities. After a while, the revelations of ineptitude presented in this book no longer cause surprise, but only anger.

The terrorists may have known that America was largely a paper tiger before 9/11. But that revelation still surprised many in the U.S., especially as they became familiar with the litany of missed opportunities.

And we were certainly a country distracted. Terrorism happened somewhere else, not here. We were instead entertained and alternately repulsed by O. J. Simpson, JonBenét Ramsey, the booming stock market, Monica Lewinsky, and a host of matters that seem particularly shallow in light of 9/11. While many of America's best reporters chased hanging chads and butterfly ballots in Florida after the 2000 presidential election, Mohamed Atta and Marwan al-Shehhi were also in the state, learning to fly the planes they would turn into giant bombs.

It is true that mistakes are often obvious only after an event. While that is the case here, most readers will still be surprised at this story. The errors America made should have been evident much earlier.

Could the attack on America have been prevented? Yes. September 11 did not need to happen.

WHY AMERICA SLEPT

CHAPTER 1

THE

TAKEOVER

Adecade before 9/11, the worldwide surge in Islamic fundamentalism and its virulent hatred of the West was largely unrecognized in America. We did not notice when some of the most prominent radicals moved to this country and set up operations just across the river from the World Trade Center. Those early militants, ignored in their new chosen homeland, would become the role models and inspiration for some of the World Trade Center and Pentagon hijackers in 2001.

Brooklyn's Atlantic Avenue is only thirty minutes away by the Number 4 train from the World Trade Center. Before September 11, a nearby waterfront promenade offered postcard views of the twin towers. But these two New York neighborhoods might as well be different countries. The sterile and overbuilt financial center on the tip of Manhattan that was rendered into a giant open-air cemetery covered by tons of twisted debris is quintessentially American. The mile stretch of Brooklyn seems a much closer cousin to downtown Cairo than Wall Street. It is a neighborhood overcrowded with the city's densest concentration of Arabs.

If someone just arrived from Lebanon or Syria, they might feel at home along those gritty and packed streets. Many Muslims, in traditional robe and turban, crowd near the Islamic community centers and bookshops, Middle Eastern restaurants, grocery stores and bakeries, smoke shops, translation services, and hairdressers. Some men gather in small groups at outdoor cafés, sipping minted tea and smoking from bubbling hookahs, large, standing water pipes filled with fruit- and herb-infused tobacco. Women in layered skirts and head-covering scarves, babies in tow, walk several paces behind the men. Quavering Arab music blares from several record stores. On Fridays, the Muslim day of prayer, when the mosques fill, overflow crowds by the hundreds throw down small prayer rugs on the sidewalk and prostrate themselves toward Mecca.

The mosques range from lavish Ottoman-style buildings to basements of car service garages. But the best known house of worship is Masjid al-Farooq, located on several floors of a run-down commercial building. The second-floor sanctuary is bathed in a soft light, tinted green from jade-colored walls and worn purple-and-emerald-colored carpet. Worshipers line up shoulder to shoulder, creating human stripes across the carpet, all facing Mecca and praying. Incense sticks resting in cracks in the plaster walls fill the room with a sweet smell. Racks along the back wall hold a collection of workingmen's shoes: Nike sneakers, paint-spattered construction boots, worn-out wing tips, scuffed thick-soled shoes of civil servants. Among the crowd of émigrés are African-Americans, young men with knitted skullcaps or baseball caps turned backward.

The imam, the mosque's prayer leader, stands in a simple brown robe behind a plain wooden lectern, reading verses from the Koran. Many of the faithful—men in their twenties from Yemen, Egypt, Jordan, and the West Bank—gather in the hallway after the service. They trade information about jobs at cab companies and at construction sites, and pass along tips on cheap rooms for rent and religious activities for Arabic-speaking newcomers. Some discuss the attack on the World Trade Center three days ago, but when they see a stranger approach, they revert to Arabic.*

This Arab mecca in the heart of New York is not a recent phenomenon. The migration had started in the early 1900s as Arabs fled persecution in the Ottoman Empire. Some set up shop not far from their stop at Ellis Island—on Manhattan's Washington Street and Brooklyn's Atlantic Avenue. In the 1930s, and again after World War II, there were

---

*A prominent Yemeni cleric, Sheikh Muhammad Ali Hassan al-Mouyad, and his assistant, Mohammed Mohsen Yahya Zayed, were arrested in March 2003 and charged with providing Osama bin Laden recruits, weapons, and more than $20 million in donations collected from the al-Farooq mosque before September 11. According to affidavits filed by federal prosecutors, Sheikh al-Mouyad boasted to an FBI informant that he was bin Laden's spiritual advisor and that he had worked for years to provide him money and arms for a terrorist "jihad."[1]

waves of new immigrants. Manhattan's high prices drove most new-comers to Brooklyn. "This area is known as an Arab enclave throughout the world," boasts Sam Moustapha, a co-owner of the family-run Oriental Pastry and Grocery Company.

It is a neighborhood where Arabs are not timid about embracing political sentiments that often seem continents removed from nearby Manhattan. Many of the local businesses have long displayed prominent anti-Israeli, pro-intifada signs and banners. Even in the immediate wake of 9/11, a flyer posted outside al-Qaraween's Islamic bookstore, next to a mosque, declared, "Allah is great—may justice come to the infidels." At the nearby Fertile Crescent, a Middle Eastern market, pictures of Israeli prime minister Ariel Sharon were stamped over with the crosshairs of a sniper's rifle scope.

A small convenience store had a half dozen posters plastered on the wall behind the counter. They were grainy black-and-white blowups of young men, all holding weapons, wearing kaffiyehs wrapped around their heads and covering their faces like Bedouins in a sandstorm. All that was visible were the intense stares of angry young Arab militants that Americans have now come to know too well. Arabic writing was scrawled on the posters. They were tributes to suicide bombers. Each of the men on the wall had blown himself apart in a terror attack against Israel. When asked about the posters and why they were on display, only miles from where thousands of Americans and foreigners lay dead from a suicide mission, the clerk pretended he did not speak English. More questions were answered only with grunts and dismissive waves.

Further down the block, at the sixty-five-year-old Damascus Bread and Pastry, Arab men have been eating and arguing politics for decades. The showcases are packed with displays of sticky dates, nut-filled pastries, and an amazing assortment of pita bread, some of which is put to good use right outside by a falafel vendor. Inside the tiny room, dense with thick and heady smoke from hours of chain-smoking, Egyptians, Syrians, Jordanians, and Lebanese sit, packed elbow to elbow, discussing the terror attacks. Many have lived through years of crises, including four Arab-Israeli wars, the arrests of local Hamas bomb makers, the nearby murder ten years earlier of radical Jewish activist Rabbi Meir Kahane, the Gulf War, and the now legendary neighborhood tales of the first World Trade Center bombers who lived and worshiped along these very streets.

Five young men at the counter, cradling cell phones and packs of cigarettes, were not as reticent as the others to talk to a stranger. Yes, the
World Trade Center attack was terrible. But America must have known
how hated it was, and that such a strike was surely coming. One
slammed the Formica counter so hard with the palm of his hand that his
demitasse of mudlike coffee flipped over. How could America support the
terror state of Israel, he asked, and then cry foul when the underpow-
ered struck back?

On this unusually warm autumn day, only days after the September 11
attacks that pushed America into a world it did not seek nor for which it
was prepared, walking along Atlantic Avenue, one can still see the buildings that once served as rallying grounds for the neighborhood's militants. These were the places that fueled the activism that eventually led
to attacks like 9/11.

At one end of a block, where the elevated subway train casts deep
angular shadows over the intersection of Foster and McDonald avenues,
an Arabic chant blares over a loudspeaker every Friday, sounding the
call to prayer at the Abu Bakr Siddique mosque. Except for a fortresslike
entry, the building doesn't look much different from other wood-frame
houses nearby. But it was here that Sheikh Omar Abdel Rahman, the
blind extremist Egyptian cleric now serving a life sentence for seditious
conspiracy for the "day of terror" plot intended to blow up New York City
landmarks, tunnels, and bridges, preached his violent rhetoric.[2] Rahman had immigrated to the United States in 1990 and inexplicably
cleared Customs although he was on a domestic terrorist watch list.

Virtual solitary confinement in a federal prison hospital in Rochester,
Minnesota, evidently did little to temper his hatred. In 1998, from his
cell, he smuggled out a fatwa, a religious order, urging his followers to
"cut all links with the United States. Destroy them thoroughly and erase
them from the face of the earth. Ruin their economies, set their companies on fire, turn their conspiracies to powder and dust. Sink their ships,
bring their planes down. Slay them in air, on land, on water. And with
the command of Allah, kill them wherever you find them. Catch them
and put them in prison. Lie in wait for them and kill these infidels. They
will surely get great oppression from you. God will make you the means
of wreaking a terrible revenge upon them, of degrading them. He will

support you against them." That fatwa has become part of the curriculum in more than thirty thousand Islamic religious schools in Saudi Arabia, Pakistan, and Yemen.

At the other end of the block, just a few hundred yards from the mosque, is a simple red-brick house at the corner of Ocean Parkway and Foster. One cannot tell from the outside that until 1997 it was the headquarters of Kahane Chai, the militant Jewish group. That was the same year the State Department branded it a terrorist organization. Kahane Chai was devoted to the teachings of Rabbi Meir Kahane, gunned down in Manhattan by an Arab immigrant in 1990. The rabbi preached a strident racism that attracted adherents in local Jewish neighborhoods. Among them was a young doctor, Baruch Goldstein, the former Brooklyn resident who in 1994 slaughtered twenty-nine Muslims while they prayed in a West Bank mosque.

But on this day, with the sun setting in less than an hour, the interest is in the remnants of the Alkifah Refugee Center, Sheikh Rahman's old preaching grounds. The center used to be nestled behind one of the ordinary-looking storefronts along Atlantic Avenue. Its stated purpose was to raise money so local Muslims could join the fight against Soviet forces in Afghanistan. Federal officials say the now shuttered center was a gathering place for Islamic terrorists, the first American base for Osama bin Laden and his al Qaeda network. The center was where key personal relationships were forged between men of different nationalities who shared bin Laden's extreme interpretation of Islam.

In the mid-1980s, the Alkifah Center was a neighborhood hub on Atlantic Avenue. It started out as a single desk in the al-Farooq mosque around 1986 and then moved into a grungy second-floor apartment in a building a few doors away at 566 Atlantic Avenue, above what is now a perfume factory. That tiny space had barely enough room for a desk, a few chairs, a phone, and a fax machine. Although many in the neighborhood recall that the Alkifah Center ran on a shoestring, documents submitted in U.S. court cases revealed that tens of thousands of dollars flowed through its bank accounts during its heyday of the late 1980s and early 1990s.

The center's director was Emir Mustafa Shalabi, a young Egyptian immigrant with a shock of red hair. Shalabi was infused with the same religious fervor for the Afghan cause that roused many young Muslims who regarded it as a holy war to liberate an Islamic country from com-

munist domination. Neighbors began calling Alkifah the "jihad office."*
Shalabi invited Sergeant Ali Mohamed, a former Egyptian army officer
and U.S. Army Green Beret, to the center's basement offices under the al-
Farooq mosque. Armed with official U.S. Army videotapes and military
documents marked "Top Secret," Mohamed conducted a series of weekend "training" classes and a two-week-long intensive seminar. Almost
all the volunteers were Arab immigrants. They bought $600 one-way
fares as a sign they were willing to give their lives for Islam.

At those training classes were such future terrorists as El-Sayyid A.
Nosair, the Egyptian immigrant later charged with killing Rabbi Kahane;
Mohammed Salameh and Clement Rodney Hampton-El, convicted in the
first World Trade Center bombing in 1993; and Mahmud Abouhalima,
Sheikh Rahman's part-time driver, found guilty of conspiracy in the
1998 East Africa embassy bombings that killed fifty-nine and wounded
more than five thousand. Sergeant Mohamed himself would eventually
plead guilty to conspiring to bomb the East Africa embassies.

Even when the Soviets humiliatingly withdrew from Afghanistan in
1989, the turmoil of the civil war to which Afghanistan fell victim
echoed in Brooklyn, and Shalabi kept Alkifah open. The religious fury of
many young Arab men who had fought the Soviets now turned against
secular Arab governments and, ultimately, America, with its military
presence in the Persian Gulf and its support for Israel. Also, the mujahedeen, or holy warriors, in Afghanistan were now fighting to create a
strict Islamic state admired by many of the younger men in Brooklyn.

The turning point for the Alkifah Refugee Center came in 1990 when
Sheikh Omar Abdel Rahman arrived in Brooklyn. An almost legendary
cleric whose extreme rhetoric had incited the assassination of Egyptian
president Anwar Sadat, Rahman had been to Pakistan and Afghanistan,
and was a friend of the wealthy Saudi mujahedeen leader, Osama bin
Laden. As word of Rahman's interest in the center spread in the Muslim
community, hard-core fundamentalists flocked to it.

*Jihad is a rallying cry for modern-day Islamic fundamentalists, and is usually
interpreted by Westerners to mean "holy war." In fact, it literally translates as "striv-
ing," and encompasses the violent struggle that is the duty of all Muslims to wage to
extend conservative Muslim rule to non-Muslims as well as to lands with large Muslim populations ruled by secular governments. The United States is the most popular
target for jihadists. In 1991, Ahmad Khomeini, the ayatollah's son, explained why
America was Islam's new enemy. "We should realize that the world is hostile to us
because of Islam. After the fall of Marxism, Islam replaced it, and as long as Islam
exists, U.S. hostility exists, and as long as U.S. hostility exists, the struggle exists."

Emir Shalabi, who was the American representative of the Afghan Services Bureau, a recruiting organization cofounded by bin Laden, had sponsored Rahman's entry into the country.[3]* Shalabi took the blind sheikh into his house, gave him a part-time driver, helped him move to an apartment in Bay Ridge, and even paid for his food and telephone bill. He also made the sheikh an integral part of his Afghanistan campaign. And when the al-Farooq needed a new imam, the fifty-two-year-old Sheikh Rahman, with the support of Shalabi, was selected, and started delivering the fiery sermons that condemned anti-Islamic practices and tyrannical foreign governments. Before long he denounced other mosque members, including some Yemenis who sold pork, beer, and pornographic magazines in local grocery stores.

Not long after the sheikh's arrival, there was a power struggle at the Alkifah Center. Rahman wanted to channel some of the jihad office's donations to his militant supporters in Egypt. Shalabi refused. He remained loyal to the man who had originally inspired him, Abdullah Azzam. A Palestinian professor of Islamic studies in Jordan, Azzam was a mentor to Osama bin Laden. Azzam had visited America often in the 1980s, urging support for the war in Afghanistan.

Others in the tightly knit Arab community in New York and Jersey City, where the sheikh moved after feuding with Shalabi, say there were rumors that Shalabi had stolen money from the jihad office and might be involved in counterfeiting. Despite the whisper campaign, which Rahman fostered, Shalabi refused to relinquish control of the fundraising. Rahman's supporters began complaining that Shalabi had become "an internal problem." A vicious quarrel over political direction and leadership—the organization's very soul—was under way. The fight worsened when Rahman publicly denounced Shalabi at a local mosque, accusing him of mishandling Arabs' money. Flyers appeared urging Muslims not to give any more money to Shalabi.

Emir Shalabi knew that the newcomers to Brooklyn, and some of those returning from battling the Soviets in Afghanistan, were dangerous. He began sleeping with a knife under his pillow and a pistol on a nearby dresser. Obsessed with his dawa, the internal call of devotion to

---

*Bin Laden did not control the office when Shalabi was director, but he wielded influence there. Federal prosecutors disclosed in 2000 that it was Shalabi whom bin Laden called in 1991 when he needed help moving to Sudan (this according to Ali Mohamed, who turned federal witness).

Islam, he grew quiet and protective. In early 1991, not able to withstand the campaign against him any longer, he announced he would return to his native Egypt, and he sold his household possessions.

The night before his flight to Egypt, Shalabi was in his empty rented house on Neptune Avenue, packing for the journey that would reunite him with his wife and child. It was just after 7:00 P.M. on a cold February evening. A light snowfall muffled the sound of cars moving through the Sea Gate neighborhood in southern Brooklyn. Someone pressed his front door buzzer. Shalabi, a tall, muscular forty-one-year-old, was wearing only a galabiya, a casual robe, when he opened the door. Whoever was standing on the other side was armed with a pistol and a knife. Before Shalabi could run, his murderer jammed the serrated-edged blade into the side of his neck, causing blood to spurt across the worn beige carpeting. Shalabi turned to flee. But his assailant again plunged the knife, this time deep into his back, puncturing his lung and shattering his shoulder bone. Shalabi crumpled to the floor. His executioner walked over to the emir, who was weakly trying to crawl away, as the trail of smeared blood on the carpet later revealed. The murderer put the nozzle of the pistol a few inches from his victim's forehead and fired.

Shalabi's body would not be discovered for three days, when a neighbor walked into the blood-splattered apartment to find out why he could not get any answer on the telephone. The murder made no news. No one was ever arrested for it. Shalabi became another statistic, one of 2,153 murders in New York that year, many unsolved and forgotten when investigative trails run cold after a few months. City residents were worried about 1991's near record murder rate, but the headlines were either about drug murders—mostly gangs spraying streets with bullets in vicious turf wars, killing innocent bystanders—or about teenagers carrying guns into schools as casually as they did pens, with three students dying during shootouts.

Today, federal and Egyptian investigators believe that Sheikh Abdul Rahman, with some of the other terrorists who were part of the first World Trade Center attack, had decided to kill Shalabi. His death served as notice that Brooklyn's jihad office was in the hands of Rahman and his radical followers and that no one should dare cross them. Depending on whom you believe along Atlantic Avenue, the killing was ordered only after Sheikh Rahman issued a fatwa. People in the Middle East had long known about fatwas. People in America had yet to learn.

CHAPTER 2

THE INTELLIGENCE WAR

If CIA analysts had been aware of the radical sermons given by Sheikh Rahman to his growing following in Brooklyn and New Jersey, the rhetoric would not have surprised them. The U.S. government had been acutely aware of the fundamentalist movement for almost twenty years by the time Shalabi was murdered.

"We knew that the Islamic threat was the next security problem for the U.S., and we had known it since the 1970s," says former CIA officer Duane "Dewey" Clarridge.[1]

Clarridge was only twenty-three when he joined the Agency in 1955. Over the next thirty years, he was a key covert operative, serving tours of duty in Nepal, India, and Turkey before returning to CIA headquarters in Langley in the 1970s. From 1973 to 1975 he was chief of operations— the Agency's covert division—for the Near East Division, and later served as the deputy chief for Arab operations, the Latin American Division, and as station chief in Rome. It was Clarridge who in 1986 persuaded Director William Casey to establish the CIA's Counterterrorism Center (CTC).*

During his tenure as deputy chief of Arab operations from 1975 to 1978, Clarridge became familiar with many of the key players in Islamic terror, men who later became household names in the U.S.

---

*Clarridge wrote a book, *A Spy for All Seasons: My Life in the CIA*, in 1997, and it had to be approved by the CIA's Publication Review Board. They eliminated any classified information from the manuscript. Now retired, Clarridge met my wife and me at his West Coast home—after September 11—for extensive interviews. No restrictions were imposed by him on frank discussions about the CIA's successes and failures countering Islamic terrorism.

"At the time," he recalls, "we were running operations in Beirut against an alphabet-soup of Palestinian terror groups, including George Habash's PFLP [Popular Front for the Liberation of Palestine], Ahmed Jibril's offshoot of the PFLP, Yassir Arafat's PLO [Palestinian Liberation Organization], and Al Fatah's Black September. At the same time, Carlos the Jackal was running around Europe, pulling off stunts like trying to use a grenade launcher to down an El Al airplane at Orly, or shooting his way into the Vienna OPEC meeting, killing three, and kidnapping the Saudi and Iranian oil ministers. We had our hands full."[2]

Two days before Christmas 1975, the CIA's Athens station chief, Richard Welch, was murdered by Greek terrorists who ambushed him in his driveway. Welch's execution prompted an internal CIA debate over ways to more aggressively fight the new terror threat. But the Agency's timing was poor. The CIA was embroiled in turmoil on Capitol Hill that was largely the making of its former director, William Colby. President Gerald Ford had fired Colby in January 1976 and appointed George Bush as his replacement. Colby's dismissal had been prompted when, during his congressional confirmation hearings, he made public a report he had compiled about the CIA's possible past violations of federal law and its own charter. The Colby report, which the press dubbed the "family jewels," prompted congressional hearings, named after the cochairmen, Senators Frank Church and Otis Pike.

The revelations during the coming months included sordid details about the Agency's early 1960s Castro assassination plots, mind-control experiments, and failed foreign coups. When Senator Frank Church, then chair of the Senate Intelligence Committee, declared the CIA "a rogue elephant," morale at the Agency was at an all-time low. "The Church-Pike hearings permanently changed the way Clandestine Services operated," says Clarridge. "It changed the rules of the game for us."[3]

Congress established a process for review and approval of all covert actions, requiring the CIA to submit all plans to a committee chaired by the president. If the plans were approved, the president would then issue a presidential finding, and Congress would be notified within sixty days. Moreover, permanent congressional oversight committees were established. And on February 18, 1976, President Ford issued Executive Order 11905, forbidding U.S. government agencies from undertaking assassinations.

The new restrictions abruptly halted, says Clarridge, the campaign under consideration in the wake of Welch's murder. Instead, the Agency changed course and decided to actually make overtures to some of the terror groups, hoping that it might ultimately defuse their anger at the U.S. while benefiting from an informal partnership. The first opportunity presented itself in mid-1976 during the spiraling chaos of the Lebanese civil war.

Through an intermediary, recalls Clarridge, "we established a relationship with Ali Hassan Salameh."[4] Salameh, a.k.a. Abu Hassan, was Yassir Arafat's protégé, and the commander of Al Fatah's elite Force 17, Arafat's personal bodyguards. Salameh had earned his notoriety as the architect of the 1972 Black September kidnapping and murder of eleven Israeli athletes at the Munich Olympics.

The U.S. embassy in Beirut had been in touch with Salameh about local security, and by 1976 when CIA officers attached to the embassy put out feelers to him, he signaled a willingness to forge a better relationship with the U.S. Unknown outside of a small handful of CIA officers, when the navy's Sixth Fleet used landing craft to evacuate the country's remaining Americans (the airport was closed because of shelling), Salameh's Force 17 provided security. When the embassy itself was abandoned, Force 17, with Arafat's blessing, supplied perimeter protection and security again at the evacuation points.[5]

"Salameh may have been a bad guy," says Clarridge, "but he was good to us. He helped us and probably saved many lives during our evacuations from Lebanon. We owed him, and he and Arafat knew it. Word spread inside the radical groups that you could work with the Americans and we could be trusted."[6]

That abruptly changed on January 22, 1979, when Salameh was killed by a powerful car bomb that exploded as his armed motorcade sped past. "I suppose the Israelis did it," concludes Clarridge. But from the Arab perspective, the United States, as Israel's main benefactor, was to blame.

"We got reports back that Fatah viewed it as a straight double cross," Clarridge says. "They thought we had used them when we needed them in Beirut, and then when they were no longer helpful, we turned them over to the Israelis, who were all about an 'eye for an eye.' It didn't matter we had nothing to do with Salameh's death. We had taken the blame in the Arab world, and that meant whatever progress we were making at inroads into the militant groups ended right there."[7]

In 1983, the U.S. embassy in Beirut was destroyed by a terrorist bombing. CIA Director Casey immediately dispatched a team to conduct an investigation. They had conflicts from the start with an FBI team that had also been sent to Beirut. Veterans at the CIA and FBI were not surprised because the two premier American crime-fighting and intelligence-gathering agencies had a long, turbulent history of clashes, disagreements, and competition. In Beirut, the two sometimes got into screaming and shoving matches. The FBI team returned home early, frustrated and angry over its treatment by the CIA.[8] Eventually, to mend fences, the CIA's new Beirut station chief, William Buckley, allowed an FBI team to return to Lebanon and conduct an investigation unhindered by their CIA counterparts. Free of interference, they solved the case, tracing a fragment of a truck axle used on the bombing truck to an Iranian factory, and eventually finding a link to the Iranian-backed Popular Front for the Liberation of Palestine.

But by the time the FBI reached that conclusion, Buckley himself had been kidnapped by Iranian-sponsored terrorists in April 1984. President Reagan approved the creation of the Restricted Interagency Group for Terrorism. The CIA's director of covert operations was the chairman, and there was one representative each from the CIA, FBI, and the National Security Council. All selected were risk-takers. Casey chose Dewey Clarridge for the CIA. The FBI's man was Oliver "Buck" Revell, the assistant director for criminal investigations. And the NSC's selection was a marine lieutenant colonel, Oliver North.

The new anti-terror group quickly developed some high-risk plans for getting Buckley back safely before he could be tortured and give up CIA secrets. North wanted to use Drug Enforcement Administration informants—heroin traffickers—who claimed to be able to deliver Buckley for a $2 million ransom. To avoid U.S. laws against paying money to drug dealers, Texas billionaire Ross Perot was ready to finance the rescue. But the FBI strenuously objected and finally convinced North that the drug informants were unlikely to deliver Buckley. A second idea, this one from North and Clarridge, was to kidnap a Lebanese Shiite cleric, the head of Islamic Jihad, the organization holding Buckley. The proposal was to trade the cleric for the CIA station chief. Again, the FBI's resistance was so fierce that the plan was scuttled.

Frustrated by the FBI's intransigence, Clarridge kept lobbying Casey to give the Agency more control. On January 1986, with Ronald Reagan's authorization, Casey created the Counterterrorism Center. Clarridge was chosen as its chief. He had a support staff of two hundred CIA officers, mostly analysts, and ten people loaned from other agencies. CTC had no field agents, however, and had to rely on CIA station chiefs abroad for surveillance, action, or informer recruitment. Clarridge knew that would not always be easy, since those station chiefs were each narrowly focused on their own geographic divisions, while terrorism was a global problem that respected no boundaries. Moreover, most of the foreign stations were running at their capacity, meaning they might not be able to easily spare resources if CTC asked for help unexpectedly. So the FBI agreed to supply most of CTC's field and operational assistance. That was not a good development for Clarridge.

"The Bureau, under Webster, was far too cautious," he recalls. And he disliked that the FBI, before committing to an operation, ran the plan past a team of Bureau lawyers to determine whether there were any legal transgressions. "No one was very excited at the prospect of sharing national security secrets with lawyers at Justice," says Clarridge.[9]

A month after CTC's creation, Clarridge developed a plan to kidnap the Islamic Jihad hijackers of TWA Flight 847 and to fly them to America for trial. Webster not only argued that the operation would likely be an embarrassing failure, but that it would also violate international and U.S. laws. Clarridge could not change Webster's mind, so he angrily shelved the plan.

Next, CTC proposed kidnapping Mohammed Hussein Rashid, a top bomb maker who had defeated airport security machines by hiding explosives in a Sony Walkman. But this time, Clarridge got some resistance, not from the FBI, but from other CIA departments. Rashid, it turned out, was sponsored by Iraq, and Casey was busy trying to woo Saddam Hussein away from his reliance on the Soviets. But Clarridge lobbied Casey and eventually got a green light. When Rashid visited Sudan, CTC tried nabbing him, but the operation failed. Clarridge blamed the FBI, whose field agents were supposed to pull off the kidnapping, while the Bureau bad-mouthed the intelligence provided by the Agency.

CTC had little to boast about in its early days. Not only had Rashid slipped through its fingers, but its special team to recover Beirut station chief Buckley had also failed.* Also, CTC's efforts to track down the ter-

---

*Buckley died after fourteen brutal months in captivity, during which he was regularly tortured. He evidently revealed all he knew about CIA operations in the Middle East before his death.

rorists who had bombed a Berlin discotheque proved fruitless. Field agent
Robert Baer had met covertly with leaders of Syria's Muslim Brotherhood
in Dortmund, Germany. He hoped to reach an agreement, as had been
done with Force 17, to keep them from using terror against the U.S. But
their request for CIA help in killing Syria's dictator, Hafiz al-Asad, was
rejected, and the Muslim Brotherhood stayed an American foe.[10]*

The FBI, meanwhile, had its own complaints about CTC's failure to
share information. The Bureau started on a whisper campaign in Washington that the CIA's jealous stewardship of CTC would be its ruination.
A task force headed by Vice President George Bush was the result. It proposed an "intelligence-fusion center" to complement CTC by collecting,
analyzing, and distributing intelligence data about terror. The task
force's recommendations were never implemented.[11]

Ronald Reagan might have named the Soviet Union as his primary foreign policy nemesis, but Islamic extremists were getting his attention and
increasingly making the United States look vulnerable and weak. From
the 1983 bombing of the marine barracks in Lebanon that killed 241
soldiers to the 1985 hijackings of TWA Flight 847 and the cruise liner
Achille Lauro, Middle Eastern terror was now on the White House's priority agenda. Senior CIA officers complained to the president's national
security team about their frustration with the FBI and warned that
America was vulnerable to Islamic terrorists entering on legal visas and
setting up sleeper cells. Reagan responded in September 1986 by forming
an interagency task force, the Alien Border Control Committee (ABCC),
whose purpose was to block entry of suspected terrorists and to deport
militants who either had come into the country illegally or had over-
stayed their visas. The CIA and FBI joined the ABCC effort.

Six months after its formation, the ABCC had its first notable success.
The CIA tipped off the FBI to a group of suspected Palestinian terrorists
in Los Angeles. The Bureau arrested eight men. But instead of being
lauded, the Bureau and the Agency came under harsh attack from civil

*Baer says that after 9/11, the FBI informed him that one of the Syrians with
whom he had discussed détente in the mid-1980s was a suspect in the international
support network that had arranged the World Trade Center and Pentagon attacks.
Baer admits that he cannot be sure that even if he had managed to form a relationship with the Syrian that it would have led the U.S. to breaking up the plot. "But clos-
ing down the channel," Baer wrote, "assured that the Syrian wouldn't lead us to
anyone. For Bonn and the CIA, it remains an unforgivable error."

liberties groups who argued that the ABCC should be banned from using any information the CIA gained from the government's routine process-ing of visa requests. Congressman Barney Frank, the Massachusetts Democrat who was a strong advocate of protecting civil liberties, led a successful effort to amend the Immigration and Nationality Act so that membership in a terrorist group was no longer sufficient to deny a visa. Under Frank's amendment, which seems unthinkable post-9/11, a visa could only be denied if the government could prove that the applicant had committed an act of terrorism.[12] Rendered toothless by the Frank amendment, the Reagan administration had virtually no way to block entry visas even when there was information linking the individuals to terrorist groups.

Meanwhile, the deteriorating relationship between the CIA and FBI hit a nadir within a couple of years when the weapons-for-hostages (Iran-contra) scandal broke. The three key figures were the CIA's Casey and Clarridge and the National Security Council's North, all involved with the Counterterrorism Center. The FBI targeted Clarridge, who they felt was withholding information from their criminal investigation in order to protect colleagues.

By the close of 1986, the FBI, and Buck Revell in particular, worried that the CIA might be violating U.S. laws prohibiting aid to the contras and also negotiation with terrorists.[13] After Casey testified to Congress, on November 21, that he did not know who was behind the sale of two thousand TOW missiles to Iran (the Agency was actively involved), Rev-ell told FBI Director Webster that the CIA director might be obstructing justice.

Casey was hospitalized in early December for a brain tumor. Although he died a few months later in May 1987, that did not stop the FBI from kicking the investigation into the diversion of Iranian arms sales and the profits to the contras into high gear. Six FBI agents retrieved critical doc-uments from Oliver North's secretary's office, even though she managed to shred hundreds of files before their arrival. Eventually, armed with search warrants, another FBI team swept into CIA headquarters in Langley. It was an unprecedented law enforcement operation against the country's premier spy agency. There, the FBI agents ordered that CIA deputy director for operations Clair George open his office safe. They found a document, with two of George's fingerprints, showing he had misled Congress. It led to a ten-count indictment against George. Three station chiefs were removed or disciplined as the FBI closed in. And as for Duane Clarridge, the decorated director of CTC, he was eventually indicted on seven counts of perjury and making false statements. ("Interestingly enough," says Clarridge, "the system never actually got around to demoting me—out of sheer bureaucratic sloth.")[14]* Even the CIA's deputy director, Robert Gates, had to withdraw his name from nomination as the Agency's next director because of pointed congressional questions about his own knowledge of Iran-contra.

Inside the CIA, there was a widespread feeling that the FBI had gone from a recalcitrant partner on joint investigations to an avowed enemy whose purpose was to destroy the Agency's hierarchy.

Most in CTC were bitter about the FBI's probe, and after Clarridge's indictment, T-shirts and buttons in his support appeared almost everywhere at Langley. But Clarridge could not survive what happened to the CIA in March 1987. While Casey was still alive, semiconscious in a Washington hospital, Ronald Reagan unexpectedly asked the FBI's William Webster to assume control of the Agency. After Gates's withdrawal and rejections of the director's job from Republican John Tower, the head of the president's Iran-contra board, and James Baker, his chief of staff, Webster had become Reagan's fourth choice. A Christian Scientist who relished his reputation as a totally honest straight arrow whose only vices were chocolate and tennis, Webster let it be known that the loose days under Casey were history. Under his stewardship, he promised to rein in the cowboys in the Operations Directorate.

"Since we at CTC had been working so closely with the FBI on terrorism," recalls Clarridge, "we had already heard a lot about Webster, and none of it was good. From the street level to the top echelons, they detested Webster because they saw him as an egotistical lightweight, a social climber, and a phony."[15]

Historian Thomas Powers remarked that the "CIA would rather be run by a Cub Scout den mother than the former head of the FBI."[16] Many in the Agency agreed. Webster had no background in foreign policy or world affairs. Whereas Casey had seemed a kindred soul, espe-

---

*The indictment against Clarridge had been handed down only weeks before the five-year statute of limitations expired. "The terrorist accused of blowing up the Federal Building in Oklahoma City had more protection of his legal rights," contends Clarridge, "and more access to counsel while being interrogated than I did." Eventually, Clarridge was pardoned before his trial by President George Bush.

cially to the covert teams, Webster was considered overly cautious, a bureaucrat hobbled by a stringent interpretation of the law and an over- whelming fear of failure. Webster's pledge to purge the CIA of anyone remotely linked to Iran-contra, and his close friendship to former CIA director Stansfield Turner, raised the specter for many agents that the Agency was in for another Carter-era cutback in covert actions. Others feared that Webster would try and turn the CIA into another FBI.

One of Webster's first moves was to replace the CIA's popular George Lauder, who had spent twenty years in the Operations Directorate, with an FBI colleague, William Baker. The choice was so unpopular that when Baker was introduced in the Agency's auditorium, no one clapped. When Baker told the assembled agents that they should study a new house manual called "Briefing Congress" and embrace the four "C's" of candor, completeness, consistency, and correctness, many in the audience audibly snickered.

"It was vintage FBI," recalls one agent in attendance. "It was what we expected."[17]

Baker was not the only FBI colleague Webster brought along. Peggy Devine, his longtime executive secretary, who had earned the nickname "Dragon Lady" while at the Bureau, joined him. Also, his FBI chief of staff, John Hotis, and a group of "special assistants" made up what CIA employees derisively dubbed either the "FBI mafia" or the "munchkins." They were soon all ensconced on the Agency's seventh floor. The assis- tants may have all had Ivy League law degrees, but they had no intelli- gence backgrounds. And they managed to effectively seal Webster off from the rest of the Agency.

Besides his insular personal staff, Judge Webster, as he liked to be called, did little himself to instill confidence that he was the right choice for the CIA. Early in his tenure, Clair George invited him to an Opera- tions Directorate staff meeting in order to familiarize him with what was going on. Each division chief presented a brief summary of what he was working on. When the discussion moved to the Middle East, Webster took out his burgundy leather Filofax and flipped to the maps in the back so he could locate some of the countries. Word that the new director of CIA "was looking for Morocco on the map" spread quickly at Langley.[18]

"We could probably have overcome Webster's ego," says Clarridge, "his lack of experience with foreign affairs, his small-town-America world perspective, and even his yuppier-than-thou arrogance. What we couldn't overcome was that he was a lawyer. All his training as a lawyer and a judge was that you didn't do illegal things. He never could accept that this is *exactly* what the CIA does when it operates abroad. We break the laws of other countries. It's how we collect information. It's why we're in business. Webster had an insurmountable problem with the raison d'être of the organization he was brought in to run."[19]*

Clarridge has personal reasons to criticize Webster. It was Webster who reprimanded him for his role in Iran-contra and, after promising to reassign him as director of CTC, forced him to resign in June 1988. But Clarridge's hostile view of Webster is not atypical. Nearly a dozen former operatives from the Directorate of Operations confirmed, on background only, that the feelings Clarridge expressed on the record were widespread at the CIA. The Agency had long prided itself on an unwritten code— Loyalty Up and Loyalty Down—and many CIA veterans felt that Webster had trashed that code by going after veterans like Clarridge.

Webster tried to earn the trust of the CIA's Operations Directorate, and to reassure the Agency's cowboys, by authorizing the post-Clarridge CTC—in an operation with the FBI—to kidnap a terrorist overseas. Within months of Webster taking charge, Operation Goldenrod resulted in the capture—in international waters off Cyprus—of Fawaz Younis, a Lebanese Shiite who in 1985 had hijacked a Royal Jordanian airliner and then blown up the plane after evacuating it. The operation—the first successful overseas extraction in the long history of CIA-FBI liaison—was announced to the press on the fortieth anniversary of the CIA's founding. It seemed to bolster Webster's claim that he would be the director capable of finally getting the Agency and Bureau to work together.

But Webster's critics were not satisfied. Younis was admittedly a small fry and was not on anyone's most wanted list of terrorists. And by treating the case as a criminal one, Webster had created complications about Younis's capture and his extended interrogation in international waters without an attorney. Although Younis was eventually convicted of air piracy, some CIA veterans thought it would have been easier merely to

---

*Clarridge was not the only one who thought Webster's legal background might interfere with running a spy agency. Pakistan's President Muhammad Zia-ul-Haq once asked Webster how it was possible for a lawyer to head the CIA. Webster did not answer.

pass Younis's location to the Israelis and let them assassinate him. Some of those sentiments, coupled with others that Webster was mistakenly applying an FBI emphasis on public image, suddenly began appearing in the press during the weeks after Younis's arrest. The comments were always attributed to anonymous intelligence sources. Some stories attacked Webster's supposed large perks or his escorting of socialites to Washington affairs instead of working late. Privately, some agents fumed about Webster blowing a sensitive operation in August 1987, when he thanked the Argentine chief of intelligence for cooperating in a case in which the Argentines were not only the target, but had known nothing about until Webster's flub.[20]

And whatever good faith Webster might have earned from giving the go-ahead on the Younis abduction, he soon lost it when he appointed his chief of staff, John Hotis, and Nancy McGregor, a twenty-eight-year-old law clerk who had been one of Webster's administrative assistants at the FBI, to rewrite the regulations for covert operations. Webster himself infuriated many veteran intelligence agents by comparing CIA covert operations to the FBI's use of undercover agents. Lawyers now became involved in every covert approval. The checklist for what had to be reviewed and approved for each proposed operation grew substantially. The fairly informal process of the past was finished. Webster's new rules tried to instill accountability in the Agency's covert work, the same framework that had existed inside the FBI—and some contend hindered their efforts—for decades.

With the new accountability in place over covert operations, and having purged the CIA of half a dozen senior officers connected to Iran-contra, Webster was subjected to a new round of criticism in the press, this time not all of it anonymous. Tom Polgar, a retired agent, wrote in an opinion-editorial in *The Washington Post* that "the new watchword at the agency seems to be 'Do No Harm'—which is fine for doctors but may not encourage imagination and initiative in secret operations."[21]

Meanwhile, the FBI's stewardship had been taken over by William Sessions, a former federal judge from San Antonio and a close friend of Webster's. With encouragement from Webster, Sessions expanded the number of FBI agents who served abroad in counterspy work. This further riled the CIA's counterintelligence department, which did not welcome the competition. Webster, to his credit, decided to make an effort to force the two longtime competitors to at least share information seamlessly. In April 1988, he announced a redesigned Counterintelligence Center (CIC). Based in Langley, its goal was to teach CIA and FBI agents how to recognize data that was useful to the other agency, and most important, to share it.

The first real test of that cooperation was not far away.

On December 21, 1988, 270 people were killed when a bomb destroyed Pan Am Flight 103 above Lockerbie, Scotland. The U.S. government never publicly revealed that three CIA officers, stationed in the Middle East, were aboard on their way home for the Christmas holidays.[22] Two weeks before, on December 5, an alert from Mossad, Israel's famed intelligence service, had been passed to the CIA. It warned that a Pan Am flight from Frankfurt to the U.S. would be bombed within two weeks. Flight 103 was a Frankfurt to U.S.–bound plane. The CIA had never passed the warning to the FBI. In an attempt to ensure the investigation's data be shared, CTC was put in charge of the probe.

The case was broken through old-fashioned police work on the ground. More than a thousand police, soldiers, and bomb technicians scoured hundreds of square miles around the bombing site. They bagged thousands of pieces of potential evidence, and in that haul was a fragment of a circuit board the size of a small fingernail. It matched an identical board found in a bomb-timing mechanism used in Togo in 1986. CTC then tracked it to a consignment of timers manufactured by a Swiss company that had sold twenty to Libya.

But the traditional disharmony between the FBI and CIA soon showed. According to one U.S. official, it was not very long before the investigation was a "chaotic mess" of noncooperation.[23] Within a few months, each had a competing theory about who was responsible. The CIA was convinced that Iran had hired a Damascus-based radical Palestinian faction to carry out the operation. Taking out the American plane was, according to Vincent Cannistraro, one of the CIA's senior CTC officers, payback for the mistaken 1988 downing of an Iranian airbus, killing 290 civilians, by the U.S. cruiser *Vincennes*. Cannistraro had become, after Clarridge's departure, the major power inside CTC, and the driving force on most missions.

Meanwhile, the FBI steadfastly believed that Libya was the sole culprit, seeking revenge for the U.S. bombings in 1986. Both agencies leaked their fight to the press. CIA officials were quoted mocking the FBI's analytical reports on the bombing as being "like essays from grade school," whereas an unidentified FBI agent said that "CIA believe they have a lot, but it's a Styrofoam brick."[24]*

Even when the Libyans became prime suspects, the two agencies differed on what should be done. The FBI wanted to wait patiently for indictments and then arrest those charged. The CIA's Webster, not surprisingly, supported that legalistic approach. But inside the CIA, especially in CTC, agents bristled because the Libyans were beyond the reach of U.S. law. Cannistraro and others argued strenuously to remove the suspects at any cost, even if that meant assassinating them or allowing the Israelis to do it on our behalf. But Webster would broker no such discussion. Frustrated with Webster's strict limits on any operations, Cannistraro abruptly resigned in September 1990, just before Iraq invaded Kuwait. "The CTC is starting to look too much like the FBI," he disparagingly told a former colleague after giving Webster his notice.[25]

A 1990 Senate panel, headed by security attorney Eli Jacobs, concluded that Webster's efforts had failed to overcome the extensive fragmentation of the government's counterintelligence efforts. The panel concluded that it was virtually impossible to cure the problems by merely insisting that the CIA and FBI drop their long-standing mutual distrust and dislike. Only by completely re-creating America's intelligence and crime-fighting apparatus might it be possible to make progress, the panel suggested.

Few people outside the government realized how deep-set the problems of mistrust and failure to cooperate between the FBI and CIA had become by 1990. The arrival in the United States of the blind Egyptian sheikh, Omar Abdel Rahman, illustrates how the internal feuding worked to the benefit of the terrorists and the detriment of the country both agencies were supposed to serve.

Although Representative Barney Frank's 1987 amendment had made it impossible to deny entry into the U.S. to someone who was a member of a terrorist group, there was a loophole that could still be used when it came to individuals who had suspected foreign intelligence con-

---

*Eventually, two Libyan intelligence officers were fingered. Libyan strong man Muammar Qaddafi finally extradited them to the Netherlands in 1999. One of them was convicted in a subsequent trial in the international court in the Hague.

nections. But this enforcement procedure could only work if the CIA and FBI shared information.

In early 1990, Rahman applied for a U.S. visa in Khartoum, Sudan, a hotbed of terrorist activity. The embassy's CIA officer processed the sheikh's request without incident. This despite the fact that Rahman was on the CIA's international terror list. The Agency had solid information that he had been on the payroll of Iranian intelligence since late 1981.[26] And during the 1980s, Rahman's Egyptian mosque, where he delivered his virulently anti-Western sermons, was a recruiting center for volunteers to wage jihad against the Soviets in Afghanistan. But the CIA officer in Khartoum evidently never saw the Agency's intelligence materials on Rahman. The CIA not only failed to make sure that information was at its own consular stations, but never passed along any warning about Rahman's background to either the FBI or the Immigration Service.*

"In the case of Rahman," FBI director William Webster later said, "none of this [sharing of information] really occurred. His name wasn't given to the FBI or wasn't recognized by the FBI, and so no objection was posed, and no vigilance exercised."[27]

Rahman was also fortunate that he passed through the visa system at a time when terror was off the CIA's and FBI's priority agenda. The Berlin Wall had fallen only months earlier and most of the focus was on the dramatic changes in Eastern Europe and what the flood of old intelligence agents from the East might mean for U.S. and European security. And in January 1990, the U.S. invaded Panama. The invasion, and hunt for Panamanian dictator Manuel Noriega, dominated the news at the start of the year. Germany reunified in March, the same month Rahman applied for his visa in Sudan.

And as is all too familiar now, despite his inflammatory sermons that attracted increasingly large crowds at mosques in Brooklyn and Jersey City, Rahman managed to stay under the radar of American law enforcement for another two years.

---

*Some critics of CIA policy have charged that Rahman's entry was so egregious that it could not be a mere human mistake, but might have been purposely allowed because Rahman had previously served as a U.S. intelligence asset. However, there is no credible evidence that the CIA had any relationship with Rahman prior to his entry to the U.S. Absent such evidence, his 1990 visa appears to be what it has long been claimed, just another bureaucratic error with significant unintended consequences.

CHAPTER 3

BIRTH OF A TERRORIST

While the Counterterrorism Center was struggling to get its footing in the incipient war on terror, a Saudi-born son of a wealthy family was trying to take spiritual control of the fundamentalist movement to free Muslims everywhere of Western influence. Osama bin Muhammad bin Laden was the seventeenth son, born in 1957, to an illiterate Yemeni laborer who had moved to Saudi Arabia in 1925.* In the quarter century before his birth, bin Laden's father went from being a bricklayer to starting one of the most prominent construction companies—the Binladen Group—in the Kingdom. The Binladen Group ingratiated itself at every turn with the royal family, and when the country's finances were hit by a sharp drop in oil prices in the late 1950s, it was the Binladen Group that helped stave off public unrest by paying the wages of thousands of civil servants. By the time the devoutly raised Osama was a teenager, the company was well on its way to today's employment of more than 37,000 people and about $5 billion in annual earnings. "It's no secret that my father was responsible for the infrastructure of Saudi Arabia," bin Laden once boasted.[1]

When Osama was nine, his father died in a plane crash while surveying a massive construction project on the Saudi-Yemeni bor-

---

*Bin Laden's father, Mohamed, eventually had twenty-one wives and fifty-four children, twenty-four of them sons, although, in accordance with Islamic law, he never had more than four wives at once. The younger bin Laden was the only son of his father's fourth wife, a Syrian woman whom his father later divorced.

der.* The royal family virtually adopted the bin Laden children. Osama received a traditionally devout Muslim education,† married his first wife (a Syrian cousin) at seventeen, and at nineteen enrolled at Jeddah's King Abdul Aziz University to study economics and business management. The 1970s, when bin Laden was at school, was a time of resurgent Arab nationalism mixed with an increasingly popular view of Islam being under attack from "infidels," the corrupting influences of the West. The restoration of Arab military honor in the 1973 Yom Kippur War waged by Egypt and Syria against Israel, followed by the Arab oil embargo of 1974, which was intended to force Western countries to pursue anti-Israel policies, had profound effects on Muslims everywhere. Osama ("young lion" in Arabic) was attracted to the growing pro-Islamic, anti-Western view.

"Every grown-up Muslim hates Americans, Christians, and Jews," he told a Syrian reporter in 1998. "It is part of our belief and our religion. Ever since I was a boy, I have been harboring feelings of hatred towards America."[2]

This view was reinforced when Saudi Arabia's King Faisal was assassinated in 1975. The assassin was the king's unbalanced nephew, Prince Faisal ibn Musaid. That Musaid was one of the most Westernized members of the royal family, and a frequent visitor to the United States and Europe, was further evidence to the fundamentalists of the corrupting influence of Western culture.

*That death is officially listed as an accident. However, Israeli intelligence files contain the results of an internal Saudi government investigation into the crash. Those files, still classified by both the Saudis and the Israelis, reveal that at the crash site, explosive residue was found on some sections of the plane's wreckage. The blast damage revealed that the impact had taken place from inside the plane prior to the crash. Saudi investigators classified the death as murder, but never pursued a thorough investigation nor made the evidence public. Retired Israeli intelligence officers familiar with the results of the Saudi investigation told the author that Mossad concluded on its own—based on its monitoring of Gulf State countries at the time—that the senior bin Laden had been killed in a fight with some members of the Saudi elite over the amount of a payback for the very project he had been surveying. "He was getting too big for his own good," said one Israeli, "and was starting to think he could do the projects and pay less to his benefactors. It's a line—money—you can't cross with the Saudis."

†The Wahhabi sect, founded by Muhammad ibn Abd al-Wahhab in the 1700s, is dominant in Saudi Arabia. It is an austere form of Islam that preaches a literal interpretation of the Koran.

The man who became bin Laden's mentor and spiritual motivator during the late 1970s was a prominent advocate inside the radical Muslim Brotherhood, Palestinian-born Sheikh Abdullah Azzam. Azzam, who had fled the West Bank after Israel's smashing 1967 military victory in the Six Day War, was a professor of Islamic law at bin Laden's university. He was a mesmerizing speaker who drew large crowds with his angry rhetoric advocating jihad to save Muslim lands from infidel encroachment. When Egypt's Anwar Sadat visited Jerusalem in 1977 and began a process that would lead to peace with Israel, Azzam rallied Islamic opposition. It was a sign of treachery, argued Azzam, and his condemnations were cited by Islamic Jihad when they eventually assassinated Sadat four years later.*

Azzam's militant view of Islamic history made him the ideological father of groups like al Qaeda. And the future about which he preached meshed perfectly with real events when in February 1979—bin Laden's last year at the university—Ayatollah Khomeini was swept to power in neighboring Iran, in the region's first fundamentalist Islamic revolution. By December of that year, the Soviet army had invaded Muslim Afghanistan to support a Soviet-sponsored communist government that was under increasing attack from a Pakistani-backed Islamic insurgency. It was the first time since World War II that a non-Muslim army occupied a Muslim country. Sheikh Azzam, then thirty-eight years old, passionately urged Islamic volunteers worldwide to travel to Afghanistan to defeat Russia's secular army. With Azzam's pleas, the mujahedeen (warriors of God) were born. And one of the first to answer was bin Laden. Within days of the Soviet invasion, instead of returning to his family's business where an executive position was reserved for him, he went to Afghanistan.[3]

"One day in Afghanistan," bin Laden later told an interviewer, "was like one thousand days of praying in an ordinary mosque."[4]

In 1980, the twenty-two-year-old bin Laden became the chief fundraiser for the Maktab al-Khidmat lil Mujahidin (Afghan Services Bureau), an organization he cofounded with his mentor, Azzam (Emir Shalabi, murdered in New York in 1991, was the bureau's American

---

*When New York police arrested El-Sayyid Nosair, the assassin of Rabbi Kahane, in 1990, among the items they seized was a box full of videotapes of Azzam's speeches, many of which urged jihad.

representative). Its purpose was to provide logistical support for the flood
of new volunteers arriving daily from Arab countries.

And while the war waged in Afghanistan, bin Laden traveled extensively to raise funds for the jihad. Through 1986, bin Laden oversaw an
operation that channeled several billion dollars from private contributors, governments, and charities to his Afghan Services Bureau. In so
doing, he established branches in over fifty countries for encouraging
recruits and raising money, organizations that would later become key
in his war against the U.S.

The CIA knew about bin Laden and initially considered him merely
"an organizer and philanthropist."[5] While the CIA ignored him, bin
Laden forged key relationships with high-ranking operatives inside Pakistani intelligence as well as the Saudi government.[6] For instance, in the
early 1980s, when the Saudi royal family was concerned about Soviet,
East German, and Cuban military advisors in the then communist South
Yemen, it asked bin Laden to create mujahedeen units to fight with
Yemeni anticommunist insurgents. The Saudis bankrolled the effort
with millions in aid, and bin Laden personally oversaw the formation of
the Arab volunteers for South Yemen.[7]

King Fahd was so delighted with bin Laden's work in Yemen that the
king, in a private audience, offered Osama a lucrative construction contract to expand the Prophet's Mosque in Medina. Bin Laden declined,
saying his commitment was first to the fight in Afghanistan, and asking
the king only to redouble Saudi Arabian support for the so-called
Afghan Arabs. The Saudis did their part. For the next ten years, the
mujahedeen were funded by nearly $2 billion in secret Saudi aid. The
money flowed through nearly two dozen Islamic charities and two banks
established by the royal family for the sole purpose of sending money to
the fighters.[8] Prince Turki bin Faisal bin Abdul-Aziz, chief of Saudi intelligence, worked directly with Azzam and bin Laden. Prince Turki had
created an Afghan department that coordinated the Saudi effort to assist
the fight.[9] As far as the Saudis were concerned, it was better to encourage young, radical Muslims to fight abroad than to direct their activism
toward the Kingdom. "Isn't it better that they go off and fight a foreign
jihad," an unidentified Saudi official told The New York Times, "rather
than hang around the mosques without a job and cause trouble in Saudi
Arabia?"[10]

Millions more in funding, arms, and technical assistance came from the U.S. through the CIA, who could not pass up an opportunity to embroil the Soviets in a long and costly conflict, even if it meant aligning the Agency with Islamic fighters who also hated America. And the third element aiding the Afghan Arabs was the dedicated commitment of Pakistan's ten-thousand-strong intelligence service, Inter-Services Intelligence (ISI). Pakistan's Zia-ul-Haq government had concluded immediately after the Soviet invasion that the crisis in their northern neighbor constituted a national security threat with which they had to deal firmly. As a result, ISI, which had sponsored terrorism against India over the Kashmir dispute since the 1970s, turned its attention to the Afghan mujahedeen. ISI provided money, training, support, and logistics. General Akhtar Abdul Rahman, chief of ISI from 1980 to 1987, was intimately involved in his service's newly created Afghan Division. He jealously maintained control over the training and supply of the mujahedeen, frequently infuriating CIA officials who wanted to be more involved in the field with the insurgent fighters.[11]

According to still classified CIA reports from the time, General Rahman personally met with bin Laden during his trips to Peshawar, in northern Pakistan. The chief of ISI, accompanied usually by several aides, provided not only cash to bin Laden, but also intelligence gathered from other sources. The CIA has concluded that in a partnership, ISI and bin Laden forced the tribal warlords who controlled much of the lucrative opium trade in northwest Afghanistan to pay them a "tax." By 1985, the CIA estimated that the "tax" provided upward of $100 million annually.[12]

In 1986, bin Laden wanted to do more than merely be the go-between for Saudi and Pakistani intelligence. And he was also weary of only raising money for the war. With the approval of his mentor, Azzam, he established his first rudimentary military training camp at Jaji. The following year, bin Laden, Azzam, and three dozen other Arabs used guerrilla tactics and their intrinsic knowledge of the surrounding landscape to hold their ground for two weeks against a larger Soviet unit. That action gave birth to al Qaeda ("the Base," in Arabic).

The Soviets, defeated, left Afghanistan in early 1989. They were replaced with a civil war fueled by ethnic rivalries and ambitious warlords anxious for power. Bin Laden and Azzam had a falling out over the future of the country. Azzam, whose rhetoric still encouraged jihad

against foreigners, thought it necessary to build alliances in Afghanistan
with moderate Islamics, including the pragmatic Northern Alliance warlord, Ahmad Shah Massoud. For Azzam, the next logical step for the
Afghan Arabs was to join the fight against Israel. But bin Laden did not
want to hear about moderation. He was convinced that the Afghan veterans should now focus on disloyal, secular Muslim regimes, and then
branch out to non-Muslim countries.

"Osama wanted to launch a guerrilla war not only in the Arab and
Islamic world, but in the whole world," Ahmed Ibrahim al-Sayed al-
Naggar, an Islamic Jihad member, told Egyptian police after his arrest
there.[13]

A year before the Soviet ouster, bin Laden had met an Egyptian doctor, who treated him for high blood pressure while on a trip to Pakistan. That doctor was thirty-seven-year-old Ayman al-Zawahiri, the
leader of Egypt's radical Islamic Jihad. Al-Zawahiri, who came from a
respected family, had become a hardened radical after spending three
years in an Egyptian jail in the early 1980s following a massive security sweep in the wake of Anwar Sadat's assassination. Al-Zawahiri
had recently moved to Pakistan to help treat Afghan refugees flooding
in from Afghanistan, and also to raise help for his own group, whose
goal was the overthrow of secular Arab leaders like Egypt's Hosni
Mubarak and replace them with strict Islamic theocracies. Six years
older than bin Laden, al-Zawahiri was uncompromising in his radical
interpretation of Islam. He and bin Laden reinforced each other's militant views, and many insiders, including al-Zawahiri's former attorney, Muntasir al-Zayat, have contended that it was al-Zawahiri who
was responsible for transforming bin Laden from a guerrilla fighter to
a terrorist.[14]

In the dispute between Azzam and bin Laden, ISI sided with bin
Laden. It had invested too much money and effort in establishing and
running the training camps for jihad to watch them just wither away.
Lieutenant General Hamid Gul, later the head of ISI, summarized why
Pakistan believed the radical training centers had to exist.

"We are fighting a jihad," he said, "and this is the first Islamic international brigade in the modern era. The communists have their international brigades, the West has NATO, why can't the Muslims unite and
form a common front?"[15]

On November 24, 1989, in Peshawar, Sheikh Azzam was driving to a local mosque with his two sons and one of their friends when his car evaporated in a giant explosion caused by forty-five pounds of TNT, activated by remote control. Azzam's murder removed the only rival bin Laden faced in assuming control of the jihadist movement.*

*No one was ever charged with Azzam's death, and some early erroneous reports said that he had merely had the misfortune of running into one of the region's many land mines. ISI, whose file on Azzam is probably the largest of any intelligence agency, concluded that six members of al-Zawahiri's Islamic Jihad carried out the murder as a favor to bin Laden. A Palestinian al Qaeda member, Muhammad Saddiq Odeh, told his Pakistani, and later American, interrogators that bin Laden had "personally ordered the killing of Azzam because he suspected his former mentor had ties with the Central Intelligence Agency." Al-Zawahiri—who delivered the eulogy at Azzam's funeral—told bin Laden that he thought Azzam was an American agent.[16]

CHAPTER 4

THE
FIRST SHOT

Sheikh Rahman's murder of Emir Shalabi in Brooklyn in 1991 was not the first murder on American soil by Islamic militants. The first was a year earlier and, in contrast to Shalabi's death, had attracted widespread attention.

The banquet room of Manhattan's Marriott Eastside Hotel was filled with followers of the fifty-eight-year-old Rabbi Meir Kahane, the founder of the radical Kahane Chai and a former legislator in the Israeli parliament, on the night of November 5, 1990.* There was enthusiastic applause for Kahane's standard speech exhorting the expulsion of Palestinians from Israel. Kahane seemed pleased with the reception. New York was the one place, he had told aides earlier that evening, where he felt most at home outside Israel.

When Kahane finished, he stepped from the podium and took a seat at a small table as a throng of supporters surged around him. No one noticed two men lingering in the rear of the ballroom. Both were dark-skinned and appeared to be Sephardic Jews. One, a thirty-four-year-old Egyptian, El-Sayyid Nosair, wore a yarmulke so he could mingle with Kahane's supporters. With his Arab colleague, Bilall Alkaisi, Nosair had attended many of Kahane's public appearances for nearly a year. The pair had promised each other that if the opportunity presented itself, they would kill the rabbi.

As Kahane lingered in the front of the ballroom, Alkaisi left to go to

---

*Kahane's rhetoric was so inflammatory—he often referred to Arabs as "dogs"—that Israel banned him from running for reelection to the Knesset in 1988.

the bathroom. While he was gone, Nosair draped a coat over his arm and drew a .357 Magnum from his waistband. Then he strolled toward the front of the hall and stood at the edge of the crowd. Without uttering a word, Nosair seemed to smile before suddenly whipping the coat off his arm and firing the revolver twice. A bullet hit Kahane in his neck, exiting his right cheek.

There was chaos as Nosair sprinted for the doors, screaming, "It's Allah's will!" A seventy-three-year-old Kahane supporter, Irving Franklin, tried tackling him, but Nosair shot him in the leg. He raced through the elegant marble lobby and, once outside the thirty-two-story hotel, jumped into a taxi. His escape had been planned, and the curbside taxi was supposed to be driven by another Egyptian, Mahmud Abouhalima. But unknown to Nosair, hotel security had shooed Abouhalima away from the front entrance less than five minutes before the shooting. The taxicab that Nosair had jumped into belonged instead to a bewildered Hispanic driver, Frank Garcia, from the Bronx.

Dozens of Kahane's followers poured onto the streets looking for the shooter. Nosair was hunched down in the rear of the taxi, which made it one block before Garcia stopped for a red light. Nosair jumped out and ran down the street, waving his gun. A postal inspector, Carlos Acosta, standing near the entrance to Grand Central Station, saw an armed man running toward him. Acosta drew his gun. Nosair fired first, hitting Acosta in his bulletproof vest. Acosta fired back, striking Nosair in the neck. The chase was over.

Nosair arrived at Bellevue Hospital only minutes after Kahane had been wheeled into the emergency room. Although Nosair's jugular had been ruptured by Acosta's shot, the doctors managed to stabilize him. Kahane, however, was pronounced dead at 9:57 P.M.

The New York police assigned to work the case felt from the start that there was more to the Kahane murder than one angry Arab shooter. In Nosair's wallet, they found clippings from Jewish newspapers listing prominent local events and three New Jersey licenses with different addresses, but all with his picture. Six hours after the murder, when detectives arrived at one of the addresses, two Arab men were at the apartment.* One was Mahmud Abouhalima, the taxi driver who was

---

*Nosair had used a string of nearly ten addresses over three years, and also maintained a private post office box in a trading and check-cashing company called the Sphinx, located in the same building as his mosque.

supposed to be Nosair's getaway driver, and the other was a Palestinian, Mohammed Salameh, who it turned out had also been in a nearby car (Salameh would later be part of the 1993 plot to blow up the World Trade Center). Both admitted to police that they knew Nosair and that they had been at the hotel at the time of Kahane's murder.

As for Nosair, he had rented a house in Cliffside Park, New Jersey, just across the George Washington Bridge from Manhattan. The police located that house the day after the murder. When they searched it, they recovered sixteen boxes of evidence that included bomb-making manuals, maps of New York landmarks, instructional booklets from the U.S. Army Special Forces, a list of names of prominent Jewish leaders and pro-Israeli politicians,* and a receipt for a case of 1,440 rounds of 7.62mm surplus ammunition, the type used in assault rifles like the Soviet-made AK-47.[2] Many of the documents were handwritten in Arabic.

In one of the great investigative mix-ups on the early trail of terror in America, the sixteen boxes of evidence were removed from New York police custody by local FBI agents three days after the shooting. Two days after that, Manhattan district attorney Robert Morgenthau asserted local jurisdiction over the case, elbowing the FBI out of their controlling role and moving the material to his own office. However, no one informed the precinct commander, Lieutenant Eddie Norris, that the files had been returned to police jurisdiction. So they remained in the district attorney's basement until Nosair's trial. Since the prosecution's case against Nosair was eventually presented through eyewitnesses and forensics, the political dimensions were largely ignored. As a result, the Arabic notes were not considered important. They were not translated and the information they contained, a virtual outline of further terrorist activity in New York, went unheeded.[3]

*The list included New York congressman Gary Ackerman; Howard Adelman, a columnist for *The Jewish Press*; and two federal judges, Jack Weinstein and Edward Korman, as well as a former assistant United States attorney, Jacques Simmelman, all of whom had played significant roles in the extradition to Israel of Mahmoud Atta (a.k.a. Mahmoud El-Abed Ahmad), a member of the Abu Nidal terrorist organization. Atta had been wanted for a deadly terror attack in 1986 on a bus in Israel, and his extradition was set for only a week before Nosair killed Kahane. A month after the Kahane murder, Abu Nidal's radical Palestinian group issued a statement from Beirut offering to pay for Nosair's defense.[1] However, according to the FBI, Nosair's defense was actually paid for by bin Laden, who gave money to Nosair's relatives, who traveled to Saudi Arabia for that purpose. Nosair's defense lawyer was social activist and leftist William Kunstler.

The case seemed straightforward. The Egyptian-born Nosair had immigrated to the United States in July 1981, and a year later was attracted to Islamic fundamentalism at a local mosque in Pittsburgh. There he married an American woman who converted to Islam—and with that marriage Nosair managed to obtain a permanent resident alien card and applied for U.S. citizenship.

When he moved to New Jersey in 1985 he settled into the Masjid al-Salaam, a radical mosque that included among its members an Egyptian, Sultan Ibraham el-Gawli, who had served time in federal prison after being arrested by U.S. Customs for attempting to smuggle 150 pounds of C-4 explosive, 100 blasting caps, remote detonators, and a 9mm pistol with a silencer to the Palestinian Liberation Organization.[4] Nosair was also a regular at Emir Shalabi's Alkifah Refugee Center.

Nosair's radicalization was rapid. By 1987 he had formed his own cell of four Muslims, and they began training for an eventual jihad, attending paramilitary classes in upstate New York and practicing at rifle ranges on Long Island and in Connecticut. A year after that, Nosair began communicating with Sheikh Rahman, who was then still in Egypt. Nosair was proud he knew Rahman and recorded some of his telephone conversations to play for others at his mosque. He bragged to friends that Rahman had given his cell a blessing.*

In June 1989, the FBI's New York field office received an anonymous tip that some Palestinians associated with the Alkifah Center were plotting to blow up several Atlantic City casinos. The FBI assigned a few agents to keep an eye on the center. During that surveillance, the Bureau tracked Nosair and several other Arabs to the Calverton Shooting Range on eastern Long Island and observed them training with a small arsenal, including shotguns, AK-47 assault rifles, and .357 Magnum and 9mm handguns. In August, the Bureau canceled its surveillance, since there had been no attack against any casino. No effort was made to identify any of the Arabs photographed by the FBI agents. And the FBI did not pass along concerns about the men to the INS. So the Immigration Service routinely approved Nosair's application for U.S. citizenship that September, months after the FBI had begun watching him.

Nosair, meanwhile, had landed a $30,000-a-year job with New York

---

*The tapes Nosair recorded of his calls to Rahman were also included in the boxes of evidence seized by police from his New Jersey apartment. But they, like most of the other material in Arabic, were not translated for nearly three years.

City, maintaining heating and air-conditioning units at the Criminal Courts Building. Leads not followed up in the original investigation reveal that Nosair might have obtained the job at a city building so that he could have access to other government sites in New York, study their construction, and analyze their weak points for an attack.*

On December 8, 1989, less than a year before Nosair killed Kahane, a policeman had given him a warning citation for throwing a can of soda at the motorcade of visiting Soviet premier Mikhail Gorbachev. At the time, no one knew that it contained a small explosive, which fortunately did not go off.[6] By the following April, however, Nosair had improved his bomb-making talents, enough so that he was able to explode a small device in an unlikely target: a West Village bar, Uncle Charley's. The six-inch pipe bomb blew up just after midnight, injuring several patrons. It was a crude device without a timer, so Nosair had to be there in order to trigger it. But he managed to do that and still flee undetected.

Through the spring, Nosair was desperate to find a target worthy of his personal jihad. He followed a U.N. official, tried tracking officials assigned to Egypt's U.N. delegation, and constantly exhorted his fellow cell members to stay true to the cause of Islam.

Within hours of the Kahane murder, two FBI agents, John Anticev and Louie Napoli, had located the Bureau's 1989 surveillance photos taken at the Calverton, New York, shooting range. They immediately realized Nosair was one of the men. But once the case was transferred back to the New York City police after a few days, the FBI agents dropped their investigation and no one in the police learned of the Calverton lead. It took another six months before the Bureau got around to identifying the other

---

*This information is from confidential documents related to the City of New York's 1991 investigation into a scheme in which Local 1795 union officials were bribed to facilitate fraudulent employment histories so people could qualify for union membership and city jobs. One of those who used the false information to get a city job was Nosair.[5] The individual who taught Nosair how to make the fraudulent application that landed him his job inside the Criminal Courts Building was another worker of Arab descent, Mohsen Mahmoud, who admitted to investigators that he had used the same false documents to get his own employment. Although this investigation was conducted prior to Nosair's trial, none of it was used because prosecutors did not want to raise questions of a wider conspiracy that had not been adequately investigated by the police or FBI.

men photographed with Nosair. One was a young African-American Muslim, Clement Hampton-El, and the others were Arabs, Mohammed Salameh, Nidal Ayyad, and Mahmud Abouhalima. Hampton-El would later be convicted of conspiring with Sheikh Rahman to blow up New York landmarks, and the other three would all be arrested for roles in the first World Trade Center attack.

The day after the Kahane murder, Lieutenant Eddie Norris, the commander of the 17th Precinct, who was responsible for investigating the murder, drove to One Police Plaza, the department's headquarters, for a meeting with Joe Borelli, the chief of detectives,* along with their aides and some FBI agents from the interagency Joint Terrorism Task Force.†

"Can you tell me this was the work of one man?" Borelli asked Norris.

"Absolutely not," Norris said. He then explained how some leads that could point to a wider conspiracy had not been thoroughly investigated.

Borelli interrupted him. "You shut up." The room fell silent. "You do murder cases," Borelli continued. Then he pointed to the FBI agents. "They do conspiracies." Despite Norris's protests, Borelli ordered him to free Abouhalima and Salameh for lack of evidence.

At a press conference later that day, Borelli told the packed room of journalists that all the available evidence indicated that the Kahane murder was that of a "lone, deranged gunman."[7] The next day, Borelli went even further. "We interviewed coworkers, his wife, people at the mosque. No one has come to us and indicated in any fashion that he [Nosair] had any dislike for or hatred of the rabbi. . . . Nothing has transpired that changes our opinion that he acted alone. There isn't anything we've found that indicates he was involved with any group of others. Based on that, we are under the opinion that he acted alone. . . . Why he did it, we may never know."[8]

Some agents in the FBI's New York field office saw it quite differently. They thought that Nosair was not only part of a plot, but that he also provided a rare glimpse into the radical Muslim community then flour-

---

*Borelli had earned fame over a decade earlier when he led the task force that successfully tracked down the Son of Sam serial killer, David Berkowitz.

†The JTTF was formed in 1980 as a way to pool the resources of the FBI and the New York Police Department.

ishing in New York. Shortly after the Kahane murder, unidentified FBI
sources leaked stories to *The New York Times* and other publications that
groups such as the Egyptian-based Muslim Brotherhood, which were
associated with New Jersey's Masjid al-Salaam, "might be capable of terrorist activities" inside the U.S.[9] But no one in the New York office was
able to get permission from Washington to conduct an investigation into
the radicals that had come to their attention as a result of the Kahane
murder. Top FBI officials were not persuaded that these groups posed
any threat worthy of investigations that would consume the Bureau's
resources. Not even inflammatory comments to local newspapers from
the imam of the New Jersey mosque to the effect that the killing of
Kahane "was not a violation [of Islam] in the sense that Kahane adopted
a position against all Arabs and Muslims" seemed to raise much concern.[10]

Neil Herman, the FBI agent who ran the New York office of the Joint
Terrorism Task Force, was one of those convinced that Nosair was part
of a larger conspiracy. "But you couldn't get anybody to take terrorism
seriously," he said. "Even after Kahane, nobody felt it could happen here,
nobody wanted to believe it could happen here."[11]

On Saturday, December 21, 1991, more than a year after Kahane's
murder, a Manhattan criminal jury composed of six whites, five blacks,
and one Hispanic stunned the prosecution by acquitting Nosair of
Kahane's murder and the attempted murder of postal inspector Acosta.
Nosair was only found guilty of minor gun possession and assault
charges. When the acquittals were announced at 8:15 P.M. in Room
1313 of the State Supreme Court, several dozen Muslim supporters
broke into applause and cheers. Nosair turned to one of his defense
lawyers: "All praise is due to Allah!"[12]

The prosecution had presented fifty-one witnesses, including eyewitnesses who identified Nosair as the killer. Nosair's defense was built
around a conspiracy theory. Although no witnesses were introduced to
support the theory that Kahane's followers would want to frame Nosair,
the defense team claimed that he was framed by one of Kahane's own
followers in a money dispute inside the rabbi's organization. Nosair, said
his lawyers, had been in the back of the room during Kahane's talk, and
had run away after the shooting simply because he was scared. As for
the murder weapon found on him, his lawyers claimed it had somehow
been planted by Kahane's followers.

The day following the verdict, lead defense attorney William Kunstler left for a vacation in Puerto Rico. From there, he told reporters that he had succeeded in getting Nosair an acquittal because he managed to keep "yuppies, establishment types, and those who supported Israel" off the jury. "This was a jury of third world people," gloated Kunstler. "It was a legal victory for Mr. Nosair and a political victory for the nation's poor and oppressed minority groups."[13]*

At the New Jersey mosque where Nosair had worshiped, Masjid al-Salaam, there was jubilation and chants of "Allah is great" when news of the acquittal arrived. Some of those who watched the celebration spill out into the streets in Jersey City included the area's large community of Coptic Christians, many of whom sport small indigo tattoos on their hands or wrists. One Egyptian shopkeeper looked out his window at the giddy festivities of the Muslims down the block. He shook his head. "They want to destroy America. They are a bad group." Few people were listening.

*One person who was outraged with the jury's decision was the presiding judge, Alvin Schlesinger, who gave Nosair the maximum for each count on which he was convicted and ordered the sentences be served consecutively, adding up to seven and a half to twenty-two years in prison.

CHAPTER 5

THE
SECRET
DEAL

While the New York police were failing to connect the dots in the Kahane murder, halfway around the world bin Laden had set about his incredibly ambitious goal of creating an empire of the world's one billion Muslims. Although bin Laden did not like the Saudi royal family, he had formed strong relationships with leading officials like intelligence chief Prince Turki, and he knew that Saudi Arabia had been indispensable in helping the Afghan Arabs prevail against the Soviets. Turki urged him to come home, which he did shortly after the murder of his longtime mentor, Azzam.

Bin Laden had become something of a local folk hero, a well-to-do son of a prominent family who had given up his luxurious lifestyle to rally Arabs to successfully battle the Soviets. Prince Abdullah, next in line to the Saudi crown, personally greeted bin Laden on his return.

But the honeymoon was short-lived. When Saddam Hussein invaded Kuwait in August 1990, bin Laden offered the royal family the services of thousands of his Afghan Arabs to defend the kingdom in case Iraq had any designs on it. The royal family stunned bin Laden by not only turning down his offer, but instead allowing 300,000 American troops onto Saudi soil.*

---

*The Saudi royal family's power, based on the very strict Wahhabi interpretation of Islam, absolutely forbids non-Muslims from entering the holy mosques of Mecca and Medina. Nonbelievers are not encouraged to even live in the country. But after Iraq conquered Kuwait, the Saudis feared for their own safety. The royal family prevailed on the grand mufti to issue a temporary exception for American troops invited

Almost overnight, bin Laden went from an ally of the Saudi rulers to an opponent. He lectured against the decision to bring in the Americans and accused the royal family of desecrating Islam's birthplace. Anti-Americanism became a growing element in his talks. Tapes of his speeches were widely circulated.[1] Meanwhile, bin Laden more intensively recruited volunteers for his Afghan training camps, sites where they could learn the basics of guerrilla warfare for the upcoming jihad he envisioned.*

The Saudis have a pervasive internal secret service. It monitored bin Laden's dissent with alarm. Had he not had the backing of powerful members of the Saudi royal family, he might well have just disappeared into a Saudi prison, never to reemerge. According to a still classified American intelligence report, Turki—with the apparent blessing of the royal family—helped broker a deal in early 1991 with the thirty-three-year-old bin Laden. In a secret agreement, bin Laden and the Saudis concocted a public fraud that would serve both their interests. Bin Laden would be allowed to leave Saudi Arabia with his four wives and his growing family (as of 2003 he has fifteen children) on a one-way visa. Whatever assets he left in the country might be frozen once he left.[2] The Saudis would publicly disown their favorite son as a radical gone bad. Bin Laden could keep preaching his jihad, however, so long as it was not directed at the Kingdom. In return, the Saudis would provide him with enough money to keep his Afghan Arabs well supplied, again, with the understanding that they would never be used against Saudi Arabia. Turki has admitted an early contact with bin Laden. He once told a reporter that "Osama was a model, we wanted more of him. He was very upright, a very friendly and amenable fellow in the 1980s." He has nevertheless steadfastly denied any improper relationship or arrangement with bin Laden.† Such an arrangement, however, would have made sense for the Saudis, since they knew it was impossible to stamp out fun-

---

into the Kingdom to protect it. The presence of military units of the infidel in the holy land of Saudi Arabia was a great affront to many devout Muslims. It was not until April 2003, after the war in Iraq, that the United States and Saudi Arabia agreed to the withdrawal of most American military personnel stationed in the Kingdom.

*This was the time when the CIA's Counterterrorism Center first learned of bin Laden, as his name frequently surfaced in reports about threats to Saudi security.

†Requests for a comment from Prince Turki through the Saudi Embassy in Washington went unanswered.

damentalism. It presented an opportunity to direct the wrath of the
movement away from their own country. As for bin Laden, whether he
was serious in agreeing to direct the jihad away from his native country
or merely buying himself millions in financing and some extra time, the
CIA believes he was amenable to the pact. And he was evidently not willing to wait for the Saudis to change their mind. He left Jeddah and first
returned to Afghanistan to collect some of his best fighters and then
moved to Sudan. There, the radical National Islamic Front had seized
power in a coup two years earlier, and they were in the midst of trying to
create a pure Islamic government. Bin Laden and his fighters were wel-
comed as honored guests.

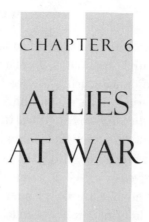

CHAPTER 6

ALLIES
AT WAR

While the Gulf War incensed radicals like bin Laden, it offered the CIA's Counterterrorism Center—which had been struggling—a chance to redeem itself. The CTC's performance during the Gulf War was admirable. Analysts doubled their efforts at reviewing cables and monitoring satellite intercepts of communications searching, for hints of terror attacks. The CTC convinced Director Webster to expel a number of suspected Iraqi businessmen, students, and diplomats. A New Jersey man, Jamal Wariat, was arrested for plotting to kill President Bush, several Palestinian terrorists in New Jersey were arrested, and an Iraqi intelligence agent was apprehended before executing a plot to kill a dissident in California.

But when the brief war finished in January 1991, there was little praise for CTC. Rather, the focus was on why the CIA had failed to notice that Saddam Hussein was building up to invade his neighbor. The Agency was rightly under attack because although an analyst had predicted an invasion the previous June, Webster had not conveyed it to the White House until August 1, only hours before Iraq invaded Kuwait. And even as the U.S. geared up for war, the CIA again stumbled, incorrectly predicting that the Soviets, who maintained more than one thousand military advisors in Iraq, would stand against us and complicate the war. Instead, Gorbachev cooperated with the coalition, and for the first time since 1945, the Americans and Soviets were temporarily allies.

Webster resigned in July 1991, only six months after the end of the Gulf War. "It was hard to find the time to attend all the little 'get lost' parties held in the next couple of weeks," recalled one former CIA official.[1] Webster was replaced with Robert Gates, the former CIA deputy director, who was serving as National Security Advisor Brent Scowcroft's assistant. Only four years earlier, Gates's own nomination to head the CIA had to be withdrawn when he was engulfed with questions about his role in Iran-contra. While those same questions again delayed a vote on Gates for months, the former analyst from the CIA's Directorate of Intelligence was finally approved by a 64–31 Senate vote in November 1991.

From his prior stint at the CIA, Gates knew what could happen if agencies did not share information in complicated investigations. The Bank of Credit and Commerce International (BCCI)—known derisively to regulators as the Bank of Crooks and Criminals—was a Pakistan-based bank that looted investors of billions of dollars while simultaneously running an international organized crime operation. BCCI's president was former Saudi intelligence chief Kamal Adham, and besides offering a Federal Express service for narcotics, it dealt in bribes, extortion, and murder, as well as being involved with terrorists and illegal arm shipments. BCCI had facilitated Iraqi smuggling of parts for its nuclear weapons program by providing fake letters of credit and false customs valuations. The Iraqis paid for those documents with cash bribes of bank officials. Another client was terrorist Abu Nidal.

The CIA, although aware of many of BCCI's transgressions for nearly a decade, never shared the information with the FBI or U.S. banking regulators. Instead, the CIA had decided to use BCCI as an asset. The bank eventually provided details about its Iraqi transactions, as well as allowing the CIA to use its Panama City branch to disburse Agency payments to Panama's strong man, Manuel Noriega. Even the anti-Sandinista rebels were covertly funded through a BCCI branch. Some CIA officials, however, were bothered by the extent of the bank's crime spree and the arrogance that allowed bank officers to boast they were the "black network."

Gates had been one of the CIA officials troubled by BCCI's brazen activities. In 1988, when he was the deputy director, he had informed U.S. Customs about BCCI's money-laundering role for drug cartels. But neither the CIA nor Customs notified the FBI, which had sole responsibility for investigating domestic bank fraud. The CIA also knew that BCCI secretly owned a Washington bank, First American, but again did not alert the Bureau.

As Gates took control at the CIA, the Agency was trying to weather some blistering congressional criticism for its mishandling of the BCCI matter, which had recently become public. Gates began to implement policies that would ensure that no matter what the CIA's interests were in an operation, the FBI would be notified of possible illegalities.

In February 1992, Gates also publicly backed a plan proposed by Oklahoma senator—and Senate Intelligence Committee chairman—David Boren to "bring about the most sweeping changes in the U.S. intelligence community since the CIA was created in 1947."[2] Boren proposed a National Intelligence Center (NIC), with a new cabinet-level post as director—to whom both the CIA and FBI directors would report. Few agents in the CIA or in the FBI, however, relished the idea of having a super-agency monitor their efforts. Leaks to the press from those unhappy with NIC soon raised a specter of a national secret police resulting in government intrusion into daily life with a loss of privacy for many Americans.[3] Boren backpedaled. As his plan died, Gates proposed a slightly modified one, but it also went nowhere.

No sooner had the Boren and Gates plans been shelved than a new scandal broke, caused by the continuing lack of cooperation between the FBI and CIA. It was about another bank, this time the Atlanta branch of Italy's Banco Nazionale del Lavoro (BNL). Since 1974, the CIA, MI6 (British Intelligence), and Mossad had a joint project called Operation Babylon to infiltrate Saddam Hussein's nuclear weapons program. In 1981, when the Western powers feared that the Iraqis were getting close to developing a bomb, the CIA used satellite intelligence to guide Israeli warplanes on a surgical strike against Iraq's main reactor at Osirak. While that strike put the Iraqi program back ten years, Hussein remained defiantly committed to his nuclear program. Much of the material Iraq needed was purchased through a struggling British machine tools company, Matrix-Churchill, which the Iraqis had covertly bought with BNL funds in 1987. Most of that money came from the BNL branch in Atlanta; that was fortuitous, because under U.S. law, since the bank was foreign-owned, the CIA had the authority to intercept all its communications.

By 1989, Operation Babylon, with its secret window through the Atlanta BNL branch, had penetrated the Iraqi nuclear program and was able to monitor whatever progress Saddam made toward acquiring a bomb. But the fifteen-year effort to track the Iraqis was virtually scuttled in 1989 when the FBI raided the BNL branch in Atlanta.

Independent of the CIA, the FBI had focused on the BNL bank only four months before the raid. In the aftermath of the S&L bank failures, there was pressure in the Bureau to concentrate on financial crimes. When the Atlanta FBI office was tipped off by a disgruntled BNL employee about "off-the-books" loans, the Bureau jumped on the case. To ensure they were not disrupting anyone else's investigation, the FBI checked with a local Customs office, the Federal Reserve, the U.S. Attorney, and even the Treasury Department. No one, however, evidently thought of putting out a feeler to the CIA.[4]

When the FBI stormed the twentieth-floor suite of BNL on Friday, August 4, 1989, they seized the file cabinets and secured all paperwork before any could be destroyed. They even found a set of secret gray books. That evidence revealed that not only had BNL illegally loaned more than $4 billion to Iraq, but it was funding Iraqi nuclear procurement. Because of the espionage implications, the Atlanta FBI office immediately apprised the Bureau's counterintelligence desk in Washington of the developments. Finally concerned that they might have stumbled onto a CIA operation, the U.S. attorney in Atlanta inquired whether the Agency had any role or interest in BNL. The CIA decided not to respond.

After the Gulf War, the FBI complained to Congress that not only had the CIA permitted Iraqi agents to leave the United States rather than be arrested by the Bureau for their role in the BNL fiasco, but the Agency had insisted that Matrix-Churchill's Cleveland office be permitted to remain open for the duration of the military action against Iraq, even though that office was integral to the financial fraud uncovered by the Bureau. As the congressional probe widened, the CIA admitted it had withheld documents, but said it did so at the request of the FBI. The FBI director, William Sessions, responded by announcing that the Bureau was undertaking its own probe of the CIA's role in the BNL matter. Three days later, the Justice Department announced that Sessions was himself being investigated for ethics violations, and a series of anonymous government officials began denigrating his competence to lead the Bureau.

Iraq-Gate, as it was dubbed by the press, dogged George Bush in his reelection bid, and Bill Clinton and Al Gore made good use of it politically. The CIA, whose image had been battered, particularly by the news that it had withheld critical documents from a criminal investigation, was incensed that the FBI had stumbled into their operation and not given any warning. Many in the Bureau, meanwhile, were infuriated that the CIA had ignored their early requests for information and then had gone on the offensive and hobbled the FBI's criminal probe of BNL. By the beginning of the Clinton administration, January 1993, there was deep-seated animosity between officials at both agencies. The timing for such disharmony could not have been worse.

CHAPTER 7

SHELTER
IN SUDAN

As CIA-FBI relations were reaching a nadir, bin Laden had settled comfortably into Khartoum, Sudan's capital, where he was operating openly. His offices were in a nine-room complex in El Mek Nimr Street, and he lived in a three-story al Qaeda guesthouse in the capital's Riyadh City neighborhood. Bin Laden established a currency company (Taba Investments), a trading firm (Laden International), and a large holding company (Wadi al-Aqiq). These firms were involved in legitimate businesses, including airport construction, building roads, growing sunflowers, and even importing bicycles. But Saudi intelligence, which continued to monitor him, knew he also used his al-Hijira (sometimes spelled Al-Hijrah) subsidiary to import explosives under the guise of construction work, the al-Qadurat trucking venture to transport his fighters in and out of the country, and his al-Mubaraka fruit and vegetable farms to provide cover for military training camps.*

While in Sudan, bin Laden had the blessing of a Sorbonne and London University–educated Islamic scholar, Dr. Hassan al-Turabi, who shared bin Laden's dream of creating a unified and pure worldwide Muslim government. Al-Turabi was the spiritual leader to the ruling National Islamic Front, and he convinced the Sudanese government that bin Laden's generosity and Islamic purity were great assets for the

---

*Bin Laden paid $250,000, for instance, for a large parcel of land in Soba, north of Khartoum. It was a training camp whose cover operation was as an agricultural farm.

country (in 1993, bin Laden handed al-Turabi a $2 million check, drawn on one of his personal accounts, to acquire supplies for Afghan Arab veterans in Sudan and elsewhere).[1]

Using Sudan as a safe haven, and influenced by al-Turabi to try and overcome doctrinal differences with other Muslim groups in order to unite against a common enemy, bin Laden attended terror conferences in other countries to discuss ways to cooperate in expelling foreigners from Islamic lands.* He envisioned himself as the director of a clearing-house for Islamic terrorism, which would not only undertake its own operations but would also train and supply far-flung radical groups, weaving homegrown plots into a worldwide crusade. Bin Laden person-ally supported radicals in Jordan, fundamentalists in Eritrea, helped establish the Abu Sayyaf terror gang in the Philippines, and sent money to Pakistani militants through the religious Jamiat Ulema Islamiyya party.[2]

It was during this time that bin Laden merged al Qaeda with Islamic Jihad, the organization run by his friend, the Egyptian doctor, Ayman al-Zawahiri. Bin Laden appointed al-Zawahiri as his second-in-command, responsible for military operations. Many of al-Zawahiri's Egyptian loy-alists became bin Laden's closest aides.[3] Bin Laden also redoubled the money he provided for his terrorist training camps in Sudan. Those camps quickly attracted new recruits as word of bin Laden's efforts

---

*Conferences on international terror, featuring many of the most militant lead-ers, were somewhat commonplace during the 1990s. During the early 1990s, for instance, after bin Laden resettled in Sudan, he attended several key meetings. From April 25 to 28, 1991, a congress of terror organizations met in Khartoum. The result was the creation of the Popular International Organization (PIO), a council of fifty members, one representative from each of the countries where an Islamic strug-gle against infidels was considered necessary. On October 18, 1991, Iran hosted the International Conference in Support of the Islamic Revolution of the People of Palestine, in Tehran. Four hundred delegates attended, vowing to work with Iranian and Syrian intelligence to cooperate in building secure cells, fighting government security forces, planning operations, and building more powerful weapons. Only three months later, Tehran convened another summit, this one attended by eighty senior leaders of almost two dozen terror organizations. Iranian intelligence urged the representatives to unite in a war of liberation. The keynote speaker, a colonel in Sudanese intelligence, spoke about the necessity of "striking fear into the heart of the West." Although the CIA monitored these conferences as part of their surveil-lance of Syrian and Iranian intelligence, they kept the information compartmental-ized along geographic lines, and did not centralize it into a global terror analysis until the late 1990s.

spread among militant Muslims. There they learned to fire Stinger missiles, wage guerrilla warfare, and build truck bombs, and all the while
were indoctrinated with the goal of jihad against the infidels. They also
were taught to create false passports, and how, when traveling on an
operation, to disguise their Muslim backgrounds by wearing Western
clothes, being clean-shaven, and carrying a pack of cigarettes (strict
Islamic interpretation bans smoking). Ali Mohamed, the former Green
Beret who was later a government witness in the foiled 1994 plot to
bomb New York City landmarks and tunnels, told investigators that he
instructed volunteers how to establish undetectable sleeper cells that
could be used in operations.[4] Bin Laden regularly visited the camps to
rally the recruits, and to give what had become a standard lecture about
America being the head of a snake. Al Qaeda, he told the recruits, had to
cut off its head.

On December 9, 1992, American troops waded ashore in Somalia, one
of Sudan's neighbors. The U.S. intervention (dubbed Operation Restore
Hope) was part of a United Nations mission to prevent humanitarian aid
from falling into the hands of rival warlords and to get it instead to starv-
ing Somalis. Televised images of the Somali famine had fueled an outcry
for the West to act before a natural catastrophe left tens of thousands
dead. But according to Sudanese who were with bin Laden, he condemned the American operation as a pretext for the U.S. to spread its
influence in the Horn of Africa.[5]*

Bin Laden dispatched Muhammad Atef, the second-in-command of
al Qaeda's military unit, to Somalia to meet with local militants.† Al
Qaeda's Abu Talha taught Somalis how to use mortars. Muhammad

---

*Bin Laden was not alone in his extremist interpretation of American motives.
The Egyptian-based Muslim Brotherhood contended that the Somali mission was a
long-established U.S.-Israeli conspiracy to prevent the popular growth of Islam in
the Horn of Africa. Palestinian militants argued that the move into Somalia was
only a prelude to a full-scale American attack on Sudan.

†Bin Laden was not the only one to provide military assistance to the Somali warlords fighting the U.S. Iran sent some Stinger missiles and some of its own Afghan
Arabs—associated with Tehran's Al-Qud forces—to the region. Senior aides to the
most troublesome Somali warlord, Muhammad Farrah Aidid, attended sessions in
Khartoum where more than a dozen Iranian terror experts helped them develop a
strategy for fighting the Americans in the capital's close quarters:

Odeh, another Afghan veteran, trained Somali units in explosives.[6] Al Qaeda's help was soon evident in Aden, a southern port staging area for U.S. troops, where a bomb killed three and wounded five.

In June 1993, Sudan's spiritual leader, al-Turabi, hosted a special session of the People's Arab and Islamic Conference in Khartoum. U.S. "genocide" against Muslims was publicly condemned. Al-Zawahiri represented bin Laden, while ranking Iranian intelligence officers and other terror leaders met with Aidid and his aides. The CIA now believes that this may have been one of the first conferences in which direct attacks on American soil were discussed (it was about the July 4 series of New York bombings coordinated by Sheikh Rahman that the FBI narrowly averted).[7]*

The U.S., meanwhile, had decided to go beyond the goals of the original humanitarian mission and to try and capture Aidid, the most meddlesome warlord. Radical Muslims saw this as an opportunity to embarrass the U.S. On October 3, 1993, eighteen Americans were killed and seventy-five wounded in fierce firefights in Mogadishu. Hundreds of Somalis were killed.[†]

*After the first World Trade Center blast, Egyptian intelligence informed the CIA that one of their New York–based informants had reported that a terror cell associated with Rahman intended to assassinate Egyptian president Hosni Mubarak during a scheduled April 1993 visit to New York and the U.N. In this instance, the CIA did pass the information to the FBI. While trying to get details on the assassination plot, a New York Muslim informant, Emad Salem, who had been rejected as an informant by the FBI because he was not deemed to be worth the $500 per week that he wanted, told a New York City detective that he had been approached by Rahman's translator and sometime bodyguard to participate in an upcoming string of bombings. The plan called for simultaneous attacks on the United Nations, the Holland and Lincoln tunnels, and the federal building in lower Manhattan. For two months, the Joint Terrorism Task Force monitored Salem's movements, having fitted him with a body recorder. On June 24, the FBI raided a garage where five suspected terrorists were mixing bombs. In three other simultaneous raids, the FBI arrested another three cell members. Among those arrested were Hampton-El, the black Muslim the FBI had under investigation for gun running. He had been under surveillance as early as 1989 when the FBI followed him and others to local gun ranges with a small arsenal of weapons. But the probe had been stopped when the Bureau's chiefs thought there was too little progress to justify its cost and time.

†The battle was a widely publicized setback for American forces and cast a pall over many subsequent Clinton administration decisions concerning the use of military force. American intelligence did not learn of al Qaeda's role in the ambush for several years. The firefight was later popularized in the best-selling book, and a movie of the same name, Black Hawk Down.

Bin Laden would not publicly admit to his role in Somalia for another four years.[8] What was critical to bin Laden was not taking credit, but rather what he learned from America's reaction to the Mogadishu battle. President Clinton, convinced there was no public support for continued military action in Somalia, withdrew all troops almost immediately. The signal to bin Laden was that the U.S. was not strong and that it would run at the first sight of real warfare. It was clear that Americans did not have any stomach for casualties, something Muslims had noted in 1983 when Ronald Reagan had responded to the deaths of 241 marines in the Beirut barracks truck bombing by withdrawing U.S. troops from Lebanon.

"We believe that the United States is a great deal weaker than Russia," bin Laden later boasted to a Pakistani journalist for the newspaper *Dawn*. "We have learned that from our brothers who fought in Somalia. They saw wonders about the weakness, feebleness and cowardliness of the U.S. soldier. Hardly eighteen of them were killed, when they fled in the dark of the night, despite the uproar that was created worldwide about the New World Order."[9] To a reporter from Britain's *Independent* newspaper, bin Laden praised Allah for empowering a holy war to defeat the Soviet army in Afghanistan, and said, "Now we ask God to use us one more time to do the same to America, to make it a shadow of itself. We also believe that our battle against America is much simpler than the war against the Soviet Union, because some of our mujahedeen who fought in Afghanistan also participated in operations against the Americans in Somalia—and they were surprised at the collapse of the American morale. This convinced us that the Americans are a paper tiger."[10]

Bin Laden, in concluding that the United States could be terrorized into abandoning a Muslim country, had made a significant mistake in judgment that would lead to grandiose operations like 9/11.

CHAPTER 8

"WHO THE HELL IS SEEING HIM?"

W hen the Clinton administration took power in January 1993, many around the new president, even veterans from Jimmy Carter's tenure, were hopeful about overcoming Washington's traditional pitfalls. "Clinton's transition team declaimed against turf battles," said former House Judiciary counsel James H. Rowe. "And it was a true measure of their liberalism that they believed intelligence infighting, like human nature, or government itself, could be overcome, or improved, if only certain 'infrastructures' were 'reinvented.' "[1]

While the new administration's intentions were admirable, the problem was that foreign policy was low on the presidential agenda. That was evident even in the way the CIA director was selected by Clinton. His choice, James Woolsey, was a conservative Democrat and, like Clinton, a former Rhodes Scholar, and an attorney. He had served as undersecretary of the navy in the Carter administration, then as a U.S. arms negotiator in Geneva before returning to his private Washington law practice. Although Woolsey had endorsed Clinton early in the campaign, he had only met him twice, once at Washington power broker Pamela Harriman's house in late 1991, and the second time early in the presidential campaign when he had accompanied Indiana congressman Lee Hamilton to Little Rock to brief Clinton and Gore on some European policy issues, primarily Bosnia.

A few days before Christmas 1992, Woolsey received a call around 9:00 P.M. from the soon-to-be secretary of state, Warren Christopher.

"Could you come to Little Rock and talk to Clinton about the CIA job?"

"I thought," Woolsey told me, "that he wanted me to talk to Clinton about who I thought should get the director's job."[2]

"Can I come after New Year's?" Woolsey asked. He was exhausted from managing a multibillion-dollar lawsuit and looked forward to a few days of rest with his family.

"No, I think you better come today."

Woolsey took an 11:00 P.M. flight and arrived in Little Rock at 12:30 A.M. Despite the late hour, Clinton was waiting for him, and the two met alone for nearly an hour.

"He was a great, charming guy," recalled Woolsey. "And of that hour, we spent about ten minutes talking about the CIA. The rest of the time we basically shared stories about growing up in Arkansas and Oklahoma. I left that meeting still without a clue that he was considering me for the CIA post."[3]

By the next morning at 9:00 there could be no doubt that Woolsey was being considered for some appointment. He was told to visit Webb Hubbell, a close Clinton confidant and law partner of Hillary Clinton's. Hubbell had a file on Woolsey and flipped through it during their thirty-minute meeting. He kept asking Woolsey whether he had any conflicts of interest or skeletons in his closet.

Back at his hotel, Woolsey got a call from a campaign staffer. It was an abrupt call. "There's going to be a press conference at 12:30. We'll pick you up at noon."

Woolsey called Christopher. "They're picking me up in twenty minutes. Is it to be director of the CIA?"

"Yes," Christopher confirmed.

"No one has asked me," Woolsey said. "And I've never said yes."

Christopher was silent for a moment. "Don't worry. Come to the press conference and we'll straighten it out."

"I think I'd like to know before that," replied Woolsey.

Christopher said he would call Clinton and get back in touch. A few minutes later the phone rang. It was Christopher.

"Yes, that's what he wants," Christopher told Woolsey.

"Okay, I guess."[4]

A limo picked up Woolsey and brought him across town to join the Clintons, most of his future national security team, including Madeleine Albright and Les Aspin, and also advisor George Stephanopoulos and press secretary Dee Dee Myers. Twenty minutes before the press conference, Stephanopoulos and Myers began reviewing possible questions.

"What if someone says you are just a bunch of Carter administration retreads?" asked Stephanopoulos.

"I was in the Bush administration," Woolsey chimed in.

"I didn't know you were in the Bush administration, Admiral," said a genuinely surprised Myers.

"I'm not an admiral," said Woolsey, not missing a beat. "I never got above captain."

Myers looked at Stephanopoulos and then shook her head. "Oh, really? Well, we better change the press release fast." She scurried from the room.[5]

If Woolsey thought that little attention was paid to him and the CIA during the selection process, once he was confirmed and took over at Langley, he quickly discovered that the administration's lack of interest now extended to what the Agency was doing.

"Clinton was just all domestic the first couple of years," recalled Woolsey. "The top lists were health care, education, NAFTA. Foreign policy and counterintelligence just weren't on the president's radar."

The three foreign policy issues that the Clinton administration had to confront under Woolsey's tenure at the CIA—1992 to 1994—were Bosnia, Haiti, and Somalia. "Each one became part of the policy agenda," said Woolsey, "but not because we chose them, but rather they were things that couldn't be avoided.* No one wanted to address them until they couldn't be ignored. The directive from the White House was unmistakable—'the United States should look decisive but don't get anyone killed.' "[†]

On January 1, 1993, the CIA was focused, however, on a very dif-

---

*Woolsey said that Clinton thought that Haiti's president, Jean-Bertrand Aristide, was "the Thomas Jefferson of Haiti. He just loved him. But we knew at the CIA that Aristide had taken psychotropic drugs, prescription, but nevertheless, he relied on these. And he had killed people. Not a lot, but still he had killed people. He wasn't an angel, but no one in the White House wanted to hear any bad reports about him."

†The lack of focus on foreign policy meant that sometimes the Clinton administration flip-flopped on key issues, such as how to deal with Saddam Hussein, Iraq, and the U.N. sanctions in place since the first Gulf War. President Bush had repeatedly insisted he would not lift U.N. sanctions on Iraq until Hussein was removed from power. But on January 13, 1993, President-elect Clinton surprised many Iraq watchers when he signaled in a *New York Times* interview that he might be ready to change U.S. policy. Clinton told the *Times* that he would not insist on Saddam's removal as a condition for normalizing relations with Iraq. "I am not obsessed with the man," said Clinton. "I always tell everybody I am a Baptist. I believe in deathbed

ferent foreign policy threat than the three that concerned the White House. A group of fundamentalist Islamic clerics from Egypt, Afghanistan, Algeria, Sudan, and Iran issued a communiqué that was joined by Libya's Muammar Qaddafi and Iraq's Saddam Hussein. It ominously announced a jihad against all Christian nations, urging devout Muslims worldwide to strike out against corrupting Western and Christian influence. During the next few weeks there was a dramatic upsurge in Islamic violence. Busloads of tourists were shot in Egypt and archaeological sites there were bombed. In Latin America, Iranian-backed terrorists blew up dozens of American-owned oil pipelines. Moderate Muslim opponents to the surge in Islamic militancy were assassinated in Turkey and Italy. In Langley, two CIA employees were killed and another two wounded, and a contract worker to the Agency was also wounded. The gunman, who fled in the pandemonium after the attack, was identified as Mir Aimal Kansi, a twenty-eight-year-old Pakistani immigrant who was angry about the U.S. treatment of Muslims in Bosnia and U.S. policy in the Middle East. He had recently boasted to coworkers and acquaintances that he would "make a big statement" by shooting up the White House, the Israeli embassy, or the CIA.[7]*

---

conversions. If he wants a different relationship with the United States and the United Nations, all he has to do is change his behavior."[6]

There was immediate criticism that Clinton's suggestion might be perceived by Washington's Gulf War allies and Arab states as weakness. On the day the *Times* article ran, Clinton used a press conference to claim the paper had never asked him about normalizing relations with Saddam and that he was "astonished" it had come to the conclusion that he would consider doing so based on his remarks. "There is no difference between my policy and the policy of the present administration," he insisted.

Immediately after the press conference, in the face of transcripts showing the *Times* had specifically asked him about normalizing relations with Iraq, Clinton reversed himself through spokesman George Stephanopoulos. "He inadvertently forgot that he had been asked that specific question about normalization and he regrets denying that it was asked," said Stephanopoulos.

*Another sign of how different security responses were before the 9/11 attacks to a terror incident like the shooting at the CIA is how easily the shooter, Kansi, was able to leave the country, without making much of an effort to hide his escape. He walked into a small Arab-owned convenience store, the Crescent Groceries, only a few miles from CIA headquarters, eight hours after the attack. He asked the owner, Mohammad Yousaf, if the store sold airline tickets. Yousaf, also a Pakistani immigrant, later told authorities the request did not seem strange to him. Although a

And finally, on February 26, Islamic terrorists detonated a bomb at the World Trade Center in the hope of bringing it down.

That explosion killed six and wounded more than one thousand New Yorkers. Clinton had only been in office thirty-eight days, and his public response was low-key, urging citizens not to "overreact." Privately, he ordered the Justice Department to make the case its top priority. But Janet Reno, who was nominated after the Zoë Baird fiasco, was still awaiting Senate approval. The Justice Department, meanwhile, was run by a lame-duck Bush holdover. At Reno's Senate hearings, the World Trade Center attack was not mentioned by the senators nor by the nominee. And the FBI was headed by William Sessions, who would soon be forced out.

But fortunately, the agents in the field seemed oblivious to the political turmoil. The day after the blast, James Fox, the assistant director in charge of the FBI's New York office, and Neil Herman, who ran the FBI-directed Joint Terrorism Task Force (JTTF),* convened a meeting of

---

description fitting Kansi had been put out by the police, Yousaf said it was so general that he never thought the calm young man in front of him was the terrorist. So he called an acquaintance at another store he owned in Arlington, Virginia, and that associate called a travel agency, Super Travel, also owned by a Pakistani immigrant. The cost for the one-way ticket to Pakistan was $740, and Kansi paid in cash and promised to return the following day. When he showed up at Yousaf's store the next afternoon, he had no luggage. "I don't need anything," he told Yousaf, who then drove him to the airport. As investigators were passing out thousands of sketches of a dark-haired killer described by witnesses, Kansi—who bore a striking resemblance to the sketch—boarded a TWA flight at 5:00 P.M. without raising any suspicions at the airport about his one-way, cash ticket or his lack of luggage.

Kansi, who had fought the Soviets in Afghanistan during the 1980s, was from a prominent family in Pakistan's outer provinces. The FBI's manhunt resulted in his arrest in Pakistan nearly four and a half years later. In November 2002, he was put to death by lethal injection in Virginia after being convicted of murder in the CIA ambush. When his body was returned to Pakistan for burial, nearly thirty thousand protesters joined the funeral procession, chanting, "Death to America! Death to Israel!" Kansi is now a hero among jihadists, and the anger over his execution is used to motivate and recruit new terrorists.

*By the time of the World Trade Center bombing, the JTTF had expanded to fifty investigators. Besides the FBI and New York police, by 1993 the JTTF also included representatives from the Marshals Service; the Bureau of Alcohol, Tobacco, and Firearms; the New York State Police; the Port Authority police; the Federal Aviation Administration; the Immigration and Naturalization Service; the Secret Service; and the State Department. Initially, the JTTF was suspicious that the bombing was the work of Balkan extremists. A bomb had been found in front of the American

senior representatives from a dozen government agencies that marked
the beginning of one of the largest criminal probes ever. Seven hundred
agents nationwide were assigned to TRADEBOM, as the FBI dubbed the
investigation. A team of thirty technicians worked in shifts around
the clock at the bomb site. The major break came quickly. Two days after
the bombing, while digging through the tangle of still dangerous rubble
from the blast zone, FBI investigators pulled out a twisted portion of
metal containing a vehicle identification number (VIN). Because the
forged steel axle was so damaged, the investigators correctly assumed
that it had to have been placed almost directly over the bomb at the time
of the explosion, and therefore belonged to the vehicle that had contained the explosive.[9]

The VIN belonged to a Ryder van that had been rented at a car rental
agency in Jersey City. It was likely stolen, investigators assumed, but
when they checked the records at the rental agency, they found it had
been hired by someone named Mohammed Salameh, with a local
address. The understandable assumption was that Salameh must be a
phony name, but they were proven wrong when they ran it through the
FBI's database. Salameh was listed as someone who had, a few years earlier, demonstrated on behalf of a convicted terrorist.[10]

Then the staff at the car rental agency further startled investigators by
informing them that Salameh had returned to the office to claim the cash
deposit he had left for the van. However, since Salameh said the van had
been stolen, the agency would not refund his deposit until he returned
with a police report. He promised to come back in a couple of days.*

---

embassy in Zagreb, the Croatian capital, only five hours before the Trade Center
attack. A call from someone identifying himself as the "Serbian Liberation Front"
claimed responsibility within minutes of the Trade Center explosion. And the U.S.
had just recently announced plans to send aid supplies to Bosnia, a decision that had
greatly angered the Serbs. It would take months before the JTTF would realize that a
group of militant black Muslims it had been investigating regarding gun running
and explosives prior to the Trade Center bombing, had links to some of the Arab suspects involved in the attack, including even Sheikh Rahman. However, in December
1992, less than two months before the Trade Center attack, the FBI had decided that
the JTTF investigation was taking too long and was unlikely to produce any substantive results. It was halted.[8]

*Incredibly, Salameh needed the money to make his escape from America. After
the bombing, he had used the little money he had to buy a $65 infant's ticket on
Royal Jordanian Airlines to fly to Amman on March 5 (a week after the attack). The

When he did, on the morning of March 4, the FBI was waiting for him.*

In the wake of the first World Trade Center attack, even the CIA and FBI were temporarily enthusiastic about sharing information. The Bureau set up a hot line to the CIA, and under Woolsey's encouragement asked the Agency's help in tracking down the culprits. FBI agents were able to use CIA assets in Israel and Egypt, and the CIA itself followed the money trail in Germany.[11]

Using materials seized from Salameh's apartment and tracing his phone call history, the case began coming together. Soon, the ringleader was identified as a half-Pakistani, half-Palestinian, Ramzi Yousef. Yousef had entered the United States in 1992 with a twenty-six-year-old Palestinian, Ahmad Ajaj. The two had met at a terrorist training camp in Afghanistan. They arrived at New York's JFK Airport on a flight from Pakistan, traveling on one British and one Swedish passport, both of which had been stolen from their owners the previous year. Yousef had only a small carry-on bag, while Ajaj had three large suitcases. When Customs checked his bags, they found six manuals about making bombs and Molotov cocktails, one that included diagrams about constructing firearms silencers, and videotapes on suicide bombings. Customs inspectors also found two stolen passports and other identification documents from Middle Eastern countries in the suitcases. At the same time that his suitcases were searched, Customs determined that Ajaj's Swedish passport was a fake. He was detained for illegal entry and was in jail at the time of the World Trade Center bombing the following year. As for Yousef, he had given the British passport on which he had left Pakistan to Ajaj, and it was one of those found in the suitcase. Meanwhile, he presented the INS with an Iraqi passport and asked for political asylum. Although the two men had been traveling together, the INS did not auto-

---

plane stopped in Amsterdam on the way to Jordan, which, even though it was a stopover, required Salameh to get a Dutch visa, something he couldn't do without a ticket. So he bought the child's ticket to get the visa, and then intended to use the refund on the van's security deposit to upgrade to an adult ticket.

*"Salameh was not one of the brightest people in the world," recalled a grateful Neil Herman, the FBI head of the Joint Terrorism Task Force. But a problem caused by that easy break in the case was that the Bureau might have later underestimated the threat posed by Islamic terrorists. It was believed by many that no movement that relied on someone as dumb as Salameh could be a serious problem.

matically bar Yousef's entry. Instead, he was taken to a room for an interview. But the waiting room was so overcrowded with new arrivals seeking asylum that Customs decided merely to photograph and finger-print him, and give him a date to appear in court to plead his case. Yousef never kept the court date. By the time the FBI fingered him in the World Trade Center case, he had left the country.*

Nidal Ayyad, who obtained the chemicals for the bomb, was arrested on March 10, and Ahmad Ajaj, who had given advice on building the explosive, was picked up only a week after being released from prison for illegally entering the country. But Yousef was not the only one who ini-tially got away. Egyptian Mahmud Abouhalima was traced to his native country, to which he had escaped. There were also some mistakes. When the FBI found Abdul Yasin, a graduate student at City College of New York, he convinced them he was innocent and had only taught Yousef to drive the Ryder van, but without any knowledge of the terror attack. After the FBI left, he fled to Jordan, and then to Baghdad. (A $5 million reward is still pending for Yasin.)

As the hunt for Yousef continued, investigators realized that all the suspects had one thing in common: they were Afghan Arabs, men who had fought during the 1980s with the mujahedeen in Afghanistan against the Soviets. At the CTC, there was concern that some of the fighters trained by the CIA during the Afghan war might now have turned their radicalism against the United States. Woolsey ordered that the Agency immediately review its intelligence files on all Afghan Arabs.

On April 13, a little over a month after the Trade Center bombing, Woolsey flew to Cairo with nearly two dozen CIA Middle East experts. There they reviewed Egyptian intelligence files on hundreds of Afghan Arabs.[12] Another CIA team arrived in Pakistan to meet with intelligence officers of the Federal Investigation Agency (the Pakistani equivalent of the FBI). The Pakistanis provided information that Afghan Arabs might be in the largely uncontrollable frontier region along the border of their country and Afghanistan.

In the middle of the World Trade Center investigation, halfway around the world in Kuwait, another bomb plot was under way. On April 10,

*Later, while in jail, Ajaj asked his court-appointed attorney (from the prestigious New York firm Willkie, Farr & Gallagher) to petition the federal court in Brooklyn to allow him to have his confiscated "reading" material returned. The judge agreed, and incredibly the government returned some of Ajaj's bomb-making manuals and videos to him, and he in turn gave them to Ramzi Yousef before he fled America.

1993, agents of the Iraqi Intelligence Service handed the keys of a Toyota Land Cruiser that was packed with plastic explosives to a specially recruited team. On April 13, under cover of darkness, these operatives began a secret trek across the southern Iraqi desert toward the Kuwaiti frontier. Their target was the just retired ex-president, George Bush, who was arriving with his family in Kuwait for a triumphant tour of the liberated land. On the day Bush was due to arrive, the Kuwaitis intercepted the explosive-laden Land Cruiser and rounded up the conspirators. The Kuwaitis kept the assassination attempt secret from the Bushes and the U.S. government for the duration of their trip. The Clinton administration later briefly balked at Kuwait's claim that Iraq was behind the assassination attempt. But a thorough probe by the Federal Bureau of Investigation and the Central Intelligence Agency, confirmed by detailed confessions from two key Iraqi operatives, sealed the case.[13]*

While the FBI and CIA investigated the plot to kill the former president, the finger pointing between them continued over which was responsible for failing to detect the threat against the World Trade Center. And each blamed the other for not quickly locating Ramzi Yousef.

Neil Herman, the FBI agent in charge of the Joint Terrorism Task Force, later said, "Back then, I don't think the CIA could have found a person in a bathroom. Hell, I don't think they could have found the bathroom. . . . They didn't have any information."[14] When a leading federal prosecutor, Gil Childers, visited CIA headquarters at Langley shortly after the first Trade Center attack, he was startled to discover how little the CIA agents knew. They kept asking Childers for information. "We talked in generalities for about an hour or so," recalled Childers, "but it was clear to me they didn't have a clue. Afterwards, when we got outside the building, [my colleagues and I] just looked at each other and shook our heads. It was obvious if we had to rely on these guys to find Yousef, we were in trouble."[15]

---

*Saddam Hussein and others in his inner circle were fearful that the unmasking of the plot might be construed as an act of war and give the U.S. another reason to go to war with Iraq. The problem that ensued was the difference between Clinton's forceful rhetorical reaction to Saddam's attempt to kill Bush and his weak military reaction. "The Iraqi attack against President Bush was an attack against our country and against all Americans," said Clinton. But to retaliate for an attempt to kill a former president, Clinton ordered U.S. warships in the Red Sea and Persian Gulf to fire twenty-three cruise missiles at a seven-building complex in Baghdad that housed the Iraqi Intelligence Service. The missiles were timed to hit at 2:00 on a Sunday morning, when nobody was there.

Congressional critics demanded better collaboration inside the intelligence community. Representative Charles Schumer proposed forcing the FBI and CIA to cooperate, including ways to forge closer links for sharing data in foreign capitals. Senators Joseph Biden and Orrin Hatch particularly criticized Woolsey for not having done more toward reorganizing the Agency, the way it gathered information on terrorists, and how it worked with the FBI on counterintelligence. (Congress should not have been so quick to criticize the intelligence agencies. In September, six months after the attack, when the Congressional Task Force on Terrorism published its list of several dozen "prominent figures in Islamist terrorism," bin Laden was not even on it.)[16]

Woolsey felt that the problem was not as simple as merely sharing intelligence with the Bureau. Sometimes the CIA passed along information and it sat idly in the FBI's files. A few months after the World Trade Center blast, for example, the CIA had telephone and satellite intercepts that led its analysts to conclude that two Sudanese intelligence officers, serving under the cover of United Nations diplomats, might have directed some of the Islamic extremists in the bomb plot. Woolsey gave the information to the FBI, which did not follow up.

Indeed, the FBI was concerned immediately with those physically responsible for the bombing, not who might have influenced them. And as for the hunt for the so-called mastermind, Ramzi Yousef, FBI director Sessions and the State Department arranged a $2 million reward for his capture. Wanted posters were printed and distributed throughout Asia. Nearly forty thousand matchboxes bearing Yousef's photo were dropped over the Pakistan-Afghanistan border. Instead of producing a solid lead, however, the Bureau was flooded with con artists hoping to bag the reward money.[17]

The failure to make quick progress on Yousef's whereabouts hurt Sessions's already weak standing in Washington. Under his leadership, the FBI's Intelligence Division had been largely emasculated,* the FBI had started subcontracting out background investigations it was supposed to conduct, and Sessions had waffled on setting firm rules for when and

*In 1992, Sessions had transferred 1,300 agents from the Intelligence Division to more mainstream work. The Intelligence Division was in an uproar and warned Sessions that the KGB reform he touted was a sham. Some in the Bureau's counterintelligence corps considered Sessions's cuts almost treasonous and launched their own unprecedented investigation of their boss.

how the Bureau could extract terrorists overseas. On July 19, 1993, Clinton fired Sessions, having come to the conclusion that he was a well-intentioned, but mostly inept, director. Louis J. Freeh, a wiry, boyish former FBI agent from New York and assistant U.S. attorney, was appointed director. But Freeh had little chance to focus on terrorism, because the day after Sessions was fired the FBI was engulfed in the investigation over whether Clinton aide Vince Foster's death was suicide or murder.

Nine days after he took over at the FBI, Freeh did have, however, an unexpected victory in the war on terror, and this time it was with the rare help of the CIA. The CIA had been monitoring a Palestinian terrorist, Ali Rezaq, who had been convicted in the 1985 hijacking of an Egyptian airliner in which Americans and Jews had been separated from the other passengers and then shot. Although Rezaq had been convicted by a Maltese court, he was released under strong pressure from Libya's Qaddafi. The CIA pleaded with Ghana to hold Rezaq when he stopped there, but the plans fell apart at the last minute. Rezaq, meanwhile, flew on to Nigeria for safe haven. CTC kept Rezaq under surveillance until an FBI team nabbed him in Lagos as he boarded a plane. When he appeared a day later in a Washington courtroom, the operation was hailed as a new phase of CIA and FBI teamwork.

But Woolsey felt the problems posed by Islamic terrorists were not going to be resolved through a single extraction. He favored a much more aggressive effort to fight Islamic extremists, but seemed out of step with the rest of the administration. He discovered, for instance, that there was no White House interest in conducting a wide-ranging probe to determine whether the Trade Center bombing was state-sponsored.[18] Woolsey and some of the Agency's leading analysts thought they had uncovered clues that might link Ramzi Yousef to Iraq and Saddam Hussein. But when he ran that intelligence past others on the National Security staff, he quickly heard back that the White House had no interest in pursuing those leads. When Jim Fox, the FBI agent who supervised the Bureau's Trade Center investigation, told reporters that he thought there could be Iraqi sponsorship of the plot, U.S. Attorney Mary Jo White called him and asked that he immediately stop talking to the media about that possibility.[19]*

---

*Laurie Mylroie, an advisor on Iraq to the Clinton campaign and an adjunct fellow at the American Enterprise Institute, has made the argument for linking Saddam and

"There was no desire to confront Saddam," Woolsey said. "I would not be surprised to know that the judicial inquiry into the World Trade Center bombing was constrained by a policy decision from the White House. The idea that the evidence might eventually implicate Iraq and force the United States to act was something no one in the White House wanted to even contemplate. The idea of body bags on the evening news was a frightening thought to them. 'Let's not have any bad news' was their directive."

It had taken Woolsey nearly a year as the CIA's director to discover that sometimes the White House seemed more concerned about public relations than substantive agendas, at least when it came to foreign policy and counterintelligence.

"The White House just viewed foreign issues as distractions from their domestic agenda," Woolsey recalled, "and didn't want to be bothered by what we had to talk about. Clinton is very bright and very impressive on a first meeting. But over time I came to conclude that he was 90 percent concerned about the PR and only 10 percent substantive, at least in dealings with the CIA."[20]

By the summer of 1993, Woolsey was feeling completely left out of the administration's decisions on important issues. The CIA not only did not seem to be part of Clinton's focus, but received virtually no attention in planning or strategy. Moreover, Clinton probably relied less on CIA analysis and recommendations than any other president. But at a luncheon with Defense Secretary Les Aspin, Woolsey discovered that the cold shoulder from the White House was not just directed toward the CIA. Woolsey and Aspin had known each other since the early 1970s, and they spoke frankly when they met.

"Do you see the president?" Woolsey asked Aspin.

"No."

"Neither do I."

"Do you think Chris [Secretary of State Warren Christopher] is?" Woolsey asked.

Iraq to the first World Trade Center attack. In her 2000 book, *Study of Revenge*, which has a foreword by Woolsey, she contends that the bombing was "an Iraqi intelligence operation with the Moslem extremists as dupes." She relies largely on the Pakistani identity used by Ramzi Yousef in the fake passport he used in fleeing the U.S. It belonged to a Pakistani national who had worked in Kuwait and vanished at the time of Iraq's 1990 invasion. Mylroie contends that Yousef was really a Pakistani working for Iraqi intelligence and that the passport link proves this.

"No, he's not."

"Don't you think it weird we never get together?"

The two men fell silent for a moment. Then Aspin mumbled, almost more to himself than anyone in particular, "I wonder who the hell is seeing him?"[21]

The isolation of the CIA director from the White House was common knowledge in political circles, and morale at the CIA, which had not been high at the start of the new administration—on the heels of the Banco Nazionale del Lavoro scandal—had fallen even further.

Finally, in early October, Woolsey was summoned to a priority National Security Council meeting on problems in Somalia over the deteriorating military effort to capture the Somali warlord Muhammad Aidid and obtain the release of a captured U.S. ranger. The meeting was called hastily and included most of Clinton's inner security circle. Besides Woolsey and the president, there was National Security Advisor Anthony Lake and his deputy, Sandy Berger; Defense Secretary Les Aspin; Secretary of State Warren Christopher; Admiral David Jeremiah, the vice chairman of the Joint Chiefs of Staff; David Gergen, Clinton's special advisor; and Robert Oakley, the former U.S. ambassador to Somalia and now Clinton's special envoy there. Some who settled in at the secure meeting room were surprised to also see Clinton's press secretary, Dee Dee Myers, and presidential advisor George Stephanopoulos.

"I did a double take," recalls Woolsey, "only because we had been told beforehand not to bring any assistants because the meeting was too sensitive. That meant that I had to leave behind my person who knew Somalia best. I wasn't sure what clearances or contribution Myers and Stephanopoulos might make, but since no one else said anything, neither did I."

The press was allowed in before the meeting for a photo opportunity of Clinton and his national security team. Then the reporters were ushered out and the doors closed. Woolsey was told he had five minutes for a presentation on what the group should know about the current situation in Somalia. He was partway through his presentation when Myers interrupted. She and Stephanopoulos began an earnest discussion about the best way to get a positive spin out of Oakley's upcoming trip and how it might be possible to get all the squabbling parties in Somalia to work together so that the United States could take credit for leaving the country in better condition than when troops arrived a year earlier.

Their discussion continued for twenty minutes. Finally, Woolsey raised his hand.

"Mr. President," he said loudly enough to interrupt, "I have a number of people that understand this country very well. It's had clan warfare for a long time and the chance of these bandits holding together is impossible. It's certainly not going to change because we sent them some food or went after one warlord."

There was a moment when no one said anything. Then David Gergen chimed in. "Well, if what Jim says is true, then all we've discussed is a waste of time."

Silence again for a moment. And then Myers and Stephanopoulos picked up with their earlier discussion as if Woolsey's remark had not been heard.

"I realized then," Woolsey told me, "that I had introduced a substantive break into the middle of a PR meeting. It was as if I had made a rude noise, and it seemed people just thought it was inappropriate."[22]

"The issue, Jim," Stephanopoulos said to Woolsey, "is how do we get the press off of dead rangers?"[23]

When Woolsey returned to Langley and told others about the meeting, most just shook their heads. The Somalia analysts were particularly downbeat. "It's difficult when your job is gathering all the information so that political leaders can make an informed decision," says Woolsey, "and you suddenly realize they don't care what you gather."[24]

In his two years as director of the CIA, Woolsey had only two semiprivate meetings with Clinton. "Even the invitation for Sue [Woolsey's wife] and I for the White House Christmas party arrived about two days after the party was over," remembers Woolsey. "I was on the D list."[25]

Ostracized from the White House and not part of the Clinton inner circle, Woolsey turned instead to the bureaucratic obstacles that had hindered the Agency in its long, contentious history with the FBI.[26] His efforts were initially stymied because it was four months before Janet Reno was finally confirmed as attorney general by the Senate. Soon after her appointment, Woolsey broke protocol and announced changes that allowed CIA agents to collect intelligence for criminal prosecutions. By the close of 1993, agents had helped on broad investigations into the Sicilian Mafia and the Cali cartel. But collaboration was not always possible. There were several instances—the specifics are still classified—in which the CIA fought to keep the identity of one of its assets in place when the FBI was only interested in investigating and prosecuting that very same asset.

"I learned pretty quickly," recalls Woolsey, "that there are often cross-purposes and the subcultures of each agency don't mesh that well together."[27]

The matter that would bring an end to Woolsey's CIA tenure was a tug-of-war between the Agency and FBI over the question of whether the CIA had been penetrated by a high-ranking Soviet mole. The agent's name was Rick Ames. Ames, who had risen in three decades to become the chief counterintelligence officer for the Soviet Europe Division, had been raising suspicion at the CIA since at least 1991, when there were mixed results on a periodically administered polygraph. But the CIA did not pass along its suspicions about Ames to the FBI until 1993, when the Bureau finally opened a formal investigation. After it saw the Ames file, the FBI was furious. The CIA had violated several earlier agreements it had with the Bureau to share, in a timely manner, all suspicions about its own agents. And the FBI was particularly incensed that it took nearly two years to receive the results of Ames's polygraph, a test the Bureau judged as not mixed, but showing Ames had clearly failed. Freeh pushed Woolsey for more information, but Woolsey stonewalled, claiming he was worried about exposing CIA secrets in court.

By late 1993, Freeh was so furious with the lack of Agency cooperation that he shut down the Bureau's office at CIC. A December 1993 meeting between the two agencies, intended to broker an agreement on the sharing of information, ended in an angry argument.[28] And while the cause of the division might have been over the Ames investigation, the result was that America's leading counterintelligence agencies were antagonists in the months following the World Trade Center bombing.

At the start of 1994, the Ames case seemed to consume the FBI's counterintelligence efforts. Woolsey and Freeh finally reached a tentative truce, with the Bureau agreeing to concentrate on catching Ames in the physical act of passing secrets to Russian agents. But Ames was not easy to nab. In February, when Ames scheduled a business trip to Russia, Freeh worried that he would take it as a chance to permanently defect. So on February 21, Freeh decided that he might as well quit the pretense of interagency cooperation. The day before Ames was scheduled to depart, the FBI arrested him and his wife.

Publicly, the CIA and FBI presented the Ames arrest as a model of interagency cooperation. Behind the scenes, both Woolsey and Freeh were infuriated with each other. Bob Bryant, the director of the FBI's Intelligence Division, told the Senate Intelligence Committee only a month after the Ames arrest that the FBI had conducted an extensive review and discovered that the CIA had failed to cooperate in at least a dozen significant cases of espionage since 1991.[29] (The FBI would be even more infuriated when it later discovered that Ames had seriously compromised the Bureau by telling the Soviets what the FBI knew about them.)

The CIA was under fire. No matter how Woolsey blustered, there was no denying that the CIA had hindered the FBI on the Ames case. And behind the scenes, FBI officials pushed some senior members of the Senate Intelligence Committee to come down hard on the CIA.[30] Senator Dennis DeConcini, the chairman of the committee, kicked off a public call for Woolsey to institute strict accountability within the Agency. The National Security Council reviewed the Ames case to determine how such bickering could be stopped in future joint investigations. In trying to sift through the conflicting accounts presented by CIA and FBI agents, one NSC staffer remarked that the two agencies were "acting like two teenagers."[31] The NSC eventually sided with the Bureau and floated a proposal to create a National Counterintelligence Center, run by a senior FBI official, who would report directly to the NSC. The CIA would still retain foreign counterintelligence. Woolsey reluctantly agreed to the proposal, but only because he thought if he did not, Congress would get in the act and cede all of the Agency's counterintelligence work to the FBI.[32]

But Woolsey's acquiescence to the NSC proposal was not enough to keep Congress at bay. Senator DeConcini, for instance, was so perturbed by what he learned about the CIA's failures in the Ames case that he drafted the Counterintelligence and Security Enhancements Act of 1994. It would have ceded all CIA internal security cases to FBI jurisdiction, meaning that the Bureau would have the run of Agency files. The CIA would be required to tell the FBI of any leaks of secrets, even before any suspects had been identified. Failure to share vital information—as had happened so frequently in the past—would become a felony.

Woolsey went ballistic when he saw a draft of the legislation and, in a dramatic late-evening trip to Capitol Hill, had a shouting match with DeConcini that was witnessed by almost a dozen people.

By October 1994, there were several press stories that Woolsey had had a falling out with the White House. "It was hard to have a falling out," says Woolsey, "since I was never really 'in' in the first place."[33] But he knew his position was vulnerable. He tried to argue against the DeConcini bill publicly, but that only compounded his problems. In an April 19, 1994, appearance on the *Today* show, Woolsey announced, "People should not have the impression that the Ames case is the only major counterintelligence case that they're going to see. They're going to see a number of these over the years to come. And I think all of us are sad."[34]

DeConcini turned Woolsey's own words against him. The following day, in a hastily called press conference and on CNN, the senator attacked Woolsey's appearance as a "diversion from his failure to cooperate with the FBI."[35]

On May 3, both Freeh and Woolsey testified before DeConcini's Senate committee. Both had signed off, the night before, on a final National Security Council compromise that required FBI and CIA agents to train together more closely and to periodically rotate some agents within each organization. Also, an FBI official was put in charge of the counterespionage section at the interagency CIC.

Things went smoothly before the committee until Woolsey again attacked the proposed DeConcini legislation as "unwise" and "badly drafted." DeConcini almost leaped out of his chair, and angrily denounced Woolsey's comments as prime examples of posturing. The senator charged that Woolsey had just illustrated why the FBI and CIA could not get along; each was more concerned about protecting its own bureaucratic turf than in doing the right thing for the country.

Shortly after his testimony on Capitol Hill, Woolsey went to the White House and met with Gore. ("I couldn't get an appointment with the president," he says.) Woolsey asked Gore if the president wanted him to resign. Gore said he didn't know, but would find out.

Two days later Gore called.

"No, he doesn't want you to resign," the vice president said.

"Well, that's good. But is my relationship with him going to change? Is it going to stay like this or get better?"

"It may never change."

"But I never even see him."

"Yes, I know," Gore replied. "I don't know if that will ever be different."[36]

Woolsey asked his family what he should do. They voted for him to leave the CIA. One day after Christmas 1994, Woolsey submitted a letter of resignation to the president.

While the CIA was stumbling over a lack of leadership, a chance to make major inroads into bin Laden's terror network slipped through American hands. In December 1994, INS officials detained Jamal Mohammed Khalifa, a trusted Saudi aide to bin Laden, at the San Francisco airport when they noticed that he was traveling on a fraudulent visa. Khalifa was married to one of bin Laden's daughters and acted as al Qaeda's agent for its fund-raising charities. Some investigators at the FBI wanted Khalifa held, but the INS and State Department overruled their request. Jordan had already convicted Khalifa, in absentia, of financing terrorist bombings, and a death sentence awaited him there. The government deported him to Jordan instead of questioning him. Six months later he was a free man, greeted by jubilant supporters after Jordan's state security court cleared him of all charges for "lack of evidence." (He is free to this day, last spotted in 2000 by U.S. intelligence officials in Yemen, a hotbed of terrorist organizations, where he had founded the militant Islamic Army of Aden.)[37]

And while Woolsey, Freeh, and the Senate Intelligence Committee had fought over the future of the Agency during the second half of 1994, the trail had grown cold on the Trade Center bombing's most wanted fugitive, Ramzi Yousef. During the spring of 1994, Yousef had fled to Thailand where he moved in with a group of Islamic militants. There, he oversaw a plot to bomb the Israeli embassy in Bangkok, but it failed when the driver of the truck packed with a one-ton bomb had a traffic accident only a few hundred yards from the embassy. By the time the Thai police confiscated the truck, and eventually matched Yousef's fingerprints to one on the bomb, he had fled back to Pakistan. In the summer, Yousef moved to Manila, at the behest of bin Laden, to work with Abu Sayyaf (the local Muslim terror group) in attacking Western interests in Southeast Asia. At his Philippine base, he was free and plan-
                    tacks.
                    anted to hear the bad news that the first World Trade Cen-
                    ght just be the beginning," says Woolsey.[38]

CHAPTER 9

JIHAD
IN AMERICA

There was at least one person who was not only willing to hear the bad news, but was himself trying to sound an early warning about Islamic terrorism. Months before the first World Trade Center attack, in December 1992, Steve Emerson had been a staff reporter for CNN. He was in Oklahoma City to cover a press conference for Iran-contra special prosecutor Lawrence Walsh. President Bush had recently pardoned former secretary of state Caspar Weinberger, and Walsh wanted to question the pardon publicly. On Christmas Day, with nothing to do and searching for a place to eat, Emerson wandered past the Oklahoma City Convention Center and noticed a throng of men, in traditional Middle Eastern garb, gathered outside. Realizing there was a convention under way, and with time to kill, he wandered inside the reception hall and discovered a gathering sponsored by a group he had never heard of, MAYA (Muslim Arab Youth Association).

"There were books preaching Islamic Jihad," recalls Emerson, "books calling for the extermination of Jews and Christians, even coloring books instructing children on subjects such as 'How to Kill the Infidel.' "[1]

Emerson was turned away from the hall because he was barred as a non-Muslim from attending. Outside he encountered a small group of recent converts to Islam. After a brief conversation in which he feigned interest in converting, one of them "sponsored" his admission to the convention. His newfound friend sat next to him and translated what the Arab speakers at the podium were saying.

"It was a shocking experience," he remembers.

The speakers included representatives from a Who's Who of radical Arab organizations, including Hamas. They exhorted the crowd to use jihad against Jews and the West. Emerson sat uncomfortably as those assembled around him shouted approval with cries of "Kill the Jews" and "Destroy the West!"[2]

The next day, Emerson called a friend in the FBI and asked if he knew about the Oklahoma conference. His FBI contact did not, but told Emerson that hateful rhetoric was not something the Bureau investigated unless there was also evidence of criminal activity. While the FBI might not have been intrigued at what was happening in Oklahoma City, Emerson was.

His interest was piqued the next month when the two CIA workers were killed outside the Agency's Langley headquarters. Then one month later the World Trade Center was bombed by Ramzi Yousef's cell. That attack was all Emerson needed to decide that the groups he had encountered two months earlier required serious investigation.

He began by learning as much as he could about radical Muslims inside the United States. In a Yemeni grocery store in Brooklyn, he found dozens of paramilitary training videos for Islamic militants, sold openly from a small table. One of the videos, produced by the Islamic Association for Palestine headquartered in Richardson, Texas, was the equivalent of a snuff film, showing the gruesome torture inflicted on Palestinian collaborators just before they were killed. In Texas, Florida, and New York, Emerson discovered that leaders of the radical groups did nothing to hide their activities. In Bridgeview, Illinois, a Chicago suburb, Emerson came across a mosque plastered with Hamas posters and recruiting literature illustrated with automatic weapons and daggers plunged into Jewish hearts wrapped in American flags.*

In June, Islamic terrorists were again front-page news when ten Muslims linked to the blind sheikh were arrested in New York for plotting a day of terror that was to include blowing up the Lincoln and Holland tunnels, the FBI's New York headquarters, and the United Nations.

The FBI might have been able to nab Sheikh Rahman earlier. The Bureau had received information about Rahman's terrorist links in Feb-

---

*Earlier that year, unknown to Emerson, two congregants of that mosque had been arrested in Israel for being Hamas operatives and part of a plot to transfer money from supporters in the United States to terrorist cells in the Middle East.

ruary 1992. It then took almost seven months of internal arguments over the ramifications of investigating a religious leader before head-quarters gave the green light to start an official probe. But even then, the FBI was timid. Although there was loose surveillance on Rahman's bodyguard and driver, the sheikh was never questioned. His offices were never bugged, nor were the phones he used frequently at his two favorite mosques. No subpoenas for records at either mosque, one in Brooklyn and the other in Jersey City, were ever issued.[3]

While Emerson was doing his early research, in September 1993 the first trial of four of the men originally indicted for the February bombing of the World Trade Center began. (Ramzi Yousef and Eyad Ismoil, another conspirator, were then fugitives. They were eventually arrested and went on trial separately in August 1996, before the same judge.) That trial lasted six months, until the following March. All were convicted and each received a 240-year sentence. The prosecution's case was that the Trade Center plot was homegrown among a small group of New York militants and that there was no foreign support for the attack. But prosecutors later told American Enterprise Institute fellow Laurie Mylroie that while there could have been foreign involvement, possibly even the backing of a country like Iraq, "We prosecute individuals. We don't do state sponsorship."[4]

The prosecutors knew that one of the defendants, Ahmad Ajaj, had spent four months in Pakistan before returning to the United States in 1992 with ringleader Ramzi Yousef. When he tried to enter the country, Customs had seized bomb-making manuals and radical videos and other publications in Ajaj's suitcases. At the trial, an English language trans-lation of Ajaj's bomb-making manual was introduced into evidence. But the translation included three fundamental mistakes that obscured potential links between the plotters and al Qaeda. Prosecutors thought the manual was printed in 1982 in Jordan. That was years before bin Laden founded al Qaeda, and in a country with a very small al Qaeda presence. In fact, it was published in 1989—a year after the terror group was formed—and in Afghanistan, the country where bin Laden started the organization. Also, according to the government translation, the manual had the innocuous words "The Basic Rule" on every page. But two separate translations of the document, the most recent done by *The New York Times* in late 2001, demonstrate that the heading is "The Base," the English name for al Qaeda.[5]

Missing critical links between al Qaeda and one of the Trade Center defendants meant that federal prosecutors would not even start a grand jury investigation of bin Laden for another three years.

"Had the government correctly translated the material," says Steve Emerson, "it might have understood that the men who blew up the World Trade Center and bin Laden's group were linked."[6]

And although specific pages of Ajaj's notebooks and bomb-making manuals had been submitted as evidence in the first World Trade Center bombing trial, it took another seven years before prosecutors shared the material with the intelligence community for full translation and exploitation of its information.[7]

In December 1993, ten months after the World Trade Center bombing and in the middle of the federal trial, Emerson attended another public five-day Muslim conference, this one in Detroit. He had thought that the fallout of bad publicity from the World Trade Center bombing might force the most militant groups to go underground or, at the very least, adopt a more moderate tone. Instead, he was surprised to discover that it had emboldened them. At the Detroit conference, representatives were sent from the most radical Arab organizations, including the Muslim Brotherhood, Hamas, and the Palestinian Islamic Jihad. Again, Emerson sat through dozens of fiery speeches urging Muslims to wage jihad against the West. Then, near the close of the five-day program, he was startled to learn that a local FBI agent was about to make an unscheduled appearance. The agent from the Detroit office made some brief remarks about civil rights and then asked if the audience had any questions. He was instantly peppered with hostile queries. One person asked if the agent might give the group advice on shipping weapons overseas to friends. Even in a pre-9/11 environment, it is surprising that such a question would not raise some suspicion with the agent, but evidently it did not. Emerson watched in amazement as the agent matter-of-factly told the assembled radicals that anyone who wanted to send weapons abroad should make certain they were following the guidelines set by the Bureau of Alcohol, Tobacco, and Firearms.

When Emerson later checked with the FBI to determine how it was possible that one of its agents could appear at such an extremist gathering, he was told that the agent had mistakenly believed the group was "some kind of Rotary Club."[8] The FBI protested it could do nothing about such a radical convention, citing bans on blanket surveillance of events or gatherings, rules prohibiting even the gathering of information available from public sources unless there were grounds to officially open individual investigative files, and finally regulations that forbade monitoring groups that operated under religious, civic, civil rights, or charitable monikers.*

The results of Emerson's research went into a PBS documentary, *Jihad in America*, that was broadcast on November 21, 1994. It was a groundbreaking hour of investigative journalism, focusing on issues that most people would not be concerned about for another seven years.

In the documentary, there were video clips, many taken clandestinely, of Muslim conferences, rallies, and fund-raising events, where terror organizations operated openly in the United States. One of those fingered by Emerson was a previously unknown Palestinian engineering professor, Sami al-Arian. The thirty-five-year-old al-Arian, a tenured teacher at Tampa's University of South Florida, was president of the Tampa-based Islamic Committee for Palestine (ICP) and a think tank called the World and Islam Enterprise (WISE). Under al-Arian's direction, both ICP and WISE had raised money for Palestinian causes and had also sponsored repeated appearances in the U.S. of speakers from Hamas and the Islamic Jihad, both Palestinian terror factions dedicated to the destruction of Israel.[9] Abdel Rahman had been one of the ICP's featured speakers. At least two other speakers invited by al-Arian were on the U.S. lists of suspected terrorists.[10]

One of al-Arian's cofounders in the ICP, Khalil Shikaki, was the brother of Islamic Jihad's founder. Some of WISE's members included Ramadan Abdullah Shallah, who in 1995 moved from Tampa to the Middle East, where he promptly took chief command of Islamic Jihad.[11] Another WISE member was Sheikh Rahman.[†]

---

*Despite the 1993 World Trade Center bombing, the FBI had not recognized domestic Islamic militancy as a priority problem. Rashid Baz, an Arab living in New York, opened fire on March 1, 1994, on a van carrying sixteen Hasidic students returning to Crown Heights after a prayer vigil. Baz shot at the van's passenger side, blowing out its windows and striking four students as it was slowly turning on the ramp that leads from the FDR Drive to the Brooklyn Bridge. The FBI classified the incident as simple "road rage" and the Justice Department did not investigate Baz's multiple connections to other militant Muslims in New York for another six years.

†One of al-Arian's and Shallah's assistants at the University of South Florida, Tarik Hamdi, later moved to Virginia where he aided Ziyad Khaleel, a U.S. citizen, who was the official webmaster of Hamas's Internet site. Hamdi helped Khaleel's

In *Jihad in America*, Emerson fingered the ICP as "the primary support group in the United States for Islamic Jihad." Al-Arian was interviewed in the documentary, denying any links to terror and claiming that his fund-raising was only for schools, clinics, and mosques, some run by Hamas, in the Israeli-occupied territories. When Emerson then showed him an Islamic Jihad newspaper that listed al-Arian's address as one of its U.S. offices, he shrugged it off as meaningless. Later in the documentary, Emerson showed video clips of al-Arian at some of the conferences he hosted, whipping the faithful into a frenzy: "We assemble today to . . . pay respects to the march of the martyrs, and to the river of blood that gushes forth . . . and does not extinguish from butchery to butchery, and from martyrdom to martyrdom, from Jihad to Jihad."[13]

After the documentary ran, al-Arian went on a public relations offensive. "I don't regret anything I said on that tape," he told a local Tampa reporter. "But things were taken totally out of context. I was laughing at one point."[14] Al-Arian told anyone who would listen that he, and other prominent Muslim activists shown in the documentary, were victims of a Zionist smear campaign. "It's not secret," al-Arian said. "The backers of this program have clear ties to Israeli intelligence."[15]

The University of South Florida made no effort to cut its ties to al-Arian after the airing of *Jihad in America* or limit the on-campus fund-raising and lecture sponsorship of WISE or ICP. The university president, Betty Castor, told *The Tampa Tribune* that whether the professor or his organizations had connections to foreign terrorism was "beyond the school's ability to determine." Mark Orr, the chairman of the university's Committee for Middle East Studies, told the *Tribune*, "We have no special way of investigating something like that. It's not our problem. As far as I am concerned, he's a bona fide member of our faculty."

The FBI investigated al-Arian and his organizations over the years, even searching WISE's offices in November 1995. But they never had enough information to obtain an indictment. Over time, the well-spoken

---

efforts to provide Osama bin Laden with advanced technology to pursue terrorist activities. Hamdi himself was in direct contact with bin Laden's top lieutenant in Western Europe at that time, a Saudi, Khalid al-Fawwaz. Al-Fawwaz has been in a British jail for the past three years appealing U.S. efforts to extradite him for his role in the 1998 East Africa embassy bombings.[12]

al-Arian became something of a celebrity cause for prominent journalists, academics, and civil rights advocates. Most of them thought that he was being picked on only for expressing his radical views. Nicholas Kristof of *The New York Times* published several sympathetic op-ed pieces defending him.*

Although Emerson won a George Polk Award for his investigative reporting, the Council on American-Islamic Relations (CAIR) blasted the PBS documentary for "prompting more hate crimes" against innocent Muslims, and some radical Islamists named Emerson as an "enemy of Islam," prompting him to seek police protection when death threats flowed in. There was no follow-up in the national media to his groundbreaking work.

One month after *Jihad in America* aired, events in the Philippines—which would later tie directly to 9/11—showed that Emerson was ahead of his time in investigating the growing fundamentalist threat. In Manila, six men had taken a one-month rental on Room 603 in a dilapidated transient hotel called the Josefa. Surrounded by squatter shacks and pawnshops, the men, who appeared to be Muslims to their neighbors, were secretive and would not even let the cleaning women enter

---

*In the wake of 9/11, and the authorization of more aggressive law enforcement tools in the passage of the U.S.A. Patriot Act, federal investigators returned to the al-Arian case. They used the new law to monitor almost every telephone and fax machine related to al-Arian for nearly a decade. Prosecutors believe they can now prove that al-Arian was not the innocent professor he claimed to be, but rather the global chief financial officer, governing Shura Council secretary, and senior North American representative of Palestinian Islamic Jihad. Much of the new evidence came directly from al-Arian's own words, as the FBI taped him regularly communicating with his Middle East–based colleagues in the Palestinian Islamic Jihad command council. He redrafted the last wills and testaments of soon-to-be suicide bombers and made bank transfers to the "martyred" terrorists' wives and children. FBI wiretaps caught him in such diverse activities as attempting to arrange ocean shipments of explosive precursor chemicals from Saudi Arabia to editing and circulating a Palestinian Islamic Jihad press release boasting of responsibility for a bus bombing that killed seven Israelis and a twenty-year-old American girl.

Although many of al-Arian's former defenders fell silent and felt betrayed by him after the fifty-count indictment was released—the University of South Florida successfully fired him—some still rallied to his cause. Ibrahim Hooper of the Council on American-Islamic Relations (CAIR) called the indictment the "Israelization of American policy and procedures," a police state frame-up concocted by the "attack dogs of the pro-Israel lobby." The Arab American Institute derided the charges against al-Arian as "specious." The American-Arab Anti-Discrimination Committee said there was "no evidence" against him.[16]

their room to change the sheets. They kept late hours, and were often spotted hauling large boxes and assorted empty bottles up the six flights of stairs and down the long corridor to their studio.

The men had taken their rental less than a month before Pope John Paul II was due for a five-day visit. The Philippine intelligence agencies, and the Manila police, were concerned that Islamic terrorists could strike at the pope. Their apprehensions were heightened because 1994 had been a year filled with terrorism. Islamic fundamentalists had killed more than one hundred people in fifty attacks in the Philippines, with many targets being Roman Catholic priests. Bombs had exploded in Manila at an American hamburger chain, a movie theater, and on the subway.

The studio rented by the six Muslims had a window that overlooked President Quirino Avenue, one of the streets on which it had been announced the pope would travel in his motorcade.

On the night of January 6, 1995, a week before the pope's arrival, a fire started in Room 603's kitchen and set off the building's alarms.* Firefighters and police raced to the building, but by the time they arrived, the fire had already extinguished itself. They were readying to leave when one policewoman decided at the last moment to walk inside the room in which the fire had started. There she stumbled on a terrorist bomb laboratory, the tiny space crammed with glass beakers and funnels, cans of gasoline, a pair of king-size Welch's grape juice bottles filled with liquid nitroglycerin, gallons of nitrates and acids in metal containers, one completed pipe bomb, and another partially assembled. There were books on chemistry, a shelf of Casio watches that could be used to fashion explosive timers, and large loops of electrical wire. In one corner, a box was stuffed with priests' robes and collars, Bibles, crucifixes, and maps of the pope's planned travels. A cardboard folder contained a

---

*For years, the story has been told that one of the men accidentally started the kitchen fire. A newer account, given by Philippine government officials after the September 11 attacks, was that the police started a fire in order to set off the building's alarms, thereby forcing everyone to evacuate, so they could search Room 603. They had become suspicious, according to Philippine authorities, because of the amount of boxes the men had moved in and their late hours. There is, however, little evidence to support the new government version, and subject to the release of contemporaneous Philippine police records that would prove otherwise, it appears the new explanation is merely an attempt to credit local authorities with having been prescient regarding a potential terror threat.

dozen passports. It took three police vans to carry all the evidence back to headquarters.

One of the confiscated items that police logged into the evidence room that evening was a Toshiba laptop computer. When the police eventually looked at the files on the hard drive, they discovered a series of startling terror plots, from a plan to assassinate the pope to a daring plan to put terrorists simultaneously on a dozen American jumbo jets flying over the Pacific, place homemade bombs aboard them, and blow them up. That plan—code-named "Bojinka" by the plotters—was scheduled to start on January 21, just two weeks from the date of the fire. Another plan found on the laptop was one that called for a terrorist pilot to dive-bomb an airplane into CIA headquarters. Yet another version involved hijacking a large commercial airplane and crashing it into a Washington landmark.*

One of the men who had fled the fire in Room 603 was none other than Ramzi Yousef, the mastermind of the 1993 bombing of the World Trade Center. Another who got away from Manila before the police closed in was Khalid Shaikh Mohammed. Nobody was certain then what role he played, or even that that name, found on the Toshiba laptop, was his real one. What was known at the time was that the twenty-one-year-old Mohammed had lived in Manila for nearly a year and told acquaintances he was a Saudi businessman. Although no one could recall him ever working, he had access to ready cash. He lived in a plush apartment

---

*The idea was to place micro-bombs, small enough to pass easily through airport security, but powerful enough to down an airliner, on the planes. On December 11 of the previous year, the terrorists had tried a practice run with an explosive. They managed to place a contact lens case filled with nitroglycerin under the seat of Philippines Airlines Flight 434 en route to Tokyo. The small explosive, operating with a nine-volt battery and using a Casio watch as a timer, exploded mid-flight. Although it blew a hole in the fuselage, killed the innocent Japanese passenger who had the misfortune of sitting on top of it, and tore through the aileron cables that controlled the wing flaps, the pilot skillfully managed to make an emergency landing. The test run, however, demonstrated to the terror cell that it worked. In 1995, the FBI interviewed Abdul Hakim Murad, one of Yousef's accomplices in the Philippines. It was Murad who told investigators that he had been involved in the suicide plane mission that was to be directed at the CIA. Murad also volunteered that he had attended four American flight schools in preparation for his mission. That, unfortunately, never caused anyone in the FBI to do a further check of U.S. flight schools for possible attendees with terror links, or to add flight schools to a list of places to regu- larly check for suspicious activity.

in an upscale neighborhood, dressed well in expensive Western clothes, and was a frequent visitor to Manila's adult bars and red-light district. Mohammed even rented a helicopter once to buzz a building in order to impress a girl he wanted to bed. But the Filipino police never managed to figure what his tie was to the other men in Room 603. Not, at least, until after September 11.*

*Investigators in several countries kept coming across Mohammed—or one of twelve aliases he used—repeatedly. Some reports say that Ramzi Yousef is his nephew. In 1996, he was indicted in absentia in the U.S. for his role in the unsuccessful plot to bomb American airliners over the Pacific. Within six months of 9/11, American investigators had concluded that Mohammed was the principal planner of the World Trade Center attacks. It was Mohammed, Filipino investigators now conclude, who originally concocted the idea for blowing up the dozen airliners over the Pacific in 1995. In 1996, the U.S. tracked Mohammed to Qatar. FBI director Louis Freeh met with Qatari officials and asked for permission to arrest him. As Qatar mulled a decision, the Clinton administration debated whether a commando team should be sent to capture Mohammed. Caution prevailed, and the U.S. decided to wait for a formal response from Qatar. Qatari officials instead tipped Mohammed, who left the country. Almost seven years later, on March 2, 2003, Khalid Shaikh Mohammed was finally arrested by CIA, FBI, and Pakistani intelligence agents in Pakistan. President Bush and U.S. government officials hailed the capture of the "mastermind" of 9/11 as the most significant breakthrough in the hunt for leading members of al Qaeda. Mohammed is now held by the United States at an undisclosed location and is under interrogation.

CHAPTER 10

RUSH TO
JUDGMENT

A few passersby later recalled the large yellow Ryder truck parked directly in front of the Alfred P. Murrah Federal Building in Oklahoma City early in the morning on April 19, 1995. Some thought it strange that such a large truck was left unattended, partially blocking the building's circular driveway.

At 9:02 A.M. the truck disintegrated in a giant explosion that ripped out the core of the nine-story building, blowing out windows ten blocks away. The blast was so powerful that it was felt fifteen miles from ground zero. A seven-thousand-pound homemade bomb—a potent mix of fertilizer and fuel oil—killed 168 and wounded hundreds, the worst act of terrorism on American soil to that date. With the realization that the catastrophe was man-made, the government's investigative agencies began a frenzied probe to track down those responsible.

The immediate focus was foreign terrorists. During the weeks leading up to the bombing, U.S. intelligence and law enforcement had received several explicit warnings that Islamic terrorists were seeking to strike targets on American soil. Just a month earlier, Ramzi Yousef had finally been run to ground in a flophouse in Islamabad, Pakistan. The break in the long manhunt came when a local Pakistani, who was aware of his real identity and the substantial reward for his capture, contacted the U.S. embassy and gave him away.*

---

*FBI agents flew Yousef back to New York where he was already under indictment. As the small plane carrying the hooded prisoner flew over southern Manhattan, FBI agent Chuck Stern lifted the hood and pointed toward the brightly lit World

The intelligence that prompted the terror warnings had pinpointed suicide attacks against government facilities starting sometime in late March 1995, and had been gathered from Iran, Syria, and the Philippines. The Marshals Service, for instance, had issued an alert only a month before the bombing, on March 15, to all federal courthouses.

"Iranian extremists want it made clear that steps are being taken to strike at the Great Satan," the marshals' memo said in part. "There is sufficient threat potential to request that a heightened level of security awareness and caution be implemented."

The Marshals Service concluded that Islamic extremists had issued their fatwa because of an episode at the end of the World Trade Center bombing trial in which some deputy marshals stepped on a copy of the Koran during a scuffle. The incident was accidental, but some Muslims thought it was a deliberate insult to their faith.

"Allegedly, the fatwa is being disseminated to persons in the United States who have the capability to carry it out," the memo continued. "The terrorists could be suicide bombers who may target as many victims as possible and draw as much media coverage as possible. Once the press is on the scene the new plans call for blowing up everyone."

Separately, the General Services Administration had received threats that federal buildings were targets. And the House Task Force on Terrorism and Unconventional Warfare had issued a warning earlier in February: "Iranian sources confirm Tehran's desire and determination to strike inside the U.S. against objects symbolizing the American government in the near future. . . . These strikes are most likely to occur either in the immediate future or in the new Iranian year—starting 21 March 1995" (within a month of the Murrah attack).

U.S. intelligence had monitored a several-day conference between senior terrorists from Iran, Syria, and Hezbollah in mid-February 1995 in which the subject of killing Americans on U.S. soil was discussed. During these meetings, known terrorists specifically mentioned Congress and the White House as "institutions that are great enemies of the Islamist movement."

John Gannon, former deputy CIA director for intelligence under President Clinton, recalled that that spring of 1995 was one of a handful of

---

Trade Center towers. "They're still standing," Stern said. Yousef smirked. "They wouldn't be if I'd gotten a little more money," he said.

periods in the decade when intelligence on terror threats peaked and the "chatter" among terrorists was particularly high. As a result, security patrols and screening at federal buildings had increased in the weeks before the Murrah bombing. When Gannon heard the news of the blast, he immediately assumed Islamic extremists had finally struck.

Within fifteen minutes of the bombing, the FBI asked the CIA and State Department to search all incoming cable traffic for leads to foreign terrorists. The CIA simultaneously began probing its vast databases to develop a short list of foreign candidates who had the means and motive to mastermind such an attack. All the information flowed through the Counterterrorism Center, where a team of analysts worked feverishly.

The National Security Agency started hunting for leads in its global communication intercepts. The NSA immediately supplemented its existing watch list with words related to the Oklahoma City bombing, allowing it to intercept any conversation remotely of value. The FBI also enlisted the National Reconnaissance Office (NRO) to provide satellite photography.

Still-classified documents reveal that, between reports from the CIA's stations and NSA intercepts, more than one hundred foreigners were quickly deemed possible suspects.[1]

Fearful that the Murrah attack might be the first in a wave of strikes, security officers at the White House began patting down visitors and even X-raying employees' lunch bags. In the federal courthouse in Manhattan, Omar Abdel Rahman and ten other Muslims were three months into their trial for conspiring to wage a "war of urban terrorism." From New York City to Los Angeles to Juneau, Alaska, federal buildings were evacuated and security tightened. Buildings closed in Boston; Boise, Idaho; Cincinnati and Steubenville, Ohio; Fort Worth; Omaha; Portland; Rochester, New York; and Wilmington, Delaware. A telephoned bomb threat cleared Miami's sixteen-story federal building.

Within hours of the bombing, eight terror groups—seven boasting they were Middle Eastern—had called the FBI, claiming responsibility. No one knew that the real bomber, Timothy McVeigh, had been stopped by a state trooper about seventy-five miles north of Oklahoma City, just seventy-five minutes after the blast. The trooper had pulled the car over because it did not have a license plate. The trooper arrested McVeigh when he discovered an unlicensed automatic pistol. Anti-government literature was also in the car, along with a business card having the handwritten notation, "TNT at $5 a stick. Need more."

But without any knowledge of McVeigh's connection to the attack, the investigation remained focused on uncovering a Middle Eastern link. Former FBI assistant director in charge of investigation and counterterrorism Buck Revell said, "It was very easy to think it was most likely a Middle East terrorist. It was a bona fide terrorist attack, and the modus operandi was similar to ones they had used before." By the early afternoon of the day of the bombing, the FBI asked the Department of Defense for Pentagon Arabic speakers to be included on the investigative team.

An FBI communiqué was circulated to its domestic and foreign field offices later that evening, giving credence to the theory that Islamic fundamentalists were solely to blame. The memo fingered the Iranian-backed Islamic Jihad as "the likely group," but it also proffered that Saddam Hussein might be involved. The Hussein speculation was raised in part because Iraq was frustrated with America's successful efforts at the United Nations, just the week before the Murrah blast, to foil Iraq's efforts to overturn Gulf War economic sanctions.[2]

Concerned that those involved might escape abroad, the FBI issued a general profile to police agencies and airport authorities worldwide. It emphasized young men traveling alone to the Middle East. That night, after the bombing, Abraham Abdallah Ahmed, a Jordanian-American living in Oklahoma City, was detained on a stopover at London's Heathrow Airport. Ahmed had checked in at Chicago's O'Hare International Airport on Wednesday night, less than twelve hours after the blast, for a flight to Rome with connections to Jordan. In addition to fitting the suspect profile, he was dressed in a jogging suit similar to one that a witness in Oklahoma City had reported seeing worn by a man near the scene of the explosion. His luggage had already gone on to Italy by the time it was located and searched. Against his will, Ahmed was forcibly put on a plane and returned to the U.S. by British authorities.

That a suspect of Middle Eastern origin was promptly apprehended confirmed the widely held suspicion that it was only a matter of time until a foreign terrorist group was directly tied to the bombing. "We felt," says the FBI's Revell, "that our international dragnet was starting to produce results."

Early reports that filtered in from the FBI's field investigation also bolstered the theory of a Middle Eastern connection. Within hours of the bombing, the FBI had dispatched hundreds of agents to conduct interviews in and around Oklahoma City. Some of the events from those early hours are revealed here for the first time, through a review of still classified FBI reports.[3] By the time the FBI had issued their evening communiqué to field offices warning of an Islamic link, crime scene investigators had uncovered a mangled license plate that they initially—and incorrectly—thought might belong to the vehicle that delivered the bomb. They traced it to a National car rental counter in Dallas. The Bureau then dispatched agents who interviewed a security officer in the Dallas office where National was located. The guard heightened their suspicions when he told the agents that he had noticed "a strange-looking group of men" congregating on the pavement outside the building the previous Friday night.

"They were dark-haired with beards," he continued, "and I am almost certain they were Arabs, or at least of Middle Eastern origin. There were three or four of them."

Unfortunately, there was no security camera at the National counter, so the agents could not confirm the guard's report.

Meanwhile, two Middle Eastern men were spotted driving from Oklahoma City to Dallas within hours of the bombing. The men stopped to ask directions from an Oklahoma highway patrolman. When the officer ran their plate, he discovered that it didn't match the vehicle. The plate belonged to a rented blue Chevy Cavalier, the very description of a car that at least two witnesses were then telling FBI agents in Oklahoma City that they had seen near the Murrah Building that morning. Asad R. Siddiqy, a cabdriver from Queens, along with the other two men, Anis Siddiqy and Mohammed Chafi, were taken into custody.

Meanwhile, in Oklahoma City, FBI agents erroneously tied the mystery group from Dallas to three men who had checked into the Plaza Inn motel earlier that week. The men had told the desk clerk they were Spanish, but both the clerk and a maid who cleaned their room thought they were Arabs, not only because of the way they looked, but also because they heard them speaking a different language. According to another employee, Ruby Foos, a fourth man checked into the motel a day or two later, went to his room, and emerged wearing flowing Arab robes. Adding to the brew, Douglas Boyer, the motel's security guard, recalled that a yellow Ryder truck had been parked out front. All of the men checked out a day or two before the bombing.

That prompted another FBI emergency communiqué, which went to all field offices. It said that if the Dallas group was the bomb team, they were almost certainly assisted, as in the 1993 World Trade Center blast, by local operatives. It noted that the Oklahoma City area has a prominent Islamic presence, and recounted that a national Islamic convention was held in nearby Tulsa the weekend before the bombing. Many local cabdrivers are Iranian, the memo added.

The FBI report concluded that the main conspirators might already be on an aircraft out of the country, having probably left from Dallas International Airport before the bomb even went off. Shortly after that memo was sent, Texas authorities contacted the FBI's Dallas office to report they were searching for "two men of Middle Eastern appearance driving a Cavalier or Chevrolet Blazer towards the Mexican border."

For thirty-six hours, the FBI continued finding witnesses who pointed to an Arab connection. One of those interviewed shortly after the blast was an injured woman who had been riding the elevator in the Murrah Building. She told two agents that she spotted a young Arab man wearing a backpack hurriedly pushing the buttons as if trying to get off. She had followed him outside, not suspecting anything was amiss. Moments later, she was sent sprawling to the sidewalk by the explosion.

Gary Lewis, a pressman for the Oklahoma City *Journal Record*, told FBI agents that he had stepped outside to smoke his pipe when he remembered he had left something in his car. As he walked down an adjacent alley, a yellow Mercury peeled away from its spot near the Murrah Building, jumped a concrete barricade, swerved to avoid hitting a dumpster, then bore down on him, forcing him up onto the curb (when McVeigh was arrested, he was driving a light yellow Mercury Marquis). Several minutes later, back in his office, Lewis was thrown to the floor as the building rocked from the blast's impact. As he and his fellow workers rushed outside, he noticed a peculiar sight: an Arab man standing nearby, staring at the smoldering federal building, grinning from ear to ear.

Another witness told crime scene investigators that he saw two men running from the area of the Murrah Building toward a brown Chevy pickup truck just prior to the blast. He described the two men, both with beards, as "possibly [of] Middle-Eastern descent, approximately six feet tall, with athletic builds."

A few blocks away from ground zero, Debra Burdick and her daughter had been on their way to the doctor's office. As she stopped for a light at 10th and Robinson, her attention was diverted by three vehicles. One was a blue Chevy Cavalier, the type of car investigators thought might be connected to the three Arabs detained while driving to Dallas.

"I looked across," Burdick told agents, "and there was that light blue car, it had a white interior, and there were three men in it. They were dark, but they were not black. . . . I would say they were Middle Easterners. . . . Now, I noticed the three men in the car, that guy sitting in the middle was kind of staring out. . . . I said, 'Huh, I wonder what they're looking at?' and as I turned around, I said, 'There's nothing there but buildings.' "

The other vehicles Burdick identified were a yellow Mercury, the same type of car that Gary Lewis, the *Journal Record* news worker, said had almost run him down a few minutes before the explosion. The third vehicle was a brown pickup. Burdick was now the second witness to describe that pickup, with Middle Eastern men inside, as having been in the immediate vicinity of the Murrah Building just before the blast.

More confirmation came from a witness identified in FBI documents only as Mary H. She had raced out of her office, five blocks from the Murrah Building, just after the explosion. As she stepped onto the meridian she was nearly run over by a brown pickup that came screeching around the corner. She told the agents there were three men inside and she made eye contact with the driver.

"He looked like he was in his twenties—late twenties. [He] had an angry look on his face. I'll never forget the look on his face. It just was full of hate and anger. It really struck me, because everyone else—people were coming out and they looked scared and confused, and he just looked full of anger." She said that two of the three people in the truck were Middle Easterners. (Later, when shown photos, she picked out an Iraqi, with ties to terrorist groups, as the driver.)

Within a few hours of the bombing, three other witnesses, Margaret Hohmann, her friend Ann Domin, and David Snider, a Bricktown worker, reported they had also spotted a brown pickup speeding out of town just after the explosion. As a result, a statewide APB was issued.

Dispatcher: "Be on the lookout for a late-model almost-new Chevrolet full-size pickup—full-size pickup, brown pickup. Will be brown in color with tinted windows—brown in color with tinted windows. Smoke-colored bug deflector on the front of pickup. . . . Middle Eastern males twenty-five to twenty-eight years of age, six feet tall, athletic build, dark hair and a beard—dark hair and a beard. Break."

Unidentified Officer: "Okay, is this good information, or do we not really know?"

Dispatcher: "Authorization FBI."

While government investigators were aggressively pursuing an Arab connection, the experts hit the airwaves and op-ed pages. While rescue workers were still digging through the smoking rubble looking for survivors, Steve Emerson appeared on CNN. He was asked if he thought militant Islamic groups were behind the Oklahoma blast.

Federal law enforcement officials were investigating a Middle Eastern link, he said. "This was with the attempt to inflict as many casualties as possible. This is not the same type of bomb that has been traditionally used by other terrorist groups in the United States other than the Islamic militant ones."

That evening, on Geraldo Rivera's CNBC evening show, Emerson said that FBI sources had told him that "based on the circumstantial evidence . . . it was Islamic extremists who mounted this attack."[4] The next morning on CBS, he told host Paula Zahn, "There is increasing information leading authorities in the direction of Middle Eastern–oriented attack from extremists based in the United States."[5]

"There was good reason for thinking they might be," Emerson later said. "The bombing, after all, was in Oklahoma City, where I had first encountered militant groups in 1992. Several Hamas operatives were living in the Oklahoma City area." It was at the Oklahoma City convention that Emerson's documentary had shown six thousand people cheering calls for killing Jews and infidels.

The rest of the press quickly picked up on Emerson's speculation. The network evening newscasts and CNN focused on the Islamic connection to the exclusion of almost any other possibility. Although most noted that the bombing had come on the second anniversary of the FBI's bungled raid at Waco that left eighty-two dead, a domestic link was discounted in the initial certainty that the perpetrators were Arab extremists.

William Webster, former director of the FBI and CIA, in an interview late on the day of the bombing, concluded that the bombing had all the "hallmarks" of Middle Eastern terror. Michael Cherkasky, a former Manhattan district attorney who worked on the World Trade Center bombing case, added to the growing consensus. "There is an MO that is consistent with Middle Eastern terrorists," he told reporters. "You have the car and the type of bomb. And it's consistent with the theme we saw in New York."

Wire service reports by the first evening drew comparisons to the previous year's bombing at the Buenos Aires, Argentina, Jewish Community Center, which killed eighty-five and wounded more than two hundred. In Argentina, as in New York, an abandoned vehicle packed with explosives did the damage. Radical Islamists backed by Iran were blamed and being sought by Argentine authorities.

Kenneth Katzman, author of the book *Warriors of Islam*, was already speculating about a motive. He told newspaper and television reporters that the bombing was probably in retaliation for the recent arrest in Pakistan of Ramzi Yousef.

"The West is 'under attack,' " Daniel Pipes, the director of the Middle East Forum, told *USA Today*. "People need to understand that this is just the beginning. The fundamentalists are on the upsurge, and they make it very clear that they are targeting us. They are absolutely obsessed with us."

"We were simply Islam the whole way," a FBI field office coordinator for counterterrorism said. "Anybody that tells you different either wasn't there or is lying."

Forty-eight hours after the bombing, the FBI had traced a vehicle identification number on the axle of the truck believed to have carried the bomb to a Ryder rental dealership in Junction City, Kansas. From eyewitnesses at that dealership, the FBI then prepared a composite drawing. By showing that around at nearby motels, the FBI identified Timothy McVeigh, who had been a guest at the Dreamland Motel in Junction City for four days preceding the bombing. A simple records check revealed he was already in custody in the Noble County Jail in Perry, Oklahoma.

The realization that the main suspect was an American with no known ties to foreign terrorists instantly reversed the investigation. The CIA and NSA stopped monitoring for foreign suspects. "We went from a

Middle Eastern case investigation to all-domestic on the turn of a dime,"
Buck Revell said.*

The early mistaken focus by government investigators and media
experts on Islamic terrorists had a detrimental effect on the real war on
terror.

"Within a week of McVeigh's arrest, I was pulled off a case we were
making on a Texas charity and its ties to Hamas," recalled a former FBI
analyst. "After that, we were focused almost exclusively on domestic
threats, what was happening with the violent home-bred groups. No
one officially closed the files on the Muslim extremists, it's just that they
got put on the back burner. I know when I went to headquarters [Wash-
ington, D.C.] later that year, no one was interested in hearing anything
about Arab money connections unless it had something to do with funding domestic groups. We had stumbled so badly on pinpointing the Middle East right off the bat on the Murrah bombing. No one wanted to get
caught like that again. And it certainly seemed, after Murrah, that the
more pressing threat was homegrown."[6]

The FBI was not the only agency affected. At the CIA, some in CTC felt
they had chased the wrong culprit for too long and that maybe the

---

*Many have continued to argue that hidden connections to Islamic terrorists, or
even to Iraq, were overlooked by the FBI. In the first days of the investigation, the FBI
had relied on some eyewitnesses to develop a composite sketch of a dark-
complexioned man they dubbed John Doe 2. Although McVeigh had an accomplice,
Terry Nichols, he was not John Doe 2. The FBI eventually concluded that the witnesses had been mistaken and there was no John Doe 2.

Jayna Davis, a former Oklahoma City television reporter and one of the first journalists on the scene, has claimed for years that John Doe 2 is actually Hashem al-
Jussaini, a former Iraqi soldier who was working in Oklahoma City at the time.
Al-Jussaini has steadfastly denied the charge. Larry Johnson, a former CIA officer
and deputy director of the State Department's Counterterrorism Office, still believes
there was a Middle Eastern connection that has not been uncovered. Moreover, some
conspiracy theorists have pointed out that Terry Nichols had traveled to the Philippines in the early 1990s to find a wife, the same time that Ramzi Yousef was there.
Although there is no evidence whatsoever that the two ever remotely crossed paths,
the conspiracy tales have been fueled by Edwin Angeles, a Filipino who claims to
know that Nichols and Yousef met. Angeles's story has been investigated repeatedly
by both Filipino and American investigators, who consider it a "complete fabrica-
tion." The speculation over an Islamic link to the Murrah blast revived briefly after
the arrest in June 2002 of Jose Padilla, the American accused of being part of a
radioactive "dirty" bomb plot. Nichols's first wife was named Lana Padilla. Some at
first thought there was a family connection, but there was none. Also, Padilla bore a
general resemblance to the John Doe 2 sketches issued after the blast.

greater threat was indeed American, not Arab. "It knocked the wind out of many of my former colleagues," Dewey Clarridge, the CIA officer who founded CTC in the mid-1980s, said. "There was little incentive for the Agency to fund a large operation against Arab militants when suddenly the concern was with domestic ones." Randy Weaver at Ruby Ridge, the long hunt for the Unabomber, the upcoming 1996 bombing at the Atlanta Olympics, and fresh memories of the Branch Davidians at Waco would only fuel the internal focus.*

A month after the Murrah bombing, European investigators concerned about Afghan Arabs who might be using Europe as a fund-raising and logistical base came across a CD-ROM that seemed explosive. Belgian authorities found the CD in the trunk of a car belonging to an Algerian who had been trained in Afghanistan and was now a member of an Armed Islamic Group cell in Brussels. The Belgian authorities took a few months to translate it from the Arabic. It began with a dedication to Osama bin Laden, and then launched into a detailed how-to book of such things as bomb making, including instructions on when to shake the chemicals and how to convert a common wristwatch into a detonator. In addition, there were details on how to kill with drugs, chemicals, toxins, and gases. The manual also covered diverse topics, from "psychological war in Islam" to "the organizational structure of Israeli intelligence" to "recruiting according to the American method."[7]

It was not long before different versions of the electronic manual were seized by police investigators in other European countries. What is

---

*On June 21, 1995, four months after the Murrah bombing, President Clinton signed a major policy document intended to address some confusion in the government over the precise jurisdiction and responsibilities of agencies in confronting terror strikes, including attacks involving weapons of mass destruction. Terrorism had been such a low priority before the Murrah bombing that there was not even a centralized budget to fight it. It was a good first step, and was prompted by Richard A. Clarke, the one official in the Clinton administration who was not only worried about the country's failure to confront the growing terror risk, but was vocal in constantly sounding the alarm. Clarke was chairman of the Counterterrorism Security Group (CSG), an interagency group that brought together senior representatives of the Departments of Defense, State, and Justice, as well as the FBI and CIA. Although often a lonely voice in the administration, Clarke pressed, to the irritation of many senior Clinton officials, his view that the U.S. was failing to seriously address international terror. As early as 1996, Clarke was the one senior official genuinely troubled by bin Laden, but he was not able to convince others, including the CIA, that his concerns were warranted.

remarkable, however, is that the CIA, with its reduced focus on Islamic terror, did not get its own copy for four years, until the end of 1999.

"The truth is," said Reuel Gerecht, a former CIA official, "they missed for years the largest terrorist guide ever written."[8]*

Once it was established that Islamic fundamentalists were not behind the Murrah bombing, there was widespread criticism of the fast suspicion placed on Arabs by the news media. The Council on American-Islamic Relations (CAIR) and the American Muslim Council took the offensive. Decent, moderate Muslims were the real victims of the rush to judgment, claimed the advocacy organizations.

The Muslim Council pointed to a *New York Post* editorial cartoon published two days after the bombing that showed the Statue of Liberty under siege. In the statue's shadow stood three turbaned, bearded men smiling and waving as one held a bomb and the others burned an American flag. The cartoonist had modified Emma Lazarus's poem to read: "Give us your tired, your poor, your huddled masses, your terrorists, your slime, your evil cowards, your religious fanatics . . ."

CAIR compiled statistics on hate crimes that surged against Muslims in the forty-eight hours following the bombing, and *The New York Times* now put sympathetic stories on its front page. *The Boston Globe*, ABC Television, and National Public Radio, among many others, sharply criticized the early experts who had fingered a Muslim connection.

"Even news outlets that had themselves originally reported that Muslims were the early suspects," recalls Steve Emerson, "now took the position that I was the only one who had suggested this. I became persona non grata in many places, including at CBS, which had hired me less than twenty-four hours after the bombing as a consultant. They ended up blacklisting me for five years."

"It was Emerson who misled us," Dan Rather later concluded. Rather had particular reason to be upset because it was on his newscast that Emerson suggested there might be an inherent cultural trait behind the violence: "This was done with the intent to inflict as many casualties as possible. That is a Middle Eastern trait." At the time, Rather did not challenge the statement.

*A CIA official told *The New York Times* that the Agency had had "access to versions" of the manual earlier and argued that it was "not the Holy Grail." However, inquiries with agents assigned to counterterrorism during the early 1990s indicate that Gerecht is right, that the CIA did not have the complete manual for years after its discovery.

"Of course, it wasn't as simple as Emerson and a group of us being responsible for the early speculation," said Daniel Pipes. "The major news outlets had all jumped on the Muslim speculation on their own, and within hours of the bombing the producers were calling. They were only interested in having someone on if they could discuss the possibility that Islamic radicals were involved. Then, when that turned out not to be the case, those same outlets suddenly adopted a holier-than-thou attitude, and blamed the very analysts they had so energetically courted just a few days earlier. But putting aside the question of who was to blame, one thing is certain: this mistake made the major American press gun-shy for years about chasing a terror story with an Islamic connection. If anything, it ensured that they bent over backward to show Muslims how fair they were, and as a result often failed to follow up on legitimate stories that had a Middle Eastern angle."

The press might not have even realized that it was ignoring Muslim terrorism. Most news outlets were instead concentrated on a single legal trial. In a post-9/11 environment, it would seem that the trial that might have absorbed the country was the almost nine-month proceedings of Sheikh Rahman and his ten codefendants for their day of terror plot in New York.

They had been indicted under the rarely used statute of seditious conspiracy, plotting to wage an illegal war of terrorism. One of the defendants was Kahane assassin El-Sayyid Nosair, who was charged with helping to orchestrate the plans from his jail cell. The testimony of another Muslim conspirator, Emad Salem, linked Rahman to the plot (Salem received $1.5 million for his efforts, and a new identity and relocation after the trial). Prosecutors presented 130 witnesses and more than one thousand exhibits.

"That trial," says Steve Emerson, "was a unique opportunity for the American public to learn about the true nature of the Islamic militant movement, the extent of its infrastructure in the United States, and its irreconcilable hatred for anyone it deems to be an enemy of Islam. The prosecution's case was a crash course in the precepts of militant Islam, and its vehement rejection of any separation of church and state. Unfortunately, it was a wasted opportunity."

Among the tens of thousands of documents introduced into evidence, videotapes, telephone records, and wiretaps revealed a vast, interlocking, and ongoing militant Islamic network throughout the United States that was committed to raising money and promoting hatred and violence against Jews, Christians, and moderate Muslims. Those materials also exposed how various Muslim "charities" were fronts used to support jihad worldwide. Other documents revealed that the World Trade Center conspiracy involved at least five different militant Islamic groups, and that some sources suggested a greater role for Hamas and the Sudanese than was previously thought.

"What I think happened," concluded Emerson, "was that by having the media ignore the evidence, and for the public to have so little interest in the proceedings, it encouraged Islamic militant groups to continue to expand their activities in the United States. A few of them had been caught, but no one seemed alarmed at the bigger threat."

On October 1, 1995, the defendants were convicted on forty-eight of the fifty counts, and the following January, the judge meted out sentences of life in prison and solitary confinement for Rahman and Nosair. The other eight defendants received sentences of between twenty-five and fifty-seven years. The sentencing of Rahman, who had assumed the role of al Qaeda's spiritual leader, was a setback to the organization. Although he used the U.S. as his base, he had traveled widely, preaching, recruiting, and raising funds in Southeast Asia, Europe, and the Middle East.*

But Sheikh Rahman's trial was overshadowed by another murder trial, this one in Los Angeles, that ran simultaneously over the same nine months. It was the case of football great O. J. Simpson, charged with slaying his wife and her friend. America was spellbound by the Simpson trial. CNN, MSNBC, and Court TV all tripled their ratings during the trial. Circulation for the supermarket tabloid *Star* jumped 40 percent. Cable's then top-rated talk show, *Larry King Live,* had a remarkable 146 consecutive shows on O.J. The entire trial was broadcast live on several local television and all-news radio stations. The evening newscasts of the three major networks, ABC, CBS, and NBC, devoted more airtime to the Simpson case than they gave to the first World Trade Center attack and the Oklahoma City bombing combined.

On the Internet, several Simpson chat boards rivaled the Net's top sex and dating forums in the volume of messages. In Florida, a service sta-

*Almost immediately after his arrest, his two sons, Muhammad and Ahmed (a.k.a. Abu Asim), both in exile in Pakistan, joined al Qaeda. Muhammad was killed by American bombing in Afghanistan in 2001.

tion owner installed small television monitors on his gas pumps and discovered that people pumped slightly more gas so they could watch a little more of the Simpson trial. On the high seas, during a three-day cruise exclusively for Simpson case buffs, one housewife bragged about hiring household help so she could spend more time watching the trial.

When the Simpson verdict was announced that October, the nation stood still for a few minutes. More than 100 million Americans watched the not-guilty finding live on television. Even President Clinton watched the verdict in an anteroom off the Oval Office with some aides, including White House chief of staff Leon Panetta. Congressional hearings were rescheduled. So was the daily State Department briefing. Airline flights were delayed. Long-distance calls dropped almost 60 percent. Stock trading plummeted.

During the follow-up analysis of the verdict and what went wrong for the prosecution, a short interview—the only jailhouse interview granted by Sheikh Rahman—ran in *Time* magazine the following week, but it received little notice. The sheikh laid out a blueprint for radical Muslim anger at America.

"In general," Rahman said, "everyone feels that it is Islam which has been put on trial. And that the U.S. wants to use this case to put Islam down." Rahman said his view of Islam was not a "radical interpretation," that the trial had been "unfair," that the government's chief witness against him was "Satan," and that the "press in general in the U.S. are racist . . . they are controlled [and] it is clear the media are against Islam."

Saying that he came to America to flee oppression, he now found the country "suffocating," and he defended the right of all Muslims to conduct a jihad against America, since "self-defense is legal in all religions." Rahman even went so far as to defend car bombings: "If it is taken during wartime and people are hurt and have to face violence, it is an act of exchanging violence."

Not long after Rahman's conviction, some Arabic newspapers reported that another Egyptian was vowing "to take revenge against the U.S." for the trial of the sheikh and for the American moves against radical Muslims. He was Dr. Ayman al-Zawahiri, the founder of the Egyptian Islamic Jihad Against Jews and Christians. "We are interested in briefly telling the Americans that their message has been received," said al-Zawahiri, "and that the response, which we hope they will read carefully, is being prepared. Because we—with God's help—will write it in the language that they understand."

Again, no American media reported the al-Zawahiri statement. Few inside the government even knew that the Egyptian Islamic Jihad had been merged with bin Laden's al Qaeda, and that the two men were well on their way to becoming the chief allies in a global war against America, eventually earning $25 million bounties on their heads for masterminding the September 11 attacks on America.

CHAPTER 11

SAFE HAVEN

IN

AFGHANISTAN

W hile Americans were distracted by the Simpson trial, Islamic fundamentalists continued to aggressively push their jihad against the West. In November 1995, two men parked a battered pickup truck near the three-story U.S. training mission to the Saudi National Guard in the Kingdom's capital, Riyadh. A few minutes after they left, the truck evaporated in a fireball. A 225-pound plastic explosive bomb, coupled to a secondary anti-personnel device to cause maximum casualties, was activated by remote control. Five Americans and two Indians were killed, and more than sixty—half Americans—were wounded. The attack was timed to maximize U.S. casualties, since the bomb detonated just before noon, when the Americans were at lunch in the snack bar near where the truck was parked, while the Saudis and other Muslims were in the nearby mosque for prayers. The blast blew out the front of the building, destroyed forty-five cars, and was felt over a mile away.

There had been warnings for nearly a week about a possible attack.[1] Faxes predicting a strike were sent by the Islamic Change Group to the U.S. and British embassies in Riyadh. They did not take it seriously enough to increase the alert levels at American installations in the Kingdom.

The Saudis blocked the FBI from participating in the investigation. Justice Department officials unsuccessfully appealed to the White House to apply pressure on the Saudis. By the following April, after interrogating dozens of suspects, the Saudis suddenly announced they had broken the case with the confessions of four local radicals. FBI investigators in

Saudi Arabia wanted access to the men. They had to watch, with the rest of the Saudi nation, when the confessions were played on the official television channel. The men were beheaded only six weeks after their arrests, before any U.S. investigator could talk to them.[2]

In their taped confessions, three of the men said they were inspired by fatwas personally issued by bin Laden, and one said he had met bin Laden and was one of "his men." This meant that the Saudi terror leader could no longer be ignored in the United States.[3] In early 1996, President Clinton finally signed a CIA finding that bin Laden was a threat to national security. That established a group called Alec Station, consisting of a small squad of CIA and FBI officers, whose goal was to build a case against bin Laden, find and capture him, and then prosecute him in an American court. With limited funding, it spent most of its time urging foreign intelligence services to track al Qaeda operatives and to keep the Agency informed.[4] At the same time, the Joint Terrorism Task Force based in New York assigned six full-time investigators to a new bin Laden desk.[5] Between the two—Alec Station and the JTTF unit—only one person had served abroad and only one spoke Arabic.[6]

Said a onetime operative in the Agency's Near East Division, "The CIA probably doesn't have a single truly qualified Arabic-speaking officer of Middle East background who can play a believable Muslim fundamentalist who would volunteer to spend years of his life with shitty food and no women in the mountains of Afghanistan. . . . We don't do that kind of thing."[7]*

The Justice Department convened a bin Laden grand jury in New York. Senior officials thought it important to obtain an indictment so

*The best thing that happened in 1996 in the U.S. effort to get intelligence on bin Laden was not the result of anything undertaken by intelligence agencies, but rather of a walk-in informant at the U.S. embassy in Asmara, the capital of Eritrea. A thirty-three-year-old Sudanese, Jamal al-Fadl, was not a high-ranking member of al Qaeda, but he knew a lot more about how the organization was structured and operated than anyone in the U.S. Frustrated at what he viewed as bin Laden's failure to promote him rapidly enough in al Qaeda, al-Fadl approached the Saudis and offered to cooperate. They turned him down (al-Fadl would have no way of knowing that the Saudis had maintained a secret relationship with bin Laden since 1991 and knew far more about bin Laden's operations than the low-ranking Fadl could tell them). Rejected by the Saudis, al-Fadl offered his information to the U.S. He gave U.S. intelligence its first realistic overview of the scope and sophistication of al Qaeda.

that the U.S. had a legal justification to ask for bin Laden's extradition if the opportunity presented itself. Inside the intelligence community, however, there was widespread dissatisfaction with the legal approach. Intelligence agencies traditionally dislike sharing information with grand juries because of the risk of leaks and disclosure of their own sources and means of obtaining the data. Also, any evidence gathered by FBI agents and prosecutors came under the protection of strict grand jury secrecy laws, which meant that the law enforcement side of the investigation could not tell the intelligence team what was going on. "Nobody outside the prosecutors and some in the FBI had access to what was going on in the grand jury," James Woolsey, the ex–CIA director, said.[8]

There was little objection from the intelligence agencies, however, when the U.S. finally started to press Sudan to expel bin Laden.* At a February 6, 1996, dinner in Khartoum for the Sudanese foreign minister and a State Department official and the new American ambassador, Timothy Carney, the U.S. presented a list of steps Sudan should undertake to prove it was not a terrorist state. The dinner was held on Ambassador Carney's last night in the country. Although Washington had ordered the embassy to evacuate, in part because of security concerns, the State Department thought it still worthwhile to give the Sudanese a road map that could get them off the terror sponsorship list. Among the steps Carney presented to the Sudanese were expelling bin Laden and dismantling his organization. "It was the first substantive chat with the U.S. government on the subject of terrorism," said Carney.

Less than a month after that dinner, Sudanese president Omar al-Bashir sent a trusted advisor, Major General Elfatih Erwa, then minister of defense, to the U.S. Erwa arrived unannounced at the Hyatt Arlington on March 3 and, after checking in, walked to another hotel, where waiting for him were Ambassador Carney; David Shinn, chief of the State Department's East Africa desk; and several CIA officers, including Frank Knott, the Africa division chief in the CIA's covert Directorate of Opera-

---

*That was not the case just months earlier, in 1995, when the then U.S. ambassador, Don Peterson, had delivered a secret note to Sudan's president putting the country on notice that the U.S. was aware of their sponsorship of terror and urging them to stop. Although bin Laden had been using Khartoum as his base for four years, Peterson said he did not even raise his name. "Osama bin Laden did not figure," Peterson said. "We in Khartoum were not really concerned about him."[9]

tions.[10] Knott handed Erwa a two-page memo dated March 8, 1996, titled, "Measures Sudan Can Take to Improve Relations with the United States." Second on the list was a request for information about bin Laden.[11]*

A few weeks later, Erwa told U.S. officials that Sudan was willing to have its own intelligence services monitor bin Laden, but if that was not enough, it would arrest him and hand him over to any country that had a legitimate proffer of criminal charges. This was the one opportunity, if the Sudanese were on the level, for bin Laden to be taken out of the international terror equation at a relatively early stage. Some senior administration officials doubted the sincerity of the Sudanese offer. Secretary of State Warren Christopher and National Security Advisor Anthony Lake were briefed.[†] They figured that Saudi Arabia was the most logical country to take bin Laden, although there was technically no arrest warrant for him (the Saudis would not issue one for another two years).[12]

To the rest of the world, the Saudis had "expelled" bin Laden in 1991 and had taken the highly visible steps of stripping him of citizenship in 1994, freezing his known assets, and urging his family to cut ties with him. But the Saudis had curiously never urged the Sudanese to take any action against bin Laden. This double standard, senior CIA officials now believe, was the result of the 1991 agreement between the Saudi chief of intelligence, Prince Turki, and bin Laden, in which the Saudis continued to allow money to flow to bin Laden in return for his agreement to keep his own fundamentalists deflected away from the Kingdom. That was particularly galling to CIA officials who had pressed the Saudis for cooperation on bin Laden. Although the Saudis were publicly committed to bringing bin Laden to justice—"We didn't leave any stone unturned,"

---

*The memo said specifically, "Provide us with the names, dates of arrival, departure and destination and passport data on mujahedin that Usama Bin Laden has brought into the Sudan." Knott told Erwa that the CIA suspected there were upward of two hundred people who fit that request.

†Lake, a strong critic of Khartoum, was not inclined to believe anything the Sudanese offered, in large part because just a few months earlier the Secret Service had removed Lake from his home, acting on CIA intelligence that a Sudanese assassination team was after him. After a week of heavy Secret Service protection at Blair House, the presidential guesthouse across Pennsylvania Avenue from the White House, Lake returned home. U.S. officials later came to believe it had been a false alarm.

Prince Turki would later tell *The New York Times*—they effectively had had him on their payroll since the start of the decade.

Urged by the Americans to ask the Sudanese for bin Laden, the Saudis demurred, claiming they feared a backlash from his supporters in the region. (The Saudis, however, had no fear of a fundamentalist backlash when they rounded up hundreds of militants after the November bombing in Riyadh, nor when they executed the four terrorists who carried out the attack.) The United States did not try to change the Saudis' decision. Policymakers in the administration decided ultimately not to push them on counterterrorism, since it was believed America would need to cash in any debts with Saudi Arabia to support the ailing peace talks between the Israelis and Palestinians, something dear to Clinton. Also, the Saudis were still allowing Americans to use their bases to enforce the southern no-fly zone in Iraq, and that was also considered more important than pressing them over bin Laden.

The U.S. asked the Egyptians next whether they would prosecute bin Laden. Cairo was relieved it had no reason to put him on trial.

Having failed to find a country to take bin Laden, it appears the U.S. then missed an opportunity to get bin Laden sent to America. A Sudanese overture indicating a willingness to possibly turn him over to the U.S. came from Mansour Ijaz, a New York–based Pakistani-American businessman who also fancied himself a freelance diplomat. Ijaz was a large Democratic Party donor, and as such personally knew Clinton, Gore, and Sandy Berger. He also had excellent contacts with Sudanese government officials and officers inside Mukhabarat, Sudan's intelligence service.*

Ijaz, who was one of the guests at the Clintons' 1995 Christmas dinner, claims that he personally told administration officials, including National Security Advisor Berger, that Sudan was willing to arrest bin

---

*Ijaz's critics claim he is prone to exaggeration. Susan Rice, assistant secretary of state for African affairs, in charge of Sudan, said that the Sudanese offer was not serious. "We wanted names. We wanted bank accounts. We wanted paper. We wanted the bodies themselves, the individuals to interview. And none of that was forthcoming." Rice has said that in repeated meetings with Sudanese officials, they never committed to any substantive intelligence sharing on bin Laden or on terror groups operating in their countries. "We didn't need back channels like Mansour Ijaz," said Rice, "because we had front channels, we had numerous direct, repeated exchanges with the government of Sudan on counterterrorism, none of which yielded anything."[13]

Laden in return for American aid and removal from the State Department's official terror sponsorship list. "The silence of the Clinton administration in responding to these offers was deafening," says Ijaz.[14] Berger—who just considered Ijaz a businessman who wanted Sudan off the terror sponsorship list so he could get an inside track on some business deals—denies Ijaz ever made an explicit offer and has dubbed his claim "irresponsible."

"What I tried to explain to Berger upon my return from Sudan was simple and straightforward," Ijaz counters. "Whatever the sins of their past, there was a segment of the Sudanese hierarchy that had realized their Islamic experiment had gone bad with the rise of bin Laden in their midst. They wanted to cooperate with the U.S. to find a way to contain the radical forces they had helped unleash, and I wanted the administration to at least listen to their overtures."[15]

The U.S. ambassador to Sudan, Timothy Carney, supports Ijaz's view that the U.S., which was so convinced that Sudan's commitment to terror was entrenched and that its offer must be bogus, missed a major opportunity in 1996.

"The fact is they [the Sudanese] were opening the doors and we weren't taking them up on it," he says. "The U.S. failed to reciprocate Sudan's willingness to engage us on some serious questions of terrorism. We can speculate that this failure had serious implications, at least for what happened to the U.S. embassies in 1998. In any case, the U.S. lost access to a mine of material on bin Laden and his organization."[16] Carney blames the CIA in large part for having become too political and providing weak analysis of what was transpiring in Sudan.

J. Stephen Morrison, who was then on the State Department's Policy Planning Staff and is now director of Africa programs at the Center for Strategic and International Studies in Washington, D.C., confirms Carney's version. The hard-line administration approach, he says, was "ultimately rigid and extremely vitriolic, to the point of being mindless. It was impossible to get an open debate about it in the Clinton administration."[17] According to Morrison, the administration just preemptively decided that the Sudanese overtures were bogus without making any effort to test them.

Sandy Berger claimed that the administration was, in 1996, "trying to get bin Laden with everything we had." But that rings hollow in light of what the administration decided to do, or more appropriately, not to do, about bin Laden.[18] When Sudan indicated it might be willing to turn him, about to the U.S., instead of an immediate and enthusiastic yes, the Clinton administration decided it would first determine whether he could be tried successfully in America.

"The FBI did not believe we had enough evidence to indict bin Laden at that time," says Berger, "and therefore opposed bringing him to the United States."[19]

That is not surprising. The FBI had not even opened a file on bin Laden until October 1995, only months before Berger claims the administration relied on the Bureau's decision as to whether the U.S. should seek bin Laden.* Moreover, it seems odd that the administration would rely on the FBI's judgment of whether it was possible to successfully prosecute bin Laden when, at the same time, the State Department was describing him as "the greatest single financier of terrorist projects in the world."[20] It appears instead that Berger, and Steven Simon, then director of counterterrorism for the National Security Council, believed that taking bin Laden carried too many risks, both in terms of reprisals and not obtaining a conviction. The best compromise, they concluded, was forcing him from Sudan so that it would disrupt his terror network and take him considerable time to regroup.[21]

"In the end, they said, 'Just ask him to leave the country,' " recalls the Sudanese general, Erwa. "Just don't let him go to Somalia. We said he will go to Afghanistan, and they said, 'Let him.' "[22]

On May 15, 1996, Sudanese Foreign Minister Ali Othman Taha sent

---

*When the Bureau finally created a bin Laden file, it dispatched two agents, Dan Coleman and John Liguori, of the Joint Terrorism Task Force, to the Counterterrorism Center in Langley. The two FBI agents were amazed that the CIA had forty thick file folders on bin Laden. Although much of it was raw, and often not reliable, intelligence, it was an indicator to the FBI agents of how far behind the Bureau was in focusing on bin Laden and also illustrated once again how little information the CIA had shared. It was during that October visit that the FBI agents learned the CIA was investigating Wadi el-Hage, bin Laden's private secretary and business agent, who was then in Nairobi, Kenya (he would later be convicted for his role in the 1998 East Africa embassy bombings). When the FBI agents studied the investigation files, they discovered that el-Hage had been in the U.S. in the early 1990s, having been implicated in the 1989 murder of a radical imam in Arizona, and had ties to associates of Rabbi Kahane's assassin, El-Sayyid Nosair. El-Hage had even flown from Texas to New York the day that Emir Shalabi was murdered, in the still unsolved case, in 1990. While the FBI was aware of el-Hage, no one in the CIA ever thought it necessary to alert the Bureau that el-Hage had links to bin Laden.

a fax to Ambassador Carney informing him that Sudan had officially asked bin Laden to leave the country, and that he was free to go. Carney faxed back a question about whether bin Laden would retain control of the millions in assets he had built up in Sudan. Taha did not respond. But when bin Laden left on a chartered plane three days later, he had already managed to liquidate and redirect his substantial assets to Afghanistan.[23]

Since the United States had advance knowledge that bin Laden was about to leave, it had a second chance to nab him while he was in international airspace. The CTC drew up an operations plan for such a seizure and presented it to White House officials. It eventually found its way to President Clinton, who ultimately decided not to act. He, and most of his top advisors, considered it a victory just to expel bin Laden from Sudan.

"We were just incensed," a former CIA analyst assigned to CTC told the author, "after we learned that there would be no action on our recommendation. We had clear and convincing proof of what bin Laden had done, and it would have been easy to bring him in." (After 9/11, Clinton told a New York dinner guest that his failure to get bin Laden in 1996 was "probably the biggest mistake of my presidency.")[24]

On May 18, 1996, a chartered C-130 transport plane left Khartoum with bin Laden, his wives and children, and 150 of his top aides and lieutenants. On the way to Jalalabad in eastern Pakistan, the plane had to stop to refuel in the Gulf State of Qatar. That kingdom, which has excellent relationships with the United States (it was the headquarters for the U.S. military's Central Command during the 2003 Iraq war), did not want bin Laden to land unless the U.S. gave the green light. After contacting embassy officials, the word came back that Washington said the plane was to proceed to Pakistan unhindered.

Although the U.S. had missed a chance to nab bin Laden, Mansour Ijaz, the New York–based businessman, continued his efforts to have Sudan offer something of value to the U.S. so it could be removed from the state terror sponsorship list. He advised Sudan to make an explicit offer to the Americans. On April 5, 1997, Sudan's president, al-Bashir, wrote a letter to Congressman Lee Hamilton, the ranking Democrat on the House Foreign Affairs Committee, inviting an FBI team to visit Khartoum and examine their intelligence files on bin Laden. When the FBI requested permission to examine the Sudanese files, they could not get a go-ahead from either Madeleine Albright at the State Department or Sandy Berger at the National Security Council. The FBI did not officially make another request for three years. It would not be until early 2000 that the U.S. began discussions about sending a full-time counterterrorism team to Khartoum, a squad that eventually arrived in May 2000. But even then its mission was not to examine the Sudanese intelligence files, but instead to determine if Sudan was really sponsoring terrorism.[25]

Based on information recently discovered by American intelligence, it is now believed that a month after bin Laden was safely in Pakistan he met with senior representatives of the Pakistani military, including Mushaf Ali Mir, a highly placed military officer who had close ties to some of the most pro-Islamist elements in ISI, the Pakistani intelligence agency.[26] They discussed uniting bin Laden's network and money with an Islamic fundamentalist movement of students that Pakistan was supporting in the continuing tribal warfare that had fractured Afghanistan since the Soviets had fled in 1991. The group that Mir wanted to unite with bin Laden was called the Taliban.

The Pakistanis had been taking money from the same benefactor as bin Laden—the Saudis—and using it to fund both madrassas (religious schools) and the Taliban. Now Mir offered bin Laden the protection of the Pakistani government if he aligned with the Taliban. For bin Laden, who found an ideological soul mate in the young one-eyed mullah who led the Taliban, Mohammad Omar, it was an ideal situation.* ISI helped bin Laden establish his new headquarters in an encampment in Afghanistan's Nangarhar province. It also placed one of the local radi-

---

*The madrassas, numbering in the thousands by the mid-1990s, had been started by the Pakistanis—and funded by the Saudis—for the tens of thousands of young men who filled the poverty-stricken refugee camps that had sprung up along the Pakistan-Afghanistan border during the war with the Soviets. The Saudis backed the schools because they were determined to find an outlet, as far away as possible from their own country, for the Islamic fundamentalism of their own youth. In those schools, the youngsters were taught a fierce and uncompromising form of Islam—based on an absolutist enforcement of Sharia, the Islamic religious law—that was also mixed with virulently anti-Western and anti-Semitic teachings. ISI hoped to use the madrassas not only to find radical Muslim recruits for its own state-sponsored terror activities in its long-running battle with Hindu India over the disputed region of Kashmir, but also to field a counterpower in Afghanistan to the dominant Northern Alliance, an Islamic rebel faction composed primarily of warlords drawn from Tajiks and other ethnic minorities living in northern Afghanistan. Pakistan backed the Pashtun minority in the Afghan civil war. Millions of Pashtuns lived in large tracts of northern Pakistan where the government had little effective control, and the southern portion of Afghanistan

cals, on its payroll, in the bin Laden camp. ISI had worked long and hard to control the militants in Afghanistan, and while they saw bin Laden as a useful ally, they wanted to ensure they knew what he was up to at all times.

That same month, from June 21 to 23, while bin Laden met with Mir in Pakistan, a three-day terrorist summit was held in Tehran. The Iranians hosted it to transform its client terror network, Hezbollah, into the vanguard of the radical Islamic movement. Sponsored by Iran's Supreme Council for Intelligence Affairs, it included such luminaries as Ramadan Shallah, chief of the Palestinian Islamic Jihad; Imad Mughaniya, Lebanese Hezbollah's special operations commander; Ahmad Salah (a.k.a. Salim), head of the Egyptian Islamic Jihad; Ahmed Jibril, the militant chief of the Popular Front for the Liberation of Palestine; Imad al-Alami and Mustaf al-Liddaw, general command representatives from Hamas; and Abdallah Ocalan, leader of the Kurdish terror group, the People's Party. Bin Laden sent Muhammad Ali Ahmad as his representative. Other terror organizations, like George Habash's Popular Front and the Palestinian Islamic Jihad, also sent representatives.[27]

During that conference, it was announced that there would be increased attacks against U.S. interests, especially in the Persian Gulf region. And to oversee those attacks, the conference established a Committee of Three, under the chairmanship of Iranian external intelligence chief Mahdi Chamran. And to acknowledge the importance of Sunni Muslims to the fundamentalist movement (Iranians are Shiites), two of the three committee members were Sunni—Osama bin Laden and Ahmad Salah. According to a member of the CIA counterintelligence team, the Agency did not infiltrate the conference, but instead obtained summary reports after paying someone who had been there. However, those sketchy reports did not arrive at a CIA field station in Asia for nearly two weeks.[28]

But before the CIA received anything about the conference, on June

---

was mostly Pashtun as well. The Taliban was a Pashtun movement, therefore one that naturally fit with the Pakistani desire to control the events in its northern neighbor. Mullah Omar, a popular young religious leader, had created a militia in Kandahar in September 1994. By November, ISI had forged its first ties with the Taliban and paid them to protect convoys traveling between Pakistan and Central Asia. As the Taliban attracted more recruits from the madrassas, Pakistani support—both financial and logistical—increased.

25, a couple of days after it finished, two men drove a stolen Mercedes tanker truck into the al-Khobar military housing complex in Dhahran, Saudi Arabia. The men had already tried to pass into the foreigners' compound, where U.S. troops lived, but were turned away because of the late hour. So instead they parked the truck against a concrete barrier, about one hundred feet from the compound's main building. They ran and sped away in a waiting car. One of the sentries thought their hasty exit suspicious, and he radioed a warning to the U.S. Air Force's Central Security Control. Guards shouted for people to evacuate the building. But in less than three minutes the truck disintegrated in an enormous fireball. It had been packed with five thousand pounds of military grade explosives, reinforced by an incendiary bomb that created a second huge blast. The front of the high-rise building collapsed (buildings up to a quarter mile away suffered damage). Dozens were killed—including nineteen Americans—and hundreds were wounded, many critically. Two previously unheard of groups claimed credit. One called a London Arabic newspaper and promised more such bombings unless Saudi Arabia expelled all U.S. troops. The second group, Hezbollah of the Gulf, called a Dubai press outlet and threatened more attacks unless the Americans left "holy Saudi land." Besides the public calls of responsibility, the National Security Agency intercepted two telephone calls to bin Laden on the day of the blast. One was from his friend, the founder of the Egyptian Islamic Jihad, Ayman al-Zawahiri, who offered "congratulations." The second came from Ashra al-Hadi, a member of the Palestinian Islamic Jihad, offering "solidarity."[29]

It had been seven years since bin Laden founded al Qaeda. A CIA analysis dated July 1, 1996, only six days after the Khobar bombing, was remarkable for its candor about the lack of progress the Agency had made in penetrating bin Laden's network.

"We have no unilateral sources close to bin Laden, nor any reliable way of intercepting his communications. We must rely on foreign intelligence services to confirm his movements and activities. We have no sources who have supplied reporting on Saudi opposition cells inside Saudi Arabia, and little information about those cells' location, size, composition, or activities."[30]*

*Although the CIA may have gathered little about bin Laden, they were learning some things about him through foreign press interviews. In early July, the same time as the CIA analysis, Robert Fisk of London's *Independent* newspaper interviewed bin

When Attorney General Janet Reno ordered Louis Freeh to prepare her first full briefing on bin Laden, the FBI was not capable of doing it. Instead, the CIA had to brief the attorney general, even though the Agency's information on bin Laden was poor.[31]

The FBI did, however, send a team of nearly one hundred agents and support personnel promptly to Saudi Arabia to investigate the Khobar bombing. But from their arrival, the agents were thoroughly frustrated by Saudi officials and security officers who blocked them from any substantive role. The Saudis suspected that Iran, the sponsor of the terror conference that ended only days before the blast, was behind the attack. But Saudi officials feared that if Iran was to blame, and American officials confirmed that, the U.S. might attack Iran. In several meetings between deputy national security advisor Sandy Berger and the Saudi ambassador to the U.S., Prince Bandar bin Sultan, Bandar repeatedly demanded to know what the U.S. might do with any information it received from the bomb probe. Berger maintained that whatever the U.S. decided to do, it would first consult with the Saudis. That did not satisfy them, so they continued to block the FBI.[32] FBI director Louis Freeh personally went to Saudi Arabia to lobby for access for his agents, but was also rebuffed. When the Saudis eventually detained suspects, the FBI was limited to reading interrogation transcripts by Saudi investigators.

Behind the scenes Freeh was furious, but not with the Saudis. Instead, he vented his anger toward the White House, complaining bitterly to close friends and colleagues that he believed the Clinton administration wanted to establish relations with the Iranian government. He was personally convinced that Berger and others were "unable or unwilling to help the FBI gain access" to the Saudi probe. Prince Bandar compounded the problem when he told Freeh that the White House had no

---

Laden in Afghanistan. Bin Laden said the recent bombings in Saudi Arabia were "the beginning of the war between Muslims and the United States. . . . The Saudis now know their real enemy is America." The American media did not report the interview. The American press was instead filled with stories about several different events, including the summer Olympics, the Whitewater investigation and a fight between the White House and the FBI over files, and the upcoming presidential election in the fall. Bin Laden's first American interviews would be a March 1997 CNN broadcast with Peter Arnett. Two months later he was on ABC passing along his threats to ABC's John Miller.

interest in the case and only wanted to avoid a confrontation with Iran.[33]*

What Freeh did not know at the time was that immediately after the Khobar bombing, Clinton called in his political advisor and pollster, Dick Morris, to check the mood of the public. "I was concerned about how Clinton looked in the face of [the attack]," recalled Morris, "and whether people blamed him."[34] The bombing happened in the midst of the president's reelection campaign and at the end of a month in which the White House was besieged by domestic scandals, including Whitewater and Filegate.† Morris worried that any public discontent with Clinton over terrorism might benefit Republican senator Bob Dole. While Morris worked the numbers, Clinton talked tough. On the day of the attack, he told the country, "The cowards who committed this murderous act must not go unpunished. Let me say again: We will pursue this. America takes care of our own. Those who did it must not go unpunished." The next day, the president said, "We will not rest in our efforts to find who is responsible for this outrage, to pursue them and to punish them."

Although the first overnight poll showed less support for Clinton than Morris expected, after a few days the numbers had improved. When he presented his findings to the president, public approval of Clinton's hard-line talk had caused support to climb—something Morris noted in his written agenda for the session.‡ Morris said that his polling revealed

---

*When the Clinton administration sent back-channel, positive signals to the new reformist Iranian government in 1997, Freeh told colleagues that he had been proven right that the administration had never been serious about getting the FBI into the Khobar investigation. Sandy Berger, and other Clinton aides, have denied Freeh's charges, and say there is nothing unusual about pursuing a two-track policy (cooperation and confrontation) regarding a country like Iran. Freeh later took the extraordinary step of secretly asking former president George Bush to intervene with the Saudis. Acting without Clinton's knowledge, Bush interceded. As a result, the FBI was given direct access to several Hezbollah suspects detained by the Saudis.

†The White House was consumed with a number of domestic political problems at the time of the Khobar bombing. In late May, independent counsel Kenneth Starr had convicted Jim and Susan McDougal and Jim Guy Tucker in connection with the first large Whitewater trial; in June, the Filegate story first broke publicly, and Senator Al D'Amato's committee issued its Whitewater report recommending that several administration officials be investigated for perjury. Also in June, the White House went on the defensive from scurrilous, and mostly unproven, allegations contained in *Unlimited Access*, a book by former FBI agent Gary Aldrich.

‡Morris's handwritten notations said: "SAUDI BOMBING—recovered from Fri-

that Americans supported tightening security and taking military action against suspected terrorist sites in other countries. He had even prepared a quick mock-up of an attack ad on Dole over the terror issue (it never ran).[35]

But Clinton, and his top advisors, decided that the president did not have to take any more public action regarding the Khobar attack. Morris was not surprised.

"He had almost an allergy to using people in uniform," Morris said. "He was terrified of incurring casualties; the lessons of Vietnam were ingrained far too deeply in him. He lacked a faith that it would work, and I think he was constantly fearful of reprisals. On another level, I just don't think it was his thing. You could talk to him about income redistribution and he would talk to you for hours and hours. Talk to him about terrorism, and all you'd get was a series of grunts."[36]

At the time, Morris had told him that his polling showed that successfully tackling three problems would cast him as a great president in the public's view—eliminating the deficit, making welfare reform work, and smashing international terrorism. Clinton was remarkably energetic on the first two, said Morris, but on terrorism he was "curiously uninvolved."[37]

And it was not just Morris's opinion. After the first World Trade Center blast in 1993, Clinton never visited the site, and only mentioned it once, in one of his weekly radio addresses. He did not meet privately with the CIA director for two years after that attack, and never asked for a single briefing on it.

"Clinton was aware of the threat, and sometimes he would mention it," recalled Leon Panetta, who served as the budget director before becoming the White House chief of staff later in the first term. But Panetta said the president was consumed with the "Big issues—Russia, Eastern bloc, Middle East peace, human rights, rogue nations, and then terrorism."[38]

When Congress wanted to pass sanctions on American and European companies that did business with Iran because of its backing of terror, Clinton fought the proposal, saying it would not only place U.S. compa-

---

day and looking great. Approve Clinton handling 73–20. Big gain from 63–20 on Friday. Security was adequate 52–40. It's not Clinton's fault 76–18."

nies at a competitive disadvantage, but anger our European allies. When a law was proposed that would make driver's licenses expire for aliens when their visas did, advisor George Stephanopoulos convinced Clinton that it was like racial profiling, so the president opposed it.

Throughout his presidency, Clinton refused to publish a list of charities suspected by the CIA and FBI as being terror fronts. He rejected efforts to name Hamas a terror organization for fear it might upset the Palestinians during his ongoing effort to forge a Middle East peace agreement with the Israelis. And after a commission on aviation security, headed by Vice President Al Gore, recommended dozens of changes, including the sharing of CIA and FBI information about suspected terrorists, extra travel safety precautions such as X-ray screening for baggage, federalization of security checkpoints, and the restoration of air marshals to flights, the president made no effort to implement any of the suggestions, considering them too disruptive to travel.[39]

Morris, who spoke frankly to Clinton about his place in history, believed that the president had no bad intent, but instead, "In Bill Clinton's epoch, terror was primarily a criminal justice problem which must not be allowed to get in the way of the 'real' foreign policy issues."[40]

While the FBI was trying to become part of the Khobar probe, the Tehran terror conference was followed by another terrorist summit at the Pakistani town of Konli, near the Afghan border, from July 10 to 15, 1996. This again brought some of the most important militant Islamic leaders together under one tent. They included Osama bin Laden and Ahmed Jibril of the Popular Front for the Liberation of Palestine, who some in the CIA believe to this day carried out the Pan Am Flight 103 bombing on orders from Tehran. Jibril arrived with Abdul Rasul Sayyaf, a senior representative of Iranian intelligence. Also present were half a dozen senior officers from ISI, as well as senior commanders of Hamas, Hezbollah, and other radical groups. All resolved to use whatever force was necessary to oust all foreign forces stationed on Islamic holy land.

One Arab observer with direct knowledge of the conference said the participants' resolution was "a virtual declaration of relentless war" on the U.S.-led West. Unknown to the participants, one of the Pakistani intelligence agents made an audio recording of the proceedings. It took nearly four months for the CIA to obtain a poor-quality copy. From that tape, the Agency learned that Rasul Sayyaf had warned, "The time to settle accounts has arrived." The senior representative of Iranian intelligence declared that "attack is the best means of defense." He urged a combined offensive, both in the Muslim world, particularly the Persian Gulf and Arabian Peninsula, and at the heart of the West. He repeated Iran's commitment to the cause and reiterated Tehran's willingness to provide the Islamists with all possible aid.

Another commander concurred, adding that "there is an imperative need for an integrated plan to deal a fatal blow to the international forces of arrogance." A U.K.-based fundamentalist stressed that, given the immense strategic importance of the Persian Gulf to the U.S. and its allies, the only way to compel the West to abandon the Gulf was through the infliction of so much pain that their governments would find it impossible to tolerate the public outcry and be forced to withdraw.

On July 16, 1996, a day after the Konli conference, the U.S. Senate ended weeks of debate by passing sanctions against Iran and Libya. On the day of the vote, the Movement for Islamic Change sent a fax to the London-based Arab newspaper al-Hayat, warning: "The world will be astonished and amazed at the time and place chosen by the Mujahedeen. The Mujahedeen will deliver the harshest reply to the threats of the foolish American president. Everyone will be surprised by the volume, choice of place and timing of the Mujahadeen's answer, and invaders must prepare to depart alive or dead, for their time is morning and morning is near." That fax, and a warning on July 18 by Israeli intelligence that Iran was likely to launch an attack against a U.S. aircraft, were ignored by the CIA, which did not even initially create a separate file for the Konli conference, nor pass along the Israeli warning to other government agencies.[41]

The following day, July 17, 1996, at 8:30 P.M., a TWA Boeing 747 exploded only minutes after takeoff from JFK airport in New York City. The plane disappeared in a fireball as dozens of witnesses along Long Island Sound watched in horror. All 230 people on board died. The early investigation focused quickly on a terror strike. When the plane's black box was recovered, it was learned that its recording had ended abruptly with a brief sound similar to the one audible on the recorder of Pan Am 103, the flight destroyed by a bomb over Lockerbie, Scotland, seven and a half years earlier. The TWA's transponder also ceased operating at the

same second as the black box, indicating an instantaneous and catastrophic event, a scenario that also fit a bomb blast. Within a week,
investigators were speculating about the exact makeup of what was
thought to be a twin-charged plastic explosive device, likely placed
against the forward wall of the central fuel tank.[42]

Several Islamic fundamentalist groups quickly claimed credit for
Flight 800's downing.[43] One of those, made the day after TWA 800 went
down, was from the Islamic Change Movement, the Jihad wing in the
Arabian Peninsula that had bragged about credible roles in both the
Riyadh and Dhahran attacks.

While investigators focused on a bomb, there were some witness
accounts that raised the possibility of a missile strike. People recounted
seeing a streak of smoke move *toward* the plane seconds before the explosion. Pierre Salinger, JFK's former press secretary and a reporter for
ABC, publicly speculated that a stray U.S. military missile had downed
the plane. His theory was briefly bolstered by the disclosure that a U.S.
Navy exercise was under way at the time of the explosion, only two hundred miles off the Long Island coast.

In the White House, Dick Morris was immediately directed to conduct
a new round of polling to check the public mood and gauge the right
response for the president. The polling found people increasingly agi-
tated about air travel safety and that there was a drop in support for Clinton's handling of the Khobar investigation. The number who believed
Clinton was "doing all he can to investigate the Saudi bombing and punish those responsible" was down to 54 percent, while 32 percent
believed he could do more. Morris feared that further White House inaction would create a chance for Dole to carve out an issue portraying
Clinton as soft on national security.

"We tested two alternative defenses to this attack, 'Peacemaker' or
'Toughness,' " Morris wrote in a memo to the president. For the "Peacemaker" thesis, Morris asked voters to respond to the statement, "Clinton
is peacemaker. Brought together Arabs and Israelis. Ireland. Bosnia
ceasefire. Uses strength to bring about peace." The other position was
presented as "Toughness. Clinton tough. Stands up for American interests. Against foreign companies doing business in Cuba. Sanctions
against Iran. Anti-terrorist legislation held up by Republicans. Prose-
cuted World Trade Center bombers."

People overwhelmingly preferred the "tough" view. "So Clinton talked tough," recalled Morris.[44] But he had no intention, according to Morris, of going beyond the words.[45]

The FBI and the New York–based Joint Terrorism Task Force kicked off one of the Bureau's largest investigations, surpassing the previous year's hunt on the Murrah bombing. Having just finished the Ramzi Yousef trial, they were alert to the desire of the fundamentalists to bring down commercial aircraft as a terror tool. And the missile speculation raised the fear that a Stinger missile might have fallen into the wrong hands and been fired from the water off Long Island Sound toward the climbing plane.

The Bureau was pressured by the White House to ensure that the investigation was thorough. The circumstances of the downing meant that was no simple task. Since the plane blew up over water, it was not possible, as it had been with Pan Am 103, to have a massive search to find microscopic pieces of evidence.* The main area, forward of the fuel tank, was missing and had probably disintegrated. Entire seat sections above the tank were also missing. Investigators knew from the start that nitrates, a key component of bombs, are degraded by fire and seawater. The inability to prove definitively what happened with science and forensics meant that the FBI had to keep many more agents on the case doing old-fashioned interviews with witnesses to the explosion and sifting through foreign cables to see if they could uncover a conspiracy.

By the fall, however, the growing consensus among investigators was that TWA 800 was a tragic accident, likely caused when a spark from a bad wire kicked off a spontaneous combustion of fumes that had built up in the main fuel tank. But to eliminate a bomb or missile as the cause would take another year. It was not until the end of 1997 that the Bureau felt comfortable enough to announce its final decision that the plane had exploded as the result of an accident.[†]

---

*The plotters who placed the bomb on Pan Am 103 had timed it so that it would also destroy the plane over water, complicating the investigation. However, Pan Am 103 had been delayed at Heathrow for nearly an hour before takeoff, so when the timer detonated the bomb, the plane was still over land.

†Despite the overwhelming evidence that TWA 800 was merely an accident, over twenty thousand websites still argue that it was downed by a missile, most suggesting it was a U.S. military error that the government subsequently covered up.

"That meant that our best resources were diverted for over a year into an investigation that was a dead end," a senior FBI official told me. "This was a case on which we should have been cut away early, and the NTSB [National Transportation Safety Board] should have run it. But because of the terror fears, that case sucked the life out of many other projects. Most of our best investigators were sidelined on 800."[46]

"We were stretched too thin," concluded Neil Herman, the chief of the JTTF.[47]

That was alarming for some FBI officials, like John O'Neill, the chief of the Bureau's counterterrorism desk. O'Neill, who was killed in the 9/11 attack on the World Trade Center, was increasingly concerned by 1997 that al Qaeda could strike inside the U.S. But O'Neill was an exception.[48] Overall, the FBI's focus on fundamentalist terror directed against the U.S. had been diverted for nearly three years. Domestic investigations into the 1995 Murrah blast, the 1996 Atlanta Olympic Park bombing, and the TWA 800 crash pushed foreign terrorism to a low priority at the FBI.* The trials of the first World Trade Center bombers as well as those involved in the plot to blow up New York City landmarks were finished. Many in the Bureau were convinced that the major threat from abroad had passed in the early 1990s. Almost no one from the FBI paid attention when, in the midst of the TWA investigation, on September 27, 1996, the capital of Afghanistan, Kabul, fell to Taliban forces. The civil war was over. Mullah Omar and his new-found friend and benefactor, Osama bin Laden, were about to create one of the world's most rigid Islamic societies, as well as a safe haven for terrorists.

American law enforcement's failure to recognize the growing threat from Islamic terror meant that it failed—during the middle of the TWA probe—to aggressively investigate several domestic cases and to pursue leads that might have led to other radicals.

---

*In preparation for security at the 1996 Olympics, Richard Clarke, the head of the government's Counterterrorism Security Group, worried that an airplane could carry out a chemical or biological attack on the stadium during opening ceremonies. When he asked the Justice and Defense departments if there were any conditions under which a civilian plane could be shot down if it posed a terror threat, he was told no. Clarke responded by creating a strict no-fly zone around the stadium.

In February 1997, a Palestinian gunman, Ali Hassan Abu Kamal, opened fire with a pistol on the observation deck of the Empire State Building, killing one tourist and injuring six. He then turned the gun on himself. His suicide note accused the U.S. of using Israel as "an instrument" against Palestinians and said his action was "against the enemies of Palestine."[49] FBI and local police officials downplayed any political motivation, saying instead that the attack was that of a deranged loner upset over recent financial setbacks.

In New York, on July 31, two men with Jordanian passports were arrested in a Brooklyn apartment, where police found a bomb factory. They also uncovered a plot to blow up the busy Atlantic Avenue subway station and a commuter bus. The detonator device was constructed for a suicide attack. The FBI did not have the resources to assist local prosecutors with the case, and again, as with the shooting by a single Arab of young Yeshiva students at the Brooklyn Bridge in 1994, the prosecution presented the perpetrators as isolated extremists who had acted on their own. Their friendships in the community were not thoroughly investigated and, as a result, their links to Hamas were not uncovered for nearly three years.

Yet, in another incident, a Sudanese member of the Republican Brotherhood, a group opposed to the fundamentalist Islamic government in Sudan, called journalist Steve Emerson about six months into the FBI's investigation of TWA 800. The man was now a plumber in Brooklyn and was calling from the basement of a building where he had found scores of boxes of old records from the Alkifah Refugee Center, the hotbed of radical activity from which Emir Shalabi had been murdered on the order of Sheikh Rahman. The records had evidently been moved there for safekeeping after the first World Trade Center attack.

Emerson immediately called the FBI in Washington and New York. "To our utter amazement," he recalled, "they said they couldn't do anything about it. The field agents were very interested, but when they ran it up to their superiors, they were told it wouldn't fly. We even smuggled out a few pages to pique their interest but the superiors would not budge."

"We were stretched so damn thin over [TWA Flight] 800 that we would have needed evidence of an imminent crime about to be committed on American soil," a retired FBI supervisor in charge recounted.

"That would have been enough to get an instant investigation going. But when someone was coming along with a chance to land historical papers about an investigation that was then three years old, it just wasn't going to happen. We didn't have time to get blamed for looking like we were picking on Arab-Americans."[50]

CHAPTER 12

THE MONEY TRAIL

The lifeblood of a terror organization is money. Without money it cannot train new recruits, plan operations, or buy compliance of corrupt officials. U.S. investigators have always had difficulty following the money trail abroad. However, it appears now that law enforcement was little better at penetrating the terror financing that flourished inside the United States during the years that Islamic fundamentalism was gaining popularity.

After 9/11, the broad mandates and aggressive legal tools of the October 2001 Money Laundering Abatement and Anti-Terrorist Financing Act led to the unmasking of several dozen domestic terror-financing schemes.[1] Charities sometimes masqueraded as conduits to pass funds to militant groups, and in other instances, supposedly legitimate businesses acted as fronts—similar to commonplace schemes in the narcotics trade—to funnel dollars to foreign terrorists. Terror groups funded from North America included Hezbollah, Islamic Jihad, and Hamas.[2] Law enforcement officials estimate the illegal traffic in millions of dollars annually, mostly starting in the mid-1980s.

Mohamad Youssef Hammoud may not be the biggest financier of terror nabbed by U.S. authorities in recent years, and the network not the largest, but his case—laid bare in 2000 in a U.S. District Court in Charlotte, North Carolina—provides an intimate view of not only how terror was financed on American soil during the 1990s, but also how it managed to stay under the law enforcement radar.[3]

Hammoud, a Lebanese Shiite Muslim, was only sixteen when he

received paramilitary training at a Hezbollah camp in 1990. Two years later, he entered the United States.[4] He settled in Charlotte, and there, while working at a Domino's Pizza, met other Lebanese Shiites. Over six months, he organized a small group, all Hezbollah sympathizers, including two brothers, three cousins, and several friends from his neighborhood in Lebanon. Initially, the meetings seemed harmless, consisting largely of singing Hezbollah rally songs, listening to taped speeches of radical Muslim leaders, and watching videos of Hezbollah "victory" attacks on Israel. But the group was increasingly imbued with anti-Israeli and anti-American invective, and eventually decided to do its part to contribute to Hezbollah's struggle by raising money for the terror group.[5]

They discussed several plans before settling on smuggling cigarettes, something they heard about from other Muslims in Charlotte. In North Carolina, the state levied only a 5 cent tax per pack. In Detroit, with America's largest concentration of Muslims and Arab immigrants, there is a 75 cent state tax on every pack. So by 1995, Hammoud and his cohorts began making weekly 680-mile journeys to Detroit. On each trip, they crammed up to 1,500 cartons of cigarettes, bought inexpensively at local tobacco outlets, inside a large van. They sold some of the cigarettes along the way to gas stations owned by Lebanese immigrants. Then, once in the Motor City, they sold most of the cigarettes to local Lebanese Shiite colleagues. Each trip netted up to $10,000, all of it from the taxes that their Detroit counterparts avoided paying the state of Michigan. In their first three years, Hammoud alone charged nearly $300,000 on ten different credit cards to buy cigarettes in North Carolina. By now, he had purchased his own tobacco shop in order to acquire cigarettes at bulk wholesale prices, and also opened a Lebanese restaurant to launder the flood of cash. Prosecutors ultimately concluded that the Hammoud cell sent several million dollars by courier and wire transfers to Hezbollah, as well as equipment such as night vision goggles, computers, and global positioning systems.[6]

Hammoud and his cell made little effort to hide their tracks, paying for gas on the thirteen-hour journey to Detroit with credit cards, which later allowed law enforcement to precisely patch together their movements. They also racked up driving violations, mostly speeding tickets. Sometimes those traffic stops led to searches of the van, and without any business documents, police confiscated unexplained cash and the cigarette cartons they found inside. Over five different speeding stops, police seized more than $62,000 in cash, and almost two million cigarettes. Somehow it took nearly a year before the multiple stops and confiscations raised suspicion. Finally, in 1996, North Carolina law enforcement officials, together with the FBI, ATF, and INS, began investigating the group. It would take another four years, however, before 250 law enforcement agents conducted simultaneous raids in North Carolina and Michigan, arresting eighteen people on a variety of money-laundering and racketeering charges, and most importantly, for providing material support to a known terror organization, Hezbollah.* Those arrests led to the discovery that the Hammoud cell had also stockpiled an arsenal of automatic weapons and was running an identity theft ring that supplied fake Social Security numbers and credit cards.

What was startling about the Hammoud case was not just that a Lebanese teenager could establish a fund-raising operation for Hezbollah, but how it exposed the extent to which many American government agencies were hapless in detecting such threats early on. What prosecutors learned was embarrassing in particular to the INS, and was also a reminder that Hammoud was in all likelihood not an exception.

When eighteen-year-old Hammoud had first entered the U.S. on June 6, 1992, he arrived at New York's JFK Airport on a flight from Caracas, Venezuela. He was accompanied by two male relatives. While in South America, all three had paid $200 each to obtain poor-quality counterfeit U.S. visas. INS officers spotted the fake visas as the three tried clearing Customs. But, as it sometimes did pre-9/11, the INS did not immediately put the trio on the next plane back to Venezuela, but rather allowed them to enter the country pending an investigation of their status.

Five months later, Hammoud officially requested political asylum, contending that Israel's Lebanese allies were out to get him and that it had been fear that had caused him to make the mistake in judgment of buying a false visa. It took another thirteen months, until December 1993, for an immigration judge to dismiss Hammoud's fraudulent claim. The judge ordered him deported. This was a year before Ham-

---

*The arrests made headlines in Lebanon. A Hezbollah spokesman dismissed any link between the terror group and the arrests in America, declaring that Hezbollah did not maintain any "organized" group in the U.S., and that the American authorities had concocted the link.

moud began his fund-raising effort for Hezbollah. But Hammoud appealed the judge's deportation order, which allowed him to stay in the U.S. while the appeal worked through the heavily backlogged immigration courts.

A year later, in December 1994, with his appeal still pending, Hammoud married an American, Sabina Edwards. Under INS rules then in existence—despite the standing deportation order—that marriage allowed Hammoud to apply for permanent residency status, a so-called alien green card. It took the INS another eighteen months—by which time the cigarette smuggling operation was well under way—before it discovered that both Hammoud's marriage certificate and Sabina Edwards's birth certificate were fakes. He was again ordered deported, this time within the month. But instead of leaving, he merely stayed in America and gave no forwarding address when he moved. The INS made a feeble effort to locate him. By the following May, in 1997, Hammoud married a second American, Jessica Wedel. And a few months later, in September, he married yet a third American, Angela Tsioumas.

The INS has a well-deserved reputation for horrendous recordkeeping. In Hammoud's case, it lived up to its dismal history. Based on his third marriage, Hammoud had the cheek to reapply for permanent residency. Meanwhile, the INS had misplaced its file documenting his first marriage fraud. It also overlooked that there were now two orders for his deportation, one of them almost four years old. No one in the INS noticed that Hammoud was already married to at least one other woman, nor did they realize that his third wife, Tsioumas, was herself already married. Her marriage to Hammoud was a complete fiction for which she was paid several thousand dollars.[7] In July 1998, more than a year after Hammoud had again applied for permanent residency, the INS incredibly granted him a coveted alien green card. (Hammoud was so confident by this time that the INS was incapable of uncovering his shenanigans that he did not even bother to divorce his second wife until three months after he received his permanent residency.)

Hammoud—finally convicted in 2002 and sentenced in 2003 to 155 years in prison for aiding a designated terror group—is only one of terror's independent financiers who for years slipped unimpeded through the system. And if small operators like Hammoud evaded detection so easily, it is little wonder that large foreign-based operations, often with state sponsorship, remained untouchable despite repeated warnings

from American intelligence that terror money was flowing unob-
structed.

Compared to small-time operators like Hammoud, al Qaeda is sophisticated. Similar to narcotics cartels, by employing many enterprises to
launder money and finance operations, they present daunting challenges
to law enforcement. Before 1998, al Qaeda used the U.S. banking system
for many of its transactions, trusting, as did many other investors, the
absolute reliability of the American system.[8]

But bin Laden never put all his trust in a single system. In the mid-
1990s, while still in Sudan, he capitalized the al-Shamal (North) Islamic
Bank in Khartoum with nearly $50 million (much of that, CIA analysts
believe, came from Saudi Arabia as part of its secret deal with bin Laden
to stay clear of the Kingdom).[9] Bin Laden had also helped create a
financing arm called the Brotherhood Group, an assortment of more
than one hundred wealthy contributors from Arab and Gulf State countries, which allowed money to flow undetected through their companies,
free from prying government investigators.[10]

The Clinton administration did not launch its first concerted effort to
disrupt the network's financing until after the 1998 East Africa embassy
bombings. It froze $240 million in al Qaeda and Taliban assets in U.S.
bank accounts. Clinton also froze all funds from Afghanistan's national
airline, Ariana Afghan, which had become bin Laden's personal Federal
Express for shipping arms and personnel.[11]

"It was at that point that al-Qaeda realized where it was vulnerable in
its financial structure and began to systematically move its assets to
commodities," one intelligence analyst, who specialized in al Qaeda's
finances, told a *Washington Post* reporter. "You see a move into dia-
monds, tanzanite and other commodities along with a new emphasis on
creating charities to handle the finances."[12]

The seizure of al Qaeda's U.S. assets prompted the terror organization
to hatch one of its most inventive financial schemes—cornering the diamond trade in the West African countries of Liberia and Burkina Faso,
an enterprise that returned millions annually and ensured safe haven to
some leading terrorists with the prospect of massive bribes to local officials.[13]* A lesser-known gem, blue tanzanite, which ranks second to sap-

*Investigators now believe that from 1998 to 2002, al Qaeda may have con-
trolled up to $100 million of the $10 billion annual diamond trade. An intensive

phires in popularity in the United States, is found only in a five-square-mile area of Tanzania. According to a joint intelligence investigation, the $400 million-a-year tanzanite market became a key source of al Qaeda funding, starting during the mid-1990s.[14]*

Other al Qaeda ventures included the honey trade in Yemen, the distribution of child pornography tapes in Cologne, Hamburg, and Düsseldorf,[15] gun running in Africa and Asia, and heroin smuggling out of the Golden Crescent, the remote opium-rich regions of Afghanistan, Pakistan, and Turkey.[16]

Al Qaeda efforts were assisted before September 11 by a byzantine international hodgepodge of money-laundering laws. There was no central database to provide law enforcement agencies around the world quick access to information about organizations and individuals involved in raising money for terror groups. Instead, data was shared through complex bureaucracies governed by legal assistance treaties. Few countries willingly provided anything under the old rules. Moreover, banking systems favored by al Qaeda—in Kuwait, Dubai and other emirates in the United Arab Emirates, Bahrain, and Lebanon—have for decades refused to enforce anti-money-laundering rules, despite repeated requests by the international community. Saudi Arabia approved amendments in 1999 so that its existing money-laundering regulations could be brought into compliance with international standards, but as of 2003 it had not implemented the changes.

Also, al Qaeda extensively relied on an ancient underground banking system—the hawala—prevalent in Pakistan and Afghanistan, countries without any money-laundering regulations. The hawala is almost

---

year-long European investigation into al Qaeda's financing concluded in December 2002 that Liberian president Charles Taylor received at least a $1 million bribe for harboring leading terrorists for several months after the September 11 attacks. Investigators charged that the terrorists moved between a Liberian safe house and presidential compounds in neighboring Burkina Faso. Taylor, and Burkina Faso's president, Blaise Campaore, have denied the charges.

*Tanzanite was popularized in the movie *Titanic*, where it was the stone used in actress Kate Winslet's necklace. When a *Wall Street Journal* investigation disclosed the al Qaeda–tanzanite link in 2002, the revelations prompted three of the country's largest jewelry retailers—Tiffany, Zale, and QVC—to suspend the gemstone's sales. A task force, dubbed Tucson Tanzanite Protocol, was established to work with the Tanzanian government to ensure that the gems were mined, exported, and traded legally after that date.

custom-made for terror groups, since it is cash-based and leaves behind
no written or electronic records that investigators can follow. Pakistani
bankers estimate that $2.5 to $3 billion enters the country annually
through the hawala system, compared to only $1 billion from the official
banking system.

But beyond the businesses it was running legitimately and through
criminal conspiracies, the largest source of al Qaeda money came from
its fund-raising network of Islamic charities and mosques.[17] Some of the
charities were literally nothing more than way stations for terror funds.
While many have operated freely in the United States for more than
twenty years, the richest are based in Saudi Arabia and have satellite
offices worldwide.[18]*

"For years, individuals and charities based in Saudi Arabia have been
the most important source of funds for al-Qaeda," the Council on Foreign Relations concluded in a November 2002 special report on the
financing of terror. "Saudi officials have turned a blind eye to this problem."[21] Given that al Qaeda's own membership has a disproportionate
share of Saudis, and that Saudi Arabia has the greatest concentration of
wealth in the Middle East, this might not be surprising.

"It looks bad for people in Saudi Arabia to write checks from a bank in
Riyadh to Hamas," says former federal prosecutor Mark Flessner.[22]
Instead, Saudi supporters of extremist groups use facilitators who disguise their contributions as charitable gifts to Islamic causes or bury
them under a mountain of paperwork and international transfers so the
trail of the funds cannot be followed by investigators.[23] Saudi officials
admit that between $200 and $300 million flows out of their kingdom
annually to a wide array of Saudi-based Islamic charities.[24] (Every Mus-

*A cache of documents discovered by U.S. agents in Bosnia in 2002 disclosed a
so-called Golden Chain of bin Laden's top twenty Saudi financial supporters. The list
included the families of three billionaire Saudi banking tycoons, several leading
industrialists, and one ex-government minister.[19] Saudi officials were again on the
defensive when it was discovered that a family that had befriended two of the 9/11
hijackers—Nawaf Alhazmi and Khalid al-Midhar—had received several thousand
dollars in cashier's checks purchased by Princess Haifa bint Faisal, the daughter of
the late King Faisal and the wife of Prince Bandar the Saudi ambassador to the
United States. Saudi officials explained away the money as innocent charitable contributions that were routine for royal family members. Even in March 2003, U.S.
government officials said that nine of the top ten financiers on their suspect list for
supporting terror were Saudi.[20]

lim has a religious duty to give at least 2.5 percent of his annual income to humanitarian causes.)

Before the September 11 attacks, Islamic charitable and religious organizations received little scrutiny from U.S. law enforcement. During most of the 1980s, the United States turned a blind eye to the money raised, since much of it was being funneled to the CIA-backed mujahedeen in Afghanistan.[25] The problem was that when the Afghan war ended in 1989, bin Laden easily tapped into those same sources for funding the jihad and applied them to a wider campaign against the West. The Clinton administration did send mid-level officials to Saudi Arabia, Bahrain and the United Arab Emirates, and Kuwait in 1999 to gather information about charities that might be aiding al Qaeda. But Saudi Arabia and the Emirates refused to cooperate, and while Bahrain and Kuwait promised assistance, nothing was forthcoming. "They listened carefully," said Jonathan Winer, former deputy assistant secretary of state. "The meetings were courteous, and very little happened afterwards." As memories faded regarding the East Africa embassy bombings, the Clinton administration did not press the issue.[26] Saudi Arabia, in particular, was treated "with kid gloves," according to Stuart Eizenstat, who was Clinton's deputy treasury secretary.[27]

After the first World Trade Center attack, some interest stirred among U.S. investigators to look into the problem of terror financing within America and from foreign countries. But those probes were suspended after the Murrah bombing and the shift in focus to domestic terror.

Before September 11 the Bush administration paid only slightly more attention to terror finances. But that changed dramatically after September 11 when the government moved aggressively against suspect charities. In the months after the World Trade Center attacks, so-called jump teams of American forensic accountants, money-laundering investigators, and lawyers were formed to track terror finances. Many of the new teams visited foreign countries in the hope of coordinating an international network to stop the flow of funds. Domestically, federal law enforcement officials raided the offices and seized the assets of some of the largest Muslim charities in the U.S., including the Holy Land Foundation for Relief and Development in Richardson, Texas, and the Global Relief Foundation and the Benevolence International Foundation, both of Illinois.[28] Holy Land had raised $13 million in donations in 2000 alone.

"Our foundation helps people in need," insisted Dalal Mohammed, a spokeswoman for Holy Land, responding to the news of the government raids. "We don't do a test on whether families are in a criminal situation."[29] Officials from some of the other charities raided by U.S. authorities claimed they raised money only for development and aid projects in Muslim countries, but the FBI and Treasury Department charged that in each case millions of dollars in contributions had been siphoned away to terror groups like Hamas.[30]

Again, a single case—the Holy Land Foundation—provides an insight into how effectively terror groups financed their work, and also how seldom U.S. investigators cracked such cases before 9/11. It took the FBI nine years to shut down Holy Land.

Hamas, an Islamic fundamentalist group, was founded in the Gaza Strip in 1988. Its goal was to replace Israel with an Islamic theocracy.* The following year, in Los Angeles, a group of Hamas sympathizers founded the Occupied Land Fund, with its headquarters listed at a post office box. In Arabic-language appeals in local papers such as the monthly *Ila Filastin*, the group did not hide that it was raising money for more than merely building schools and hospitals. A typical ad was one that ran in 1989: "We call you to Jihad for the sake of Allah by donating any amount you can in support of the Intifada's families in Palestine."[31]

In 1992, the organization relocated to Richardson, registered as a nonprofit group dedicated to "charitable relief for refugees and the indigent needy" among Palestinians in the West Bank and the Gaza Strip. In Texas, Holy Land became more sophisticated by dropping the explicit calls for jihad. It started using modern fund-raising tools, establishing automatic bank withdrawals for donors and setting up matching gift programs with unsuspecting prominent companies like Home Depot and American Express. Donors could make contributions through popular websites like Amazon. Borrowing a successful fund-raising tool from Christian charities, individuals who gave regular monthly donations were allowed to "sponsor" a Palestinian child and receive photos and letters from the child.[†]

---

*Hamas is an Arabic abbreviation for "Islamic Resistance Movement."

†The children's letters differed from any other charity in that they often carried a political message. Typical was that of a Palestinian girl in a letter published in the Holy Land newsletter in 2001: "I enjoy good health and I am doing very well in my studies. My father, who spent the last 13 years in Israeli prison, has recently been released, truly a mercy and blessing from God."

From its early days in Texas, the local FBI office had information from Washington that raised questions about whether Holy Land might be funneling money to Hamas. The suspicions had been raised by Israeli investigators who were then looking into the foundation's West Bank offices.

"From the start, some of us had little doubt about their connection to Hamas," Buck Revell, who ran the Dallas FBI's inquiry in the early 1990s, said.[32] Revell recalled that the FBI quickly had come across American Express records that showed the foundation had paid for travel by senior Hamas operatives to attend fund-raising events in the U.S.[33] But the Bureau was in no rush to shut down Holy Land in the early days. Instead, they wanted to follow its key members to see if they might help develop information to prevent future terror attacks in the U.S. and abroad. "To shut it down at that time," said Robert Blitzer, who was then chief of the Bureau's counterterrorism unit, "probably would not have been in the best interest of the nation."[34]

Meanwhile, law enforcement continued gathering potent evidence that it was much more than a benevolent charity. The Bureau had electronic surveillance at a Marriott Courtyard hotel near the Philadelphia airport in 1993, where three of Holy Land's leaders—chief executive Shukri Abu Baker, executive director Haithan Maghawri, and chairman Ghassan Elashi—held a summit meeting with three Hamas leaders.* They discussed violent ways to derail the Middle East peace process and to replace Arafat's Palestinian Authority with a more radical regime. And, most aggravating to the FBI agents monitoring the meeting, they talked about how the "democratic environment in the United States allowed them to perform activities that are extremely important to their cause."[35]

A year later, in 1994, with the country more alert to Islamic fundamentalism because of the first World Trade Center attack, FBI surveillance on a meeting in Oxford, Mississippi, picked up Hamas officials declaring that Holy Land had been selected as the terror group's chief

---

*According to the FBI report, the other three were Muin Kamel Mohammed Shabib, a Hamas recruiter and weapons procurer; Abdelhaleem Hasa Ashqar, a top U.S. fund-raiser for the terror group; and Mohammad al-Hanooti, the top Hamas fund-raiser in New Jersey. When the FBI later asked Elashi if he was at the Marriott summit, he denied ever being in Philadelphia. When agents then produced American Express receipts that showed he had been there, he said he did not recall ever attending such a meeting. (None of the men could be reached for comment.)

fund-raiser in the United States. The Bureau again found American Express records that showed Holy Land had now paid for another eleven fund-raising trips around the U.S. by two Hamas operatives. One of those men, Sheikh Muhammed Siyam, was chief of Hamas's military wing in Gaza, and at a Los Angeles fund-raising dinner, he urged the crowd of contributors, "Finish off the Israelis! Kill them all! Exterminate them! No peace ever!"[36]*

Word of the FBI inquiries into Holy Land found its way to reporters, and a series of articles began raising questions about the foundation and its links to terror. Holy Land was aggressive, however, in fighting any insinuation. The foundation hired public relations firms, later gave $10,000 to the city of Fort Worth after a tornado struck in order to burnish its reputation, and also engaged the power-connected Washington, D.C., law firm of Akin Gump. When *The Dallas Morning News* ran some stinging articles about Holy Land's links to Hamas, the foundation sued.

In 1995, Congress had passed a law that allowed the president to seize the assets of groups that aided terrorists. President Clinton used the opportunity to finally name Hamas a terror organization and issued an executive order freezing its U.S. assets. Holy Land was not mentioned even though the new law was drafted so broadly that it was possible to freeze an organization's assets if its funds merely "benefited" a terror group. "You didn't have to be buying bullets," said ex–FBI analyst Matt Levitt.[38]

A major reason for the FBI's inaction, according to Buck Revell, was the inherent caution in pre-9/11 Washington about aggressively pursuing probes that might involve political or religious advocacy.[39] Many senior officials in the Justice Department undeniably remembered the congressional investigations during the 1970s that exposed the FBI's illegal tactics—including spying, blackmail, and even sabotage—against leftist political and religious groups. The FBI had also had bad experiences in trying to link other groups to supporting terror. In the 1970s, it moved against the Irish Noraid (Northern Aid Committee), which raised money for Catholic widows and orphans in Northern Ireland. The FBI charged that Noraid also ran guns for the IRA, but was

*When the FBI asked Holy Land official Ghassan Elashi about such rhetoric, he replied, "I thought we had freedom of speech here." Holy Land raised $207,000 from the attendees at that meeting.[37]

unable to make a case, and eventually was castigated by some prominent politicians. In the early 1980s, the Bureau investigated CISPES
(Committee in Solidarity with the People of El Salvador), a Chicago-
based organization that backed the Salvadoran Marxist rebels. CISPES
not only denied any terror links, but sued the FBI in federal court, and
after nearly a decade, the FBI settled the case by agreeing to pay
$190,000 for CISPES's legal fees and issuing the following remarkable
statement: "The FBI shall not conduct an investigation solely on the
basis of activities protected by the First Amendment of the Constitution
of the United States, or on the lawful exercise of any right secured by the
Constitution or laws of the United States."[40]

It is little wonder that after those experiences the FBI was gun-shy
about pursuing a probe against Holy Land, which claimed to have legitimate political and charitable purposes.

The same year that Clinton passed the seizure law, Israeli authorities raided the foundation's branch office outside Jerusalem. They
found key documents tying the money flowing from Texas to the relatives of suicide bombers and Hamas operatives. That material was
summarized and sent to the Justice Department.[41] But after the Murrah bombing, the Dallas FBI field office had shelved its investigation,
and the developments in Israel did not result in anyone in Washington
restarting the probe.

During the next two years, Holy Land operated without any interference from the government. Its leaders became increasingly bold and
often appeared at fund-raising events and Islamic conferences voicing
their support for Hamas.[42] By 1997, the Israelis had collected enough
evidence for the equivalent of the Justice Department to close Holy
Land's Middle Eastern branch and seize its funds. After that closure, the
Israelis sent more evidence to the U.S. about how Holy Land diverted
money to terror groups. That new information finally prompted the
Treasury Department to propose freezing Holy Land's assets. But Attorney General Janet Reno, thinking the evidence was not strong enough,
blocked the freeze from taking place.[43]

The following year, in 1998, new evidence surfaced tying Holy Land
to Osama bin Laden, yet incredibly federal investigators still did not act.
The al Qaeda link had emerged in the FBI's investigation of the East
Africa embassy bombings that August that killed more than two hundred. The FBI discovered a diary kept by Wadi el-Hage, a bin Laden con-

fidant. Hage referred in his diary to a "joint-venture" with Holy Land, and in his address book there was the name and number of an alleged Hamas member who worked with the Texas foundation.*

In January 2001, the leadership changed at the Justice Department and FBI as George Bush took office. Nine months later—and only six days before 9/11—FBI teams raided the Richardson, Texas, office of InfoCom, a company run by relatives of some Holy Land officials and the firm that ran the Holy Land website. The Bush administration froze some company assets, but allowed Holy Land to continue to operate. No charges were filed. It would not be until December 6, almost three months after the World Trade Center and Pentagon attacks, that the FBI finally closed Holy Land.

In the first few months after September 11, 168 charities and other organizations in the U.S. responsible for funneling upward of $50 million annually to a web of terror organizations from al Qaeda to Hezbollah were either closed or had their finances blocked.[44] Thirty-one of those had been on a secret list of suspect charities distributed to American anti-terrorist specialists as early as 1996. For at least six years, the terror organizations reaped the benefits of fund-raising through charities, illegal schemes, and straight money laundering, while law enforcement and Treasury officials failed to move against them.

After September 11, the money pipeline that led from America to foreign terrorists had finally been reduced to a trickle.

*Hage's diary and address book were introduced into evidence in his trial in Federal Court in New York in 2001. He was sentenced to life in prison after being convicted of conspiring to murder Americans in the East Africa bombings.

CHAPTER 13

CAMPAIGN OF TERROR

In April 1997, ISI put out feelers to Prince Turki bin Faisal, the chief of Saudi intelligence, to determine whether Saudi Arabia had any objection to ISI's sponsorship of bin Laden. Bin Laden had become increasingly vocal in press interviews, including one in mid-February in which he said that Muslims were "duty bound to expel the unbelievers" and that the bombings in Riyadh and al-Khobar were merely warnings of what would be coming. "If someone can kill an American soldier," bin Laden said, "it is better than wasting his energy on other matters."[1]

ISI did not want any problems with the Saudis, who were generous financial sponsors. They had no idea, of course, that Prince Turki had reached his own accommodation with bin Laden in 1991. The Saudis covered well, even paying lip service to the American desire to bring him to justice. After the Khobar bombing, ISI wanted to ensure it was not making an enemy of its large southern neighbor and to check whether its public position was its real one. A few days after the ISI queries, the Saudi ambassador to Islamabad surprisingly delivered a formal reply. "Mr. bin Laden has committed no crime in Saudi Arabia. The Kingdom has never called for his arrest."[2] The secret deal between bin Laden and the Saudis was still in good standing.

Not everyone was blind to what was happening in Afghanistan. Egyptian intelligence prepared a report in early 1997 that noted that "Osama bin Laden is working behind closed doors preparing a new group of Arab 'Afghans' under the cover of the Afghan Taliban Movement, with the aim of creating fundamentalist organizations in a number of Arab and Islamic countries."[3]

By the summer of 1997, bin Laden had kicked off the long-range planning for a series of attacks against Western interests that he hoped would be spectacular. Zawahiri, bin Laden's right-hand man, was dispatched to Western Europe where he spent a month activating dormant al Qaeda cells.[4] In September, Iranian intelligence hosted another terror conference in Tehran, in which the attendees were urged "to be ready to launch an unprecedented terrorist campaign."[5] The following month, bin Laden held a war council, with senior commanders from several countries traveling to Kandahar for the meeting.

The "campaign of terror," as bin Laden referred to it, began on November 17, 1997. The Egyptian-born Zawahiri wanted to destabilize his country's secular government and had decided to start by disrupting the profitable tourist trade. A cell he directed opened up with machine guns and hand grenades on a bus of Japanese tourists in northern Egypt. After killing them, the attackers went after another bus filled with French, German, and Swiss passengers. Then they hunted down tourists in the nearby ancient temples, using knives to slaughter more. The police did not arrive for nearly forty-five minutes, by which time fifty-eight tourists were dead, and dozens wounded, many critically.

But a far more ambitious plot was under way. It was a planned double strike against the U.S. government, something bin Laden had first thought of in 1993 when he was in Sudan. That year he had dispatched Ali Mohamed, the former U.S. Army sergeant, to reconnoiter possible targets in neighboring Kenya. Mohamed returned with surveillance photos of several possible targets, including the U.S. and Israeli embassies, as well as the French cultural center.* Bin Laden picked the American

---

*The case of Ali Mohamed is one of the most embarrassing for U.S. law enforcement prior to 9/11. A former Egyptian army officer who served also in the U.S. military, Mohamed had given training seminars in the 1980s to volunteers at New York's Alkifah Refugee Center. In 1989, he trained an Islamic cell that included Kahane assassin El-Sayyid Nosair in the use of firearms. The FBI had him under surveillance, but closed the file, since they did not think any laws had been broken. Mohamed came back from Africa, where he was working with al Qaeda, in 1993. Canadian investigators questioned him that spring after his identity was used by a suspected al Qaeda member trying to enter the U.S. from Vancouver. The FBI located him near San Francisco, and the Bureau spoke to him about possibly testifying against Sheikh Rahman in an upcoming trial. Mohamed gave them some of the earliest information in government files about al Qaeda and convinced the agents he could serve them better as an informant. They let him go. He continued to carry out assignments for bin Laden, including training his personal bodyguards and sur-

embassy, and according to later testimony from Mohamed, used a pencil to draw a line where a suicide truck should attack the building.[6] Soon bin Laden dispatched another cell to Tanzania to coordinate a strike with the Kenya team. As with most al Qaeda operations, the planning proceeded over several years until all the elements were in place.

In February, bin Laden and al-Zawahiri issued fatwas against "all Jews and Crusaders." Bin Laden's focus on "Jews and Crusaders" coincided with an early 1998 visit to one of his Afghan compounds by two representatives of two leading Saudi families. They made a "donation" to bin Laden to ensure he understood that his 1991 agreement not to conduct operations inside Saudi Arabia was still intact. The donations, the Saudi representatives said, had the backing of the House of al-Saud. The CIA, relying on electronic intercepts acquired from another agency, estimated that bin Laden received more than $10 million from his Saudi visitors. Bin Laden reiterated that his Afghan Arabs would not be a threat to the Saudi regime.*

The February plea was bin Laden's strongest yet for jihad. "To kill Americans and their allies, both civil and military, is an individual duty of every Muslim. . . . And to obey God's command to kill the Americans and plunder their possessions where he finds them and whenever he can."[7] The following month, about forty Afghan ulema (clergy) convened and blessed the bin Laden fatwa—that gave him the religious imprimatur he coveted.

---

veilling possible terror targets. He traveled frequently between the U.S. and Afghanistan. His FBI handlers would later contend they had no evidence he had broken any laws. "They did a lousy job of managing him," said Larry Johnson, a former CIA agent and director of the State Department's counterterrorism effort under the administration of the first George Bush. Two months after the East Africa embassy bombings in 1998, Mohamed admitted his complicity and offered to cooperate with federal authorities. In return for his help against his codefendants, he was allowed to plead guilty to five counts. What Mohamed received for his help is not known, as the plea agreement is sealed by the court. His lawyer, and the prosecutors, refuse to comment.

*At a meeting later that year in Kandahar, Prince Turki met with senior ISI operatives, Taliban leaders, and two bin Laden representatives. This resulted in a more formal agreement that the Saudis would not ask the Taliban to extradite bin Laden to the U.S., and in return the Taliban would ensure that the Islamists would not target Riyadh. The Saudis also increased the money they supplied for Taliban weapons, as well as payments to Pakistan's ISI.[9]

In May, bin Laden traveled surreptitiously to Sudan with al-Zawahiri to meet with other regional terror leaders to discuss the final stages of an operation intended to inflict punishment on the U.S.[8] In June, in Kandahar, bin Laden and al-Zawahiri hosted an international conference of Islamic radicals, in which they announced the formation of an Islamic Front to "fight the Americans and the Israelis."[10]

In the midst of this upsurge in terror activity, U.S. Attorney Mary Jo White, in the Southern District of New York, finally filed a sealed indictment on bin Laden in June. The grand jury had been impaneled for two years, and the indictment focused on al Qaeda's role in the deadly firefight in Mogadishu, Somalia, as well as several counts charging bin Laden with conspiracy to kill Americans. The Justice Department restricted knowledge of it to a small group inside the Terrorism and Violent Crime Section. Afraid of leaks, the officials did not even tell people like Sandy Berger, Clinton's national security advisor, or Richard Clarke, the chief of the government's Counterterrorism Security Group, the central clearinghouse for coordinating the government's response to terror threats. Bypassing the CSG, which held weekly meetings in the White House Situation Room and was comprised of counterterrorism experts from the CIA, NSC, Defense Department, and the State Department, was a significant oversight. As a result, although the indictment meant that federal prosecutors were ready to proceed rapidly to trial if bin Laden was arrested, it had little effect on national security planning since few knew anything about it.

On August 7, 1998—the eighth anniversary of the arrival of American troops in Saudi Arabia—bin Laden added to the counts that could be included on any murder indictment against him. Two truck bombs exploded within four minutes of each other outside the U.S. embassies in Nairobi, Kenya, and Dar es Salaam, Tanzania, 450 miles apart. In Nairobi, the concrete-reinforced embassy partially collapsed, windows and doors blew out, and an adjacent seven-story building was destroyed. In Dar es Salaam, the blast tore off one side of the embassy. Although bin Laden was reportedly disappointed that so few Americans died (12), 259 overall were killed and 5,000 wounded. Al Qaeda had managed to pull off an attack that garnered worldwide attention.

That attention also meant that the U.S. government made bin Laden an overnight priority, right in the middle of the Monica Lewinsky scandal that was overwhelming the president.* On the morning of the attacks, Clinton said, "We will use all the means at our disposal to bring those responsible to justice, no matter what or how long it takes. . . . We are determined to get answers and justice." The CIA's response was for Director George Tenet to send a notice to his staff that fighting al Qaeda had become the Agency's top priority.

A few days after the bombings, Sudanese security forces detained two suspects who had arrived in Khartoum from Kenya. The two, holding Pakistani passports, had rented an apartment overlooking the U.S. embassy in Khartoum, and when in Kenya, they had stayed at the Hilltop Hotel, used by other members of the embassy bombing plot. Sudan believed the men were al Qaeda members and sent a cable to the FBI offering to extradite them to America.[11]

Before the FBI could reply, on August 20, Clinton ordered eighty Tomahawk cruise missiles to strike three bin Laden training camps in Afghanistan and the al-Shifa pharmaceutical plant in Khartoum, Sudan. (It was the same day the president had to submit a DNA sample to the special prosecutor in the Lewinsky matter.)

But instead of punishing al Qaeda and sending a strong message of American resolve, the strikes were largely ineffectual. When the cruise missiles hit the al Qaeda training camps, they killed twenty-six Afghan Arabs, though the real target had been bin Laden and his deputies. They were nowhere to be found, having left the camps almost immediately after the bombs had ignited at the East Africa embassies. Also, Pakistani intelligence officials, aware of the timing of the strike, had warned key Taliban and al Qaeda allies, even sending a senior ISI operative to personally tell bin Laden of the impending attack.[12]

As for the Sudanese pharmaceutical factory, which the administration believed produced materials for chemical weapons, the strike set off a debate about whether the intelligence that had led to the strike was mistaken. A series of leaks from those who opposed the strikes filtered to

*Even with the extensive coverage of the embassy bombings by the American press, a later university study showed that between the 1996 truck bomb at the Khobar Towers and the August 1998 truck bombs at the embassies, the most prominently covered news story in both newspapers and television was neither terror attack, but rather the gruesome killing of six-year-old beauty pageant queen JonBenét Ramsey.

the press. Janet Reno had pressed the White House to delay the raid to allow the FBI to have more time for its investigation. She was overruled by the White House. Three of the four joint chiefs of staff (navy, air force, and Marine Corps) were not told about the military response plans until the evening of the raids. The White House had instructed Chairman General Henry Shelton not to brief them. And the FBI director, Louis Freeh, was also frozen out, since the White House did not ask the Bureau to review the evidence supplied by the CIA.

Sudan was so furious over the military attack that it allowed the two suspects it had detained after the East Africa embassy bombings, who had been offered to the U.S., to leave for Pakistan, where they disappeared.

And an article in *The New Yorker* by investigative journalist Seymour Hersh raised substantive questions about whether al-Shifa was in fact a weapons-producing plant as the U.S. adamantly maintained.*

"There is . . . widespread belief that senior officials of the White House misrepresented and over-dramatized evidence suggesting that the Tomahawk raids had prevented further terrorist attacks," Hersh wrote.

Hersh also questioned Clinton's motives in ordering them, noting that it was only three days after the president gave evidence to the grand jury in the Monica Lewinsky case, after which he had made an angry television appearance. Might the missile strikes be Clinton's attempt to divert the country from his personal problems? Hersh wondered. That gave ammunition to Republicans, who were increasingly depicting every foreign policy move as an attempt to distract voters.

Clinton and his aides had expected that charge. But the White House thought it would be able to convince skeptics that the strikes were justified. They were wrong, and the chorus of critics grew.

Daniel Benjamin, the director for counterterrorism at the National Security Council, recalled that the months after the strikes, filled with press accusations and Republican criticisms, were "a nightmare."[13]

"Not only were they [the press] not buying it," said Benjamin, "they were accusing the administration of essentially playing the most shal-

---

*Later, more questions would be raised when Professor Thomas Tullius (chair of the Chemistry Department at Boston University) examined—with full access—the bombed-out remains of al-Shifa. He found no trace whatsoever of EMPTA, the chemical whose supposed presence at al-Shifa served as the forensic evidence that the pharmaceutical facility was manufacturing banned VX nerve gas.

low and foolish kind of game to deflect attention from other issues. It was astonishing."[14]

But the most chilling effect of the criticism was on the president himself. It made it less likely that Clinton would pursue tougher action against bin Laden.

"The dismissal of the al-Shifa attack as a blunder had serious consequences," Benjamin concluded. "That in turn meant there was no support for decisive measures in Afghanistan—including, possibly, the use of U.S. ground forces—to hunt down the terrorists."

After the outcry over the missile strikes, Clinton directed that the campaign against al Qaeda be a covert one conducted by the CIA, with an emphasis on disrupting their operations. He also authorized lethal force only if they found bin Laden or other top al Qaeda leaders.[15]

On at least two occasions (some critics say four times) over the next fifteen months, real opportunities presented themselves to eliminate bin Laden himself, but Clinton never felt comfortable enough to pull the trigger. The first intelligence identified an elaborate al Qaeda encampment pitched in an isolated region of Afghanistan, complete with a convoy of Toyota Land Cruisers and a plane nearby. When the CIA discovered the land was owned by wealthy Emiratis, and without a confirmation that bin Laden himself was there, Clinton passed. He did not want to take a chance on hitting the wrong target after the fuss over the Sudanese pharmaceutical plant.

The second time Clinton had to make the choice, bin Laden had been credibly pinpointed in an eastern Afghan city. However, he was in a densely populated neighborhood, and Defense Secretary William Cohen estimated "hundreds would die." Without certainty that bin Laden would be hit, Clinton again demurred.

After he left office, Clinton told *Newsweek* that he thought he had "a 40 percent chance of knowing he [bin Laden] could be hit. But there was a very large number of women and children in that compound and it's almost like he was daring me to kill him. And we know at the same time he was training people to kill me. Which was fair enough—I was trying to get him. I felt it would hurt America's interests if we killed a lot of Afghani women and children and didn't even get him."*

Even in late 1998, when intelligence reports showed that Abu Hafs,

---

*By the summer of 2000, CSG's Richard Clarke was pushing a new concept from the Pentagon, a forty-nine-foot unmanned flying drone—dubbed the Predator—to

an important al Qaeda operative, had been pinpointed in Room 13 at the Dana Hotel in Khartoum, the administration debated whether to strike. White House officials wanted either to eliminate Hafs or have Sudan expel him to a friendly country where he could be interrogated. By the time the CIA got White House approval to develop a plan, Hafs was gone.[16]

The following year, in August 1999, the U.S. missed yet another opportunity to capture bin Laden. According to a well-placed American intelligence analyst assigned to counterintelligence operations against foreign terror networks, starting in June, the United States had picked up increasing evidence that al Qaeda would like to commemorate the African attacks with another strike.

In order to put bin Laden on the defensive, in late July, the U.S. leaked the false story in the Arab Gulf States that it might dispatch a team of commandos to capture the world's most wanted terrorist. Initially, the fear that Special Forces might arrive in Afghanistan prompted Afghan officials to publicly announce that bin Laden was no threat.

"Bin Laden is in Afghanistan, but he is under the control of special guards," said Maulwi Wakil Ahmed Mutawakil, the Islamic militia's most senior spokesman. "Bin Laden has no military training camps in Afghanistan. . . . All of the activities of bin Laden have been stopped," he said, trying to assure the West of his good intentions.

But the U.S. accelerated the false whisper campaign to say that a commando team had targeted the terrorist's latest encampment. That evidently so rattled the Taliban that they issued a public warning that the U.S. was about to attack bin Laden. Qatar's Al Jazeera satellite television even reported that U.S. commandos had landed in Pakistan in preparation for a strike. The United States, for its part, officially denied the report.

The irony is that during the time this psychological warfare was being played out, a real chance to nab bin Laden apparently passed. According to the American intelligence analyst, a field source in Pakistan had

---

find bin Laden. If armed, it might even be able to eliminate him. But money and jurisdiction over who controlled it—the Pentagon or the CIA—meant the program limped along until 9/11. Then, used extensively in the war in Afghanistan, it was an unqualified success. In September 2001, a Predator fired its two Hellfire missiles, killing Muhammad Atef, al Qaeda's military chief for nearly a decade.

passed word through a Pakistani military officer that bin Laden was in the northwest town of Peshawar. The warning was given on August 4, 1999. For reasons still unclear, U.S. intelligence only received notification on August 7, by which time bin Laden was safely back in Afghanistan. A follow-up investigation confirmed that bin Laden had indeed been in Pakistan for at least two days, but a subsequent internal investigation at the CIA to determine how it could take three days to receive such a tip proved inconclusive.

The U.S. response after the East Africa attacks, and its whisper campaign intended to disrupt al Qaeda, did not intimidate the terror group. It was gearing up for a series of blows to the West as the millennium approached. The fear among most Western intelligence agencies was that al Qaeda would try to do something spectacular around New Year's. Tensions were heightened during this period when the NSA electronically intercepted a message within al Qaeda that bin Laden was plotting a "Hiroshima" against America.[17]

In October 1999, many in law enforcement thought the first blow happened when they heard about the crash of EgyptAir Flight 990, some sixty miles south of Nantucket, killing all 227 on board. The plane's black box recorder revealed that a moment before the crash, the copilot, Gamil al-Batouti, said "tawakltu ala Allah," which means "I put my trust in God." Then the airliner nearly nose-dived into the ocean. There was concern that al-Batouti might be the first in a series of fundamentalists who had been placed inside commercial planes to bring them down near the millennium. A lengthy investigation by the National Transportation Safety Board found no evidence of a mechanical failure, but the FBI could find no links between al-Batouti and radical Islamists either, even though it was intrigued that on the flight there had been more than thirty Egyptian military officers, including seven generals. That would have been a tempting target for fundamentalists opposed to Mubarak's secular rule. But eventually, federal authorities concluded that the crash was intentionally perpetrated by the copilot as his own personal suicide.

Several real plots meant to capitalize on the success of the East Africa bombings attack were under way, but they went awry. In Jordan's capital, Amman, an al Qaeda cell had planned to bomb the four-hundred-room Radisson Hotel, which was expected to be crammed with tourists over Christmas and New Year's. But Jordanian security officers, who had

tapped the phone of one of the cell members, monitored a call from top
bin Laden aide Abu Zubaydah giving the order to carry out the attack.
The Jordanians raided the cell's safe house in an Amman suburb and
discovered seventy-one barrels of sulfuric and nitric acids, enough to
level the Radisson.

In Yemen, a plot to attack the incoming USS *The Sullivans,* a destroyer,
with a bomb-laden speedboat failed when the terrorists overloaded their
small skiff and it sank before getting close to the U.S. ship. Although law
enforcement would not learn about the Yemeni plot until al Qaeda
records were confiscated a year later, when Jordanian authorities
thwarted the bombing of Amman's Radisson Hotel, law enforcement
was on high alert.

In Port Angeles, Washington, a customs official decided to search the
rental car of a young Arab crossing into the U.S. from Canada. The Arab,
Ahmed Ressam, was sweating profusely even though it was a cold win-
ter day. He had reason to be nervous. In his trunk Customs found 110
pounds of explosives and some circuit-board timers.

There were only fifteen days before the New Year. Had other terrorists
entered the country? And if so, what could they be planning?

Thousands of FBI agents volunteered or were assigned to the investigation, called BORDERBOM. From Seattle to Boston, they questioned
hundreds of Muslims and put dozens of suspected radicals under visible
surveillance. The agents made early morning "knock-and-talk" visits,
quizzing Muslims at their homes. They hoped the massive presence of
the Bureau's investigation might make any terrorists reconsider and
abandon their plans.

In Seattle, however, one Arab, Abdelghani Meskini, was proceeding
with his mission, for which he had been promised a fake visa that would
allow him to travel to an al Qaeda training camp in Afghanistan.
Meskini had arrived recently in Seattle and rented a car and then a room
at a run-down motel near the city's best-known tourist site, the Space
Needle. He was to meet Ressam, who had been stopped at the border
with explosives in his car.

When Ressam was two days late, Meskini flew back to his home in
Brooklyn. Meanwhile, FBI agents found Meskini's phone number written on the back of a business card in Ressam's wallet. They placed a
wiretap on his phone.

At dawn on December 30, 1999, sixteen FBI SWAT commandos tiptoed up two narrow flights of stairs to Meskini's small apartment. They smashed the door with a battering ram. Meskini was handcuffed, shackled, and driven to FBI headquarters for questioning.

"What's your name?" he was asked as the sedan screeched away. Meskini hesitated. Treasury agent Sal Emilio, the driver, exploded: "Don't make it hard! You don't know how hard we can make it." He glared at the prisoner as he swerved through the thick morning traffic. Meskini was read his rights. Already weak from fasting during the Ramadan holy days, he was interrogated for eleven hours in a ten-by-ten room, one wrist handcuffed to a steel bar on the wall.

"You're the big fish, and you're going away for twenty-five years," agents told him. Finally Meskini talked. His orders were to rendezvous with Ressam and pick up a car packed with explosives. He then intended to blow up the Seattle Space Needle in the middle of the millennium celebrations. One hundred thousand people were expected at the Needle that year. Mayor Paul Schell, who had earlier been told of the explosives seized at the border crossing, had already canceled the event, saying "the FBI can't assure us there is no risk."

Terrorists only have to succeed occasionally to sow fear in the public and to further their own aims. Ten months later, on October 12, 2000, the Yemeni terrorists got another opportunity to make up for their bungled attempt on the USS *The Sullivans*. A lighter explosive load was used on a rubber dinghy to attack the USS *Cole*, a $1 billion guided missile destroyer, in the port of Aden, killing seventeen seamen, wounding thirty-nine, ripping a forty-foot hole through the half-inch steel hull, and nearly sinking it (repairs cost $240 million). Bin Laden was ecstatic with a strike against one of America's most sophisticated ships—soon an al Qaeda recruitment video that circulated throughout the Middle East opened with footage of the wrecked destroyer.

A National Security Council memo sent to the Pentagon in 1997 had warned precisely of terror threats to American ships in port. The navy not only had ignored the warnings, but did not even have the *Cole* on higher alert when it approached Yemen, which then ranked second to Afghanistan on the State Department's list of terror-sponsoring states.[18]

Some officials inside the administration, like CSG's Richard Clarke, were convinced that after the *Cole*, the next attacks might be inside the

U.S. Clarke argued strenuously for a broad military response targeting a known list of terror training camps and Taliban support facilities.[19] But Clinton's reaction to the *Cole* attack was more muted than his tough talk on previous attacks. While he promised to "find out who was responsible and hold them accountable," he seemed disturbed that the bombing might complicate a very sensitive stage of the administration's hard-fought efforts to win a Middle East peace.* The bombing came during a new round of fighting there, and Clinton and his aides were preoccupied with defusing the escalating violence between the Israelis and Palestinians and returning them to peace negotiations.†

As in the 1998 embassy bombings, U.S. investigators quickly linked the attack to bin Laden and al Qaeda. Although Clinton would likely have had little problem in winning public support for strong military action, he opted for doing nothing. He passed in late 1998 when presented a targeted military response by General Hugh Shelton, the chairman of the Joint Chiefs of Staff, judging it too costly and unwieldy.[20] Instead, he issued an executive order seizing the assets of bin Laden and al Qaeda. None were found.

The failure to respond publicly again emboldened bin Laden and his top aides. America was capable of being struck, and the country seemed unwilling to retaliate. By the time of the *Cole* attack, bin Laden and al Qaeda were already working on the biggest terror attack ever devised. Nothing in the U.S. response made them rethink their decision to try and bring down the World Trade Center towers in New York.

---

*A CIA analyst who visited the White House as part of an Agency briefing team regarding the *Cole* told the author that nearly half of a fifty-minute meeting was taken up instead with a discussion of the violence in the Middle East. "And most of that was a discussion by the President as to whether anyone in the Agency had done any type of study to determine if Arafat abandoned his military uniform and switched to a Western suit and tie, if his image would so dramatically change that Israelis might find it easier to reach an agreement with the Palestinians. When we left there, we just looked at each other and rolled our eyes."

†Seventeen al Qaeda operatives were later arrested, convicted, and jailed by Yemen for their role in the *Cole* attack. On April 11, 2003, ten of the jailed terrorists, including ringleader Jamal al-Badawi, escaped from their Yemeni jail, and are now the subject of a massive manhunt.

CHAPTER 14

"WE GOT IT COVERED"

After the 1998 East Africa bombings and the attack on the USS *Cole*, Counterterrorism and Security Group's Richard Clarke asked the FBI if it wanted White House assistance in amending the Justice Department's restrictive rules for opening investigations and gathering information. Although it had been clear since the early 1990s that some United States mosques were centers for radical activity, under the existing rules the Bureau was prohibited from having agents attend religious services, eavesdrop on houses of worship, or open an investigation unless it had credible information that a crime was planned. Clarke kept asking the Bureau, which at first ignored him, until they finally told him that they did not require any revisions of the rules in order to successfully break up terror plots.

The FBI's stubbornness did not, unfortunately, surprise Clarke, who had come increasingly to view the Bureau, and its director, Louis Freeh, as extremely sensitive to anything it considered criticism. Near the end of 1999, Clarke saw firsthand how defensive FBI agents could be when pressed. He was overseeing one of his weekly CSG meetings. A National Security Council official told two FBI representatives, Steve Jennings and Michael Rolince, that he had been reviewing some old intelligence files and had been surprised to see that Ayman al-Zawahiri had been in the U.S. in the early 1990s for fund-raising.

"I couldn't believe it," said the NSC official. "Did you know that?"

The two agents barely nodded their heads.

"Well, if he was here, someone was handling his travel and arranging his meetings and someone was giving him money. Do you know who these people are? Do you have them covered? There are cells here and we need to know more about them."

"Yeah, yeah, we know," Rolince replied. "Don't worry about it." He waved his hand as if to dismiss any concern. "We got it covered."[1]*

However, it was evident even to some senior FBI officials that many field agents did not have "it covered" when it came to terrorism. As far back as 1998, Robert Bryant, the deputy director, had written a five-year strategic planning document in which he ranked counterterrorism a "tier one" program and predicted that growing terrorism would "directly threaten the national or economic security of the U.S." But not many shared Bryant's view then.[2]

In 1999, Dale Watson, the Bureau's anti-terrorism unit chief, had concluded that too few agents around the country were working on terror cases or even knew how to do so. In March 2000, he convened an unprecedented meeting in Washington of all supervising agents in charge of the Bureau's fifty-six field offices. Some attending mockingly called the conference "Terrorism for Dummies." But what Watson and others in the counterterrorism unit learned was that many field offices had done virtually nothing on terror investigations. Later, senior agents at headquarters had to threaten to withhold managers' raises and bonuses unless they paid more attention to the issue. (The efforts were not very successful—on September 10, 2001, there were fewer FBI agents assigned to counterterrorism than there had been in 1998 at the time of the East Africa embassy bombings.)[3]

While some in the Bureau may have appeared almost cavalier in dealing with terrorism, there was little direction from the Clinton administration that might have changed their minds. Clinton had concentrated on pushing the Taliban to dislodge bin Laden, but was not focused on preempting a potential domestic terror strike.

Through the middle of 1999, Clinton did indeed increase the pressure on the Taliban. In July, he issued an executive order freezing the assets of the Afghanistan regime and placing U.S. sanctions on the Tal-

---

*Ali Mohamed, the ex–U.S. Army sergeant, was responsible for al-Zawahiri's travel in America. At the time of the conversation, Ali Mohamed was in federal custody, having made his plea agreement over the East Africa bombings. There is no evidence that at that time anyone from the FBI had quizzed him about any role he had had with al-Zawahiri in the early 1990s.

iban. That blocked the Taliban from retrieving Afghanistan's $220 million in gold reserves on deposit with the Federal Reserve.[4]

In late 1999, Clinton was presented with the preliminary findings of a blue-ribbon panel—which he helped create—on the threat from terror. Back in 1993, after the first World Trade Center attack, Clinton had considered but decided against establishing a commission to study terrorism and how to best protect the home front from further attacks. Five years later, after the East Africa embassy attacks, House Speaker Newt Gingrich floated the same idea. Not wanting to be upstaged, Clinton joined the effort, and soon a bipartisan fourteen-member panel was empowered to make sweeping strategic recommendations on how the United States could ensure its future security. The U.S. Commission on National Security/21st Century was cochaired by ex-senators Gary Hart and Warren Rudman. They had a staff of researchers, spent nearly two years studying the problem, and visited twenty-five countries.

The preliminary report that now landed on the president's desk concluded, "Americans will likely die on American soil, possibly in large numbers." The report received no press coverage. "To this day," Hart said, "it still bothers me that not even *The New York Times* gave us even a small mention."[5]

The same thing had happened a few months earlier when the National Symposium on Medical and Public Health Response to Bioterrorism issued a prescient report about the growing threat of bioterror, including the use of anthrax. The mainstream media paid no attention.

While Hart may have been disappointed that newspapers were not paying attention to his committee's findings, some officials inside the government were equally frustrated by the White House's failure to concentrate on their own conclusions. The White House had ordered a review of American defenses, and the internal report, completed in March 2000, concluded that despite ten years of government programs to improve homeland defense, the country was vulnerable to attack. Citing the need for new joint federal-state-local terror task forces and a major effort to "detain and deport potential sleeper cells," the report also exposed how the INS was utterly ineffective in preventing terrorists from entering the country. Yet no one in the administration championed a single recommendation in that report.[6]

In April 2000, Clinton traveled to India and Pakistan, his first visit to

the subcontinent. Twice he met with Pakistan's General Pervez Musharraf. At a long meeting with dozens of aides, terrorism was barely mentioned. Clinton later said he feared raising the subject in front of
Pakistanis of unknown loyalty.[7]* Another opportunity to confront terrorism with a sponsoring state had passed by.

*Sandy Berger later claimed that in the private meeting Clinton had with
Musharraf the president had pushed "very hard," telling Musharraf to "get bin
Laden." "I will do as much as I can," Musharraf had assured him. That satisfied the
president. One of the reasons that the Clinton White House may have been more
relaxed about the terror threat was, according to Berger, that the FBI had repeatedly
assured them during 1999 that al Qaeda lacked the ability to launch a domestic
strike.

CHAPTER 15

ENTER THE HIJACKERS

While the FBI was assuring other government counterterrorism experts that they had the matter of al Qaeda cells in America "covered," nineteen young men who might have disagreed with that appraisal had begun arriving in America.

A sullen-faced Mohamed Atta landed in Newark, New Jersey, from Prague, on a temporary visitor's visa issued in Berlin on June 3, 1999. Picking up a *New York Times,* he learned what the country's newspaper of record considered important that day. A front-page story was headlined, "Canoeist Goes to Court, Fighting for Right to Curse." It was about a twenty-five-year-old computer programmer charged under an obscure century-old law with a misdemeanor for cursing when his canoe overturned. This was the society and culture that Atta and his collaborators considered salacious and insidious, and he was in the vanguard of a group that intended to disrupt it.

When later that same year Ziad al-Jarrah—the pilot of the doomed United Airlines Flight 93, which crashed in rural Pennsylvania—received his pilot's license in Hamburg, Germany, the United States was not focused on the increasingly violent anti-American rhetoric sweeping religious schools and mosques across the Middle East. Instead, the topic du jour was whether husband-and-wife actors Tom Cruise and Nicole Kidman had hired sex therapists to teach them how to make love in the film *Eyes Wide Shut.*

In April 2000, Nawaf Alhazmi turned up at the National Air College Flight School in San Diego. He wanted to fly a plane. But a school instructor questioned his limited English and he got only one lesson. In May, Alhazmi was joined in San Diego by Khalid al-Midhar. When they asked about learning to fly Boeing jets at Sorbi's Flying Club in San Diego, they were dejected when told they must first master Cessnas and Pipers.

"You can't just jump right into Boeings," the instructor said. "You have to start slower." When the instructor took them aloft, al-Midhar had trouble with rudimentary procedures. At times, he was so nervous that he prayed to Allah. Both Alhazmi and al-Midhar would be on American Airlines Flight 77, which smashed into the Pentagon.

On Memorial Day, May 29, 2000, Marwan al-Shehhi arrived at Newark Airport. Most news organizations featured a story about multiple arrests of Immigration and Naturalization officers for having coerced sex with detained immigrants and selling false entry papers at several processing centers. Al-Shehhi did not need any help from corrupt INS officials. With a tourist visa issued in the United Arab Emirates that very day, he cleared Customs in less than half an hour.

Later, al-Shehhi hooked up with Atta to check out flight schools. In June, the pair arrived at Airman Flight School in Norman, Oklahoma—the same school previously attended by another bin Laden operative. They said they wanted to be pilots, but they didn't like the school, and instead headed for Huffman Aviation in Venice, Florida.

The day before America's 224th birthday, July 3, 2000, cable news programs, talk radio, and newspaper editorials were consumed with the debate raging in the Colorado State Board of Education over whether "In God We Trust" is a religious statement. That same day, Atta and al-Shehhi, who had no doubt about what constituted a religious statement, nor any compunction about mixing policies of state with religious instruction, signed up for flight training at the 1950s-styled, one-story Huffman Aviation Center in Venice, Florida. They paid the $38,000 in fees with checks drawn from a local bank.

Atta (which in Arabic means "the gift") would be the pilot on American Airlines Flight 11, which would crash into the World Trade Center's North Tower. The twenty-three-year-old al-Shehhi would fly United Airlines Flight 175 into the Trade Center's South Tower.

Also in July, Fayez Ahmed left his home in Saudi Arabia, telling his family he was joining the International Islamic Relief Organization. He wound up on United's Flight 175. The following month, Ziad al-Jarrah, a Lebanese man with a German girlfriend, turned up in Venice, Florida, to bone up on his flying. He flew United Airlines Flight 93.

Meanwhile, throughout 2000 the cell received money, most of it wired by an accomplice in Germany. It was by far the best-funded al Qaeda project ever. Some money also came from an account in the United Arab Emirates. The incoming funds—at least $325,000 into about thirty-five American bank accounts—ranged from wire transfers as large as $69,985 to only $1,500 one week before the hijackings.[1] Zacarias Moussaoui, who would later be charged as the twentieth hijacker, returned to the U.S. from Pakistan in February, declaring $35,000 in cash to Customs. (The hijackers had so much money that in the days before 9/11, they returned almost $73,000 to foreign accounts and debit cards.)[2]

On December 21, 2000, Atta and al-Shehhi were issued pilot licenses. Florida was swarming with national journalists at the same time, but none were reporting on terrorism. The 2000 presidential election had deteriorated into an entertaining sideshow—reality television for cable news channels. And while the country enjoyed a good laugh at the expense of Florida's butterfly ballots and hanging chads, Mohamed Atta and Marwan al-Shehhi remained in Florida learning to fly jetliners. After the Supreme Court had issued the 5–4 decision that locked in a Bush victory, several thousand disputed Florida presidential ballots from Palm Beach County, which had been transported to the state capital earlier that month, were loaded into a rental truck and returned to West Palm Beach. Television crews rode near the Ryder truck, filming it live along the way. Atta and al-Shehhi meanwhile crossed the state to Opa-Locka, north of Miami, where they had reserved time on a big jet simulator at SimCenter Inc. Each spent three hours on a full-motion 727 simulator. They concentrated on turns, not landing or taking off. Each paid $1,500 cash.

Also in December, Ahmed Alnami left his home in the Asir region of Saudi Arabia, telling his family he was going on a religious pilgrimage. He ended up on United Airlines Flight 93. Hani Hanjour, a native of Taif in Saudi Arabia who had first entered the U.S. in 1996 on a student visa, traveled from the United Arab Emirates back to America. He became the pilot of the plane that crashed into the Pentagon. Waleed and Wail Alshehri left from a suburb of Abha in Saudi Arabia. They told their father that they were joining Muslim fighters in Chechnya. But on September 11, their father learned they were part of the team that hijacked American Airlines Flight 11, which destroyed the Trade Center's North Tower.

Only after September 11 would Americans learn how many mistakes had been made along the way by American law enforcement and the INS.

CHAPTER 16

"NONE OF THIS IS EVER GOING TO HAPPEN"

The word "terrorism" was mentioned only once during the presidential campaign, and that was in response to a question about the Middle East in the final debate. Recalling his career in Congress, Al Gore said, "I worked hard to . . . deal with the problems of terrorism." It was an issue that no one, from the candidates to pollsters to journalists covering the campaign to voters, considered remotely important in deciding who should occupy the White House.

Historian Robert Dallek told a live CNN audience during the campaign that the 2000 election marked a new era in choosing leaders.

"With the end of the cold war now, there is much less premium, I think, on the idea that you have to have someone with a foreign policy or military background."

"Unless there's a war, of course," remarked anchor Morton Dean.

Everyone laughed at the idea of war.

When the new administration took office on January 21, 2001, those involved in counterterrorism did not suddenly feel that much had changed from the Clinton years. Richard Clarke, who kept his job at CSG, became the only career civil servant to serve as a National Security Council senior director under three consecutive presidents. George Tenet was also kept in charge of the CIA. So the problem with the Bush administration initially was not a matter of continuity, but rather of focus. It sent mixed signals, at times appearing much tougher than Clinton on terrorism, and at other times indecisive. Its first foreign policy and military priority admittedly revolved not around terror, but around an ambi-

tious missile defense shield (when military commanders tried to fill a
$600 million gap in their first budget by diverting funds from ballistic
missile defense, Defense Secretary Donald Rumsfeld would recommend,
two days before 9/11, that the request be vetoed).

The matter of al Qaeda and terrorism was viewed largely as an intelligence problem. The administration was not initially drawn to military
options for dealing with a threat that was not front and center.

"The U.S. government can only manage at the highest level a certain
number of issues at one time—two or three," Michael Sheehan, the
State Department's former coordinator for counterterrorism, told *The
Washington Post.* "You can't get to the principals on any other issue.
That's in any administration."

Although the new administration could have ordered an armed
response for the USS *Cole* attack the previous October—Clinton had left
the decision for Bush—it did not, even though Richard Clarke presented
a detailed memo on January 25 arguing that bombing al Qaeda's training camps was simple and important. And Bush did not renew Clinton's
deployment of submarines and gunships on a six-hour alert near the
Afghan border. In a January 10, 2001, meeting in the Tank, the secure
conference room of the Joint Chiefs of Staff, President-elect Bush and his
defense team met the Joint Chiefs for their first complete briefing. The
subject of the six-hour alert force near Afghanistan was raised by General Henry Shelton, the chairman. He told Bush that he thought the
force was a waste of manpower and money. Intelligence services had
never provided him a target he could strike in time to make the deployment worthwhile. Bush's team had little problem doing away with that
force, in part because they thought that the terror problem was larger
than just removing one person, bin Laden. Instead, they told Shelton,
they intended to develop a strategy to pursue the entire network at once.

One of the things that Richard Clarke told top policymakers, like foreign policy advisor Condoleezza Rice and Vice President Dick Cheney,
was that whatever they chose to do, the *Cole* attack indicated that the old
policies had not worked and they needed something more aggressive.
When Rice first met Clarke, she peppered him with questions about al
Qaeda. She promised Clarke that the new administration's terror policy
would not continue Clinton's "empty rhetoric that made us look feck-
less."[1] Rice asked him to develop a new policy paper. Clarke did so, in a
long and detailed document, but it languished for months as the new
administration lumbered through the transition process.

One of the first chances to test their seriousness was on January 31, only ten days after the president had been sworn in. Former senators Gary Hart and Warren Rudman were wrapping up their work on the U.S. Commission on National Security/21st Century (its preliminary conclusions released toward the close of the Clinton administration had been virtually ignored). In the final report, seven Democrats and seven Republicans unanimously agreed that "the combination of unconventional weapons proliferation with the persistence of international terrorism will end the relative invulnerability of the U.S. homeland to catastrophic attack. A direct attack against American citizens on American soil is likely over the next quarter century." Such a long estimate for the timing of such an attack diluted the report's impact, however, and made it less likely that the new administration or the media would treat it as a priority.

The report included fifty suggestions for useful overhauls of government agencies to enhance domestic security and called for the formation of a cabinet-level position—to be called the National Homeland Security Agency—to combat terrorism.

The two ex-senators sent out several thousand press releases, hundreds of copies of the report, and even met with the editorial boards of *The New York Times*, *The Washington Post*, and *The Wall Street Journal*. Again, nothing made it into newspapers or onto television. "The national media just didn't pay attention," Hart says. One senior reporter from a well-known publication told one of Hart's fellow commissioners, "This isn't important, none of this is ever going to happen," Hart recalls.*

Despite failing to again garner press coverage, commission members began lobbying for their recommendations, convinced that they were important to the nation's security and might eventually save lives. Hart and Rudman met separately with Defense Secretary Rumsfeld, Secretary of State Colin Powell, and Condoleezza Rice, urging each to focus more on terrorism. In April, Hart and Rudman testified before the Senate Judiciary Committee's Subcommittee on Terrorism and Technology. Hart warned, "The prospect of mass casualty terrorism on American soil is

---

*ABC news anchor Barbara Walters, in a post-9/11 interview with Larry King, disagreed with Hart. "It's not our fault," Walters said. This despite admitting to King that before September 11 she expected only "to be doing movie stars in trouble for the next year because this is where the ratings are. . . . There was very little interest in any foreign leaders. I mean, Larry, who knew who the president of Pakistan was?"

growing sharply" and said the nation must embrace "homeland security as a primary national security mission."

Once again, there was no news coverage. And in Congress, just as some members began drafting legislation to enact some of the recommendations into law, it ground to a sudden halt in May. The White House acted as if the Hart-Rudman Commission had never existed. Administration officials said they preferred to table the final report and instead let Vice President Cheney study the problem of terrorism—which the bipartisan group had already spent more than two years studying—while assigning responsibility for domestic security to FEMA, the Federal Emergency Management Agency, headed by former Bush campaign manager Joe Allbaugh (Bush announced a new Office of National Preparedness for terrorism at FEMA, but at the same time proposed reducing FEMA's budget by $200 million).

If the Hart-Rudman Commission was overlooked, it is not surprising that another blue-ribbon panel was equally ignored. The National Commission on Terrorism (informally known as the Bremer Commission, after its chairman, L. Paul Bremer, who had served as ambassador-at-large for counterterrorism in the Reagan administration) had been established by Congress to suggest changes in the way governments battle terror. In June 2000, it released its report, suggesting wholesale changes in the way the FBI and CIA operated. But few were listening, and the recommendations were shelved to be studied at a later date. (Bremer was appointed to direct the rebuilding of postwar Iraq in May 2003.)

"And so Congress moved on to other things, like tax cuts and the issue of the day," recalled Hart. Cheney, who already had a full plate, including supervising the administration's energy plans and its dealings with Congress, was supposed to come up with a report by October 1. September 11 intervened.*

It was not that the Bush administration did not think terror was an important issue, but rather that it did not take seriously a blue-ribbon

---

*After September 11, Hart was dismayed when he saw a former Clinton administration cabinet official on TV calling for the formation of a commission to study the best ways to combat terrorism. He just shook his head in disappointment. "If a former cabinet officer didn't know we existed and what we did, how could the average man on the street?" "Human nature is prevalent in government as well," Rudman said. "We tend not to do what we ought to do until we get hit between the eyes."

panel's report that it considered better suited for a think tank discussion than for implementation as government policy. So Bush officials decided to set the administration's policy on fighting terrorism in their own time and style.

At an April 30 CSG meeting, the influential undersecretary of state Richard Armitage announced an important shift in American policy—from that point on, he said, the top U.S. priority in Southeast Asia would be the complete destruction of al Qaeda. Armitage, as is his style, was blunt. The goal of eliminating al Qaeda, he said, was more important than stopping the spread of nuclear weapons in Asia, preventing another Indian-Pakistani war, or even restoring democracy in Pakistan in the event of a coup against General Musharraf. "Only al Qaeda," said Armitage, "is a direct threat to the United States."[2]

Earlier that April, Condoleezza Rice had briefed Bush on the progress of developing a working strategy to get bin Laden. Present at the meeting were Vice President Cheney and White House chief of staff Andrew Card. Bush was visibly impatient at how slowly policy was being developed to fight al Qaeda. "I'm tired of swatting flies," the president said. "I'm tired of playing defense. I want to play offense. I want to take the fight to the terrorists."[3] But Bush did not want to repeat Clinton's mistake of talking tough publicly and then not following through with strong actions.

The administration's first four months was a quiet time on the terror front. The CIA and NSA picked up virtually nothing in terms of so-called chatter, telephone and satellite intercepts of suspected terrorist communications. It was not until May that Cofer Black, the chief of the CIA's Counterterrorism Center, had gathered intelligence indicating that Abu Zubaydah, a senior al Qaeda leader, might be planning a significant attack. Black thought the target would be overseas, most likely Israel or Saudi Arabia, although the U.S. could not be excluded.

From that point on, terror chatter picked up. As a result, the State Department issued a worldwide terror warning to American travelers and residents overseas. Embassies were placed on a higher security alert, and in the Persian Gulf, the threat condition for the U.S. military was raised to Delta, the highest.[4] The navy's Fifth Fleet left its port in Bahrain, where it was considered an easier target, and headed out to sea. All domestic law enforcement agencies received notice of a possible terror attack. July 4, a day of particular concern, passed without incident. But still the higher alerts stayed in effect. Between May and July 2001, the FBI issued three sets of warnings.

The peak concern was in July, when Egyptian president Mubarak passed along information from his intelligence service that al Qaeda planned to try to assassinate Bush and other Western leaders at the annual G-8 meeting in Genoa scheduled for July 20.[5] The Egyptians believed that a plane crammed with explosives would be dive-bombed in a kamikaze-type attack into any site where Bush might be. The summit was held with extraordinarily tight security, including antiaircraft guns at the airport, and the airspace over the city was closed.

But when the G-8 summit passed without incident, it remained difficult to maintain the high security levels that in some cases had been in effect since May. Especially for the Gulf forces, maintaining a top security level can be exhausting after a week, but this had been in effect much longer. With no new specific information, the threat level was reduced.

Richard Clarke called a CSG meeting and asked the CIA's deputy director of the CTC, Ben Bonk, to brief the gathering on al Qaeda's plans. Bonk told the officials that al Qaeda was planning "something spectacular," but there were no specifics. As if to illustrate how little the nation's top counterterrorist experts knew, CSG released a report actually titled "Threat of Impending al-Qaeda Attack to Continue Indefinitely."[6] Some of Clarke's detractors became more vocal, saying he cried wolf too often and that he had been in the job too long.

Although the CIA did reiterate in August that the threat was still active, most government officials seemed more preoccupied with starting their long August vacations than with fretting about continued general warnings about bin Laden and al Qaeda. Bush left for a monthlong break in Texas on August 4.

Originally, the National Security Council and the Counterterrorism Security Group had decided to have its first Bush administration meeting of the so-called principals—cabinet-rank policymakers—during the middle of August. But Colin Powell could not make the date, and instead of sending deputies, he wanted to be present himself. The NSC delayed the meeting to September 4. Al Qaeda would be a central topic of discussion and CSG chief Richard Clarke was slated to present a series of policy suggestions.

While the government had been on high alert over the summer due to the CIA analysis of an increased probability of a terror attack, the Justice Department had made its own small contribution. On June 22, 2001, a few days before the fifth anniversary of the Khobar Towers bombing, the new Republican Justice Department announced the indictment of thirteen Saudis and one Lebanese in that attack. Most importantly, the charges included unnamed Iranian government officials who it said were part of the conspiracy. Attorney General John Ashcroft called the case a "milestone" and promised to pursue the unnamed Iranians. For ex–FBI director Louis Freeh, who had long felt the Clinton administration had failed to pursue Khobar leads that led to Iran, the Bush move was a long overdue strike against one of the Middle East state sponsors of terror.*

As for how to deal with al Qaeda, the administration's view had evolved during its first nine months in office. Starting in July, a group of Bush's advisors began talking with Richard Clarke and other counter-terrorism experts from the CIA and Defense Intelligence Agency. In less than a month, the advisors had progressed from the concept of "rolling back" al Qaeda to "permanently eroding" the group, and then, finally, to "eliminating" them.

On September 4, 2001, one week before the World Trade Center attacks, the principals had their first counterterrorism meeting. The purpose was to agree on a National Security Presidential Directive that would set forth the new administration's policy regarding al Qaeda. Among those attending were Colin Powell, the CIA's George Tenet, Chairman of the Joint Chiefs General Richard Myers, and Secretary of the Treasury Paul O'Neill. Paul Wolfowitz represented his boss, Defense Secretary Donald Rumsfeld, and Sean O'Keefe represented the Office of Management and Budget's Mitch Daniels. Condoleezza Rice and Richard Clarke rounded out the group.

---

*When Ashcroft submitted his first budget, however, he was not nearly as focused on terrorism. Although he sought increases in funding for sixty-eight Department of Justice programs, none were related to counterterrorism. Ashcroft had the bad timing—on September 10—of rejecting the FBI's request for $58 million for 149 new counterterrorism field agents, 200 additional analysts, and 54 extra translators. September 10 was also not a good day for Vice President Cheney. That was the day his chief of staff picked to tell Senator Dianne Feinstein that that the draft legislation on counterterrorism and homeland defense that she had sent to the vice president in July might take another six months to study. Feinstein, angry at such a long delay, told him she did not think they could afford to wait six months.

During the first quarter of the meeting, they agreed to submit a proposal to the president to significantly increase the money and arms to the Northern Alliance in their fight against the Taliban.* Much of the rest of the meeting was taken up with a discussion of the armed Predator drone and a disagreement among the military, the CIA, and the executive branch as to who should have the responsibility to issue the fire order if a target was located.

But despite the long digressions from developing a new strategy, the group did decide that the Bush administration would follow a phased strategy of escalating pressure on the Taliban so that eventually the choices facing Afghanistan's Islamic rulers would be to hand over bin Laden and expel al Qaeda or face removal from power. The CIA and Pentagon were instructed to produce multiple options involving covert and overt force to accomplish that goal. The directive did not reach Bush's desk by September 11.

*The Clinton administration, fearful of involving the U.S. in a civil war that might anger Pakistan and other allies, refused any substantive aid to the Northern Alliance. Bush's national security advisors intended to present their detailed plan to the president on September 10. However, on September 9, Ahmad Shah Massoud, the charismatic leader of the Northern Alliance, was assassinated in what most intelligence observers believe was bin Laden's prelude to the World Trade Center attack. By September 11, Bush still had not received the new Northern Alliance recommendations.

CHAPTER 17

THE GERMAN CONNECTION

Less than a week after nearly three thousand people were killed in the wave of September 11 homicide attacks, investigators had unearthed enough information to realize that many leads pointed to Hamburg, Germany. Mohamed al-Amir Awad al-Sajjid Atta led a group of student acolytes when he lived in Hamburg, after moving there in 1992, when he was twenty-two, to study at the local Technical University. It was from Germany that Atta recruited two other men who also became pilots in the September 11 plot.*

However, while Atta is often credited as the U.S. mastermind, there is evidence that several other Hamburg-based Islamic extremists played more critical roles in the plot's success. Those other terrorists operated in ways that should have raised the suspicion of German police and intelligence agencies.

Yemen-born Ramzi bin al-Shibh was only twenty when Atta moved to Hamburg. Al-Shibh, whose nom de guerre was Obeida, formed a close friendship with Atta and eventually was the emissary between al Qaeda, Atta, and the other hijackers. In late 1999, almost two years before the American attacks, al-Shibh and Atta traveled to Afghanistan, where they

---

*Although Atta was registered as an engineering student at Hamburg's Technical University, when he was absent in late 1999 and early 2000 at al Qaeda training camps in Afghanistan, no one noticed, since he was not required by the university to attend classes. Six of those involved in the 9/11 attacks were students at that same university. After 9/11, German investigators began referring informally to the university group as the "Hamburg kamikazes."

encamped in an al Qaeda outpost on the edge of Kandahar.[1] It was there, during the last few months of 1999 and the beginning of 2000, that al-Shibh completed the logistical plans, especially the financing, for the September 11 attacks, according to later court testimony from Shadi Abdullah, a twenty-six-year-old confessed al Qaeda member who was arrested by German authorities after 9/11. Abdullah had been at the camp with al-Shibh. Although he did not recall Atta, he remembered al-Shibh as one of bin Laden's "close confidants" and a member of al Qaeda's "inner circle."[2] Abdullah said the encampment was teeming with hatred toward America and that bin Laden was a frequent visitor, even organizing a celebration after the bombing of the *Cole* in October 2000.*

In Hamburg, while both Atta and al-Shibh worked hard to find recruits for their cell, al-Shibh had a wider circle of acquaintances and more influence in the small Muslim community, largely because he was by far the more likable of the two. A German Muslim convert, Shahid Nickels, who knew both, told German police that Atta was severe and moralizing. Al-Shibh, on the other hand, while equally religious, commanded greater loyalty because, according to Nickels, he was "very charismatic, very charming. You could not dislike him. . . . Of the group, he was respected the most."[3]

Because American investigators early on found written instructions to the other hijackers in Atta's possessions, they assumed that he was the ringleader. One major assumption about Atta's role was based on something as simple as an incorrect interpretation of an Arabic word in a voice mail message from another hijacker, Ziad al-Jarrah. Al-Jarrah, who had also briefly lived in a Hamburg house with Atta, referred to him as "pasha," which the FBI translated as "boss." That reinforced the belief that Atta was the group leader. Instead, "pasha" is merely a common conversational term of respect between friends. Incredibly, the FBI did not learn this for nearly four months after the September 11 attacks.

What the Bureau and other early investigators did not then know was that al-Shibh had unsuccessfully made four attempts—two from Germany and two from his native Yemen—to enter the United States before 9/11. His visa requests were always denied, not because of any suspi-

---

*Abdullah recalls Zacarias Moussaoui, the so-called twentieth hijacker awaiting trial as of early 2003 in federal court, being at the same Afghanistan camp. According to information Abdullah provided his German police interrogators, Moussaoui ran the guesthouse for al Qaeda at the Kandahar airport, where he was responsible for collecting the passports of arriving recruits and giving them their assignments.

cions of terrorism, but because the bar to entry is high for Yemenis, since so many overstay their visas. These were the only government actions that inadvertently interfered with the hijackers' plans.

Some investigators now believe that al-Shibh was originally to be the twentieth hijacker, and that when he failed to gain entry to the United States, Zacarias Moussaoui was hastily substituted.[4] Al-Shibh had wired a $2,200 deposit so he could attend a flight training center in Venice, Florida, in August 2000. Ziad al-Jarrah, who piloted the plane that crashed in Pennsylvania, attended that school and tried to enroll al-Shibh.

Others believe that al-Shibh was slated to be more than just the twentieth hijacker, and that if he had gained access to the U.S., he would have led a fifth team, as well as assuming Atta's central pre-attack role.[5]

"Al-Shibh had the strongest connection to al Qaeda and with the Saudis who hijacked the planes on September 11," says a German intelligence officer involved in the Hamburg investigation. "Al-Shibh was the agent between the Hamburg cell and al Qaeda."

So while Atta and two others in the Hamburg cell reported their passports stolen in late 1999 (Atta had at least three German passports)[6] and then used their new documents to obtain tourist visas for the U.S. in mid-2000, al-Shibh remained in Germany where he became the plot's paymaster. When Atta and some of the other hijackers took flying lessons in Florida, al-Shibh made himself indispensable by arranging the money transfers—he wired funds to both Atta and al-Shehhi in Florida—and attended critical planning meetings in Germany.

Al-Shibh was spotted in Afghanistan only five months before the attacks, and in July 2001, he went to Spain when Atta flew there. Investigators believe the trip was made so Atta could receive final instructions—too sensitive for telephone or e-mail transmission—from al-Shibh.[7] Only six days before the 9/11 attacks, al-Shibh used an alias to fly to Madrid, where he temporarily disappeared.*

Besides the al-Shibh–Atta cell, Hamburg had a surging Muslim population and a growing number of radicals throughout the 1990s. One

*Al-Shibh was arrested exactly one year after the attacks in Karachi, shortly after he bragged about the planning for the September 11 attacks in an audiotape broadcast on the Arab news outlet, Al Jazeera. When Pakistani commandos, together with

man, forty-four-year-old Syrian-born Mahmoun Darkazanli, the owner of an import-export company, is a mysterious figure with ties to many of them. He has been tried on, and acquitted by German prosecutors of, money-laundering charges.[8] His overall role in the lead-up to 9/11 remains a mystery, but American intelligence analysts believe that Darkazanli is a key facilitator in the financing of al Qaeda operations, and that he had substantial contacts with the al-Shibh–Atta cell.[9] The CIA has long suspected him of being bin Laden's Hamburg "commissioner."[10] His import-export company was among the first private businesses to have its U.S. assets frozen after 9/11 because of suspicions over possible links to terrorists.[11]*

There is little doubt that Darkazanli has associated with some unsavory people. A close friend, the six-foot-five, 308-pound Mohamed Heidar Zammar, had made a hasty exit from Germany after September 11. Zammar was a militant who often railed against the West, urging jihad at his local mosque and boasting of fighting for Muslims in Bosnia and other places.[14] American officials suspect that the forty-two-year-old Zammar helped recruit Mohamed Atta. He is now in a Syrian jail, after being arrested on terror suspicions in the fall of 2001 in Morocco.[15]

In April 2002, when police arrested Mohamed Galeb Kalaje Zouaydi,

---

an FBI support squad, raided the safe house where al-Shibh was hiding, a pitched firefight broke out. But al-Shibh eventually gave up and Pakistani police units publicly pulled him through the streets after his arrest. Al-Shibh was in American custody shortly after his detention, and has been held in an undisclosed location since his apprehension. The FBI and CIA interrogators who eventually questioned him considered the way he was captured to be an important indicator as to what type of al Qaeda member he was. That he was willing to surrender instead of dying a "martyr" when police arrived to arrest him indicated to the interrogators that he was not likely a religiously motivated zealot who would die before giving up useful information. Instead, they decided to play to his own feelings of power and notoriety while trying to shake his confidence that anyone in al Qaeda had remained loyal to him. Government officials described al-Shibh as "a cooperating" prisoner, and he may eventually face trial before a military tribunal.

*Darkazanli has admitted knowing three of the 9/11 suicide pilots—Atta, Ziad al-Jarrah, and Marwan al-Shehhi.[12] After the September 11 attacks, Darkazanli still defended Atta. "No one can produce real evidence of these accusations of terrorism against the Muslim world," he told a New York Times reporter in June 2002. "It is just a big American crusade against Islam. And so is this, what is being said about me, is also only part of this conspiracy. A video photo of Atta—should this be considered evidence? Any child can manipulate these things today on a computer. . . . Bush and his people have invented everything."[13]

another Syrian-born businessman, who was charged with raising and laundering hundreds of thousands of dollars for al Qaeda cells in at least eight countries, Darkazanli's name again surfaced.[16] Spanish police uncovered records showing that Zouaydi had sent $15,240—from some of the same bank accounts from which he funded the al Qaeda cells—to Darkazanli. Some of Zouaydi's money found its way to the leader of al Qaeda's Spanish cell, Imad Eddin Barakat Yarkas, whose phone number was found in Atta's American apartment after the attacks. Yarkas, who has been charged by Spanish authorities with helping finance 9/11, is from the same small Syrian town, Aleppo, as Darkazanli. When Spanish prosecutors handed down indictments in 2002 for both Zouaydi and Yarkas, Darkazanli was named in both. Prosecutors charged he was part of "the most intimate circle of Mohamed Atta."

Darkazanli had initially come to the attention of American intelligence in 1998, at the time of the East Africa embassy bombings. An Iraqi, Mamdouh Mahmud Salim, an al Qaeda founder, was arrested in Germany on September 16, 1998, for his suspected role in those bombings. The forty-four-year-old Salim had established links to al Qaeda and other terrorists in Lebanon, and he managed terror training camps in Afghanistan and coordinated the finances for some bin Laden front companies.[17*]

According to federal prosecutors, between 1992 and 1996, Salim was al Qaeda's representative at a series of extraordinary meetings in Khartoum, Sudan, with unidentified Iranian religious leaders. The meetings were al Qaeda's attempt to put aside its differences with Shiite Muslim terrorist organizations, such as Iranian-backed Hezbollah, and reach a tripartite agreement to join forces against the United States. As part of that venture, which fortunately stalled, Salim and bin Laden also met in Sudan in 1994 with Imad Mugniyeh, the mastermind behind the terrorist attacks that took more than two hundred American lives in the bombings of the marine barracks in Beirut during the 1980s.

Salim's arrest put Darkazanli on the radar screen for American intelligence. The CIA learned that Salim had visited Germany many times,

---

*Salim is incarcerated at the Metropolitan Correctional Center in Manhattan. On November 20, 2000, while awaiting trial with four other defendants for the East Africa bombings, Salim stabbed one prison guard in the eye, another in the body, and then sprayed irritants on others during a failed escape. His trial on the East Africa embassy charges is scheduled to begin in 2003.

often just to meet Darkazanli.[18] When arrested, his cell phone had Darkazanli's private number programmed in it. In 1995, Darkazanli had held power of attorney over Salim's bank account at Deutsche Bank's Hamburg branch.

Darkazanli has admitted meeting with Salim several times, but claims it was for legitimate business reasons, including helping Salim set up a bank account to fund an Islamic radio station.[19] It wasn't long, however, before CIA counterterrorist analysts linked Darkazanli to bin Laden's personal secretary, the Lebanese-born Wadi el-Hage, who was also arrested for his role in the East Africa bombings. Darkazanli's address, phone numbers, and even his bank account number at Deutsche Bank were found in el-Hage's address book after his arrest. El-Hage's business card for his trading company listed Darkazanli's home address in Hamburg.[20]

"We passed along this information to our counterparts in German intelligence," a senior retired CIA officer confided.[21] The FBI pressed the Bundeskriminalamt (BKA), their German equivalent, to detain Darkazanli. The Germans said there was not enough evidence.[22]

German intelligence did place Darkazanli under some temporary surveillance, and even tapped his phones. That led them to the Al-Kuds mosque located in a rough neighborhood, St. Georg, near Hamburg's main rail station. Al-Kuds, a few prayer rooms on the second floor of a building where an Asian grocery store and a fitness club take up the ground floor, is a magnet for the city's radicals. Located along a street popular with drug dealers, junkies, and the homeless, Al-Kuds was the weekly Friday destination for Mohamed Atta and his friends. The boisterous giant, Mohamed Zammar, was also a regular. But before the Germans learned anything about Darkazanli's connections at the mosque, in early 2000 they dropped surveillance when a judge ruled they did not have evidence of a crime.

German authorities protest that post–Nazi era laws intended to protect civil liberties restrict them from investigating the matter more aggressively. And there is little doubt that German law enforcement was more focused on combating its domestic terrorists—neo-Nazis—than Islamic fundamentalists. Moreover, under German law at the time, it was not even a crime to plan terror attacks to be carried out in a foreign country on behalf of an organization outside Germany.[23] Frustrated, the FBI broke protocol and sent its own agents to Hamburg, without informing the Germans, to conduct its own field probe of Darkazanli. When the BKA discovered the Americans' presence, the government formally complained to the United States. The FBI team was pulled back.

If the BKA had continued to watch Darkazanli, however, they would have observed him attending the Hamburg wedding of Said Bahaji. German prosecutors now admit that Bahaji was one of two men who provided logistical support for the 9/11 hijackers, wiring some of the money so they could attend American flight training schools.* Mohamed Zammar, now in a Syrian jail, the close associate of Darkazanli's, was the best man at Bahaji's wedding.[24] Bahaji shared the second floor of the same bland, pale yellow house in a lower-middle-class neighborhood at 54 Marienstrasse with Mohamed Atta and Ramzi bin al-Shibh. When Atta wrote the first check under their new lease, on the line for "purpose of payment" he wrote in Arabic, "dar el-ansar"— "house of followers." It was here, according to investigators, that the 9/11 planning first took shape.

After his wedding, Bahaji moved to an apartment around the corner from Atta (when Bahaji's own apartment was eventually searched by German investigators, they found many books on holy war, including ninety-four copies of bin Laden's *Call to Fight the Infidels*).[25]

Despite repeated pleas from American authorities, Mahmoun Darkazanli has not been arrested since September 11. Free in Hamburg, he steadfastly maintains his innocence. While his freedom might seem puzzling, a classified CIA report completed after September 11 gives a possible answer. It concludes that the Germans have treated Darkazanli timidly in their 9/11 probe because he is likely an informant to BKA, the German FBI.[26] Ironically, it was a CIA suggestion that might have led to the arrangement between the Germans and Darkazanli. In December 1999, the CIA assigned a case officer to the U.S. consulate in Hamburg. That agent—his name withheld at the Agency's request—pressed his

---

*The other man who helped Bahaji was Mounir el-Motassadeq, a Moroccan who went on trial in late 2002 in Germany, charged with being an accessory to more than three thousand counts of murder for his logistical assistance to the plot. In February 2003 he was convicted and sentenced to the maximum under German law, fifteen years. Bahaji is still at large as of early 2003, believed to be hiding in the border region between Afghanistan and Pakistan.

German counterparts be more aggressive in investigating Darkazanli. The Germans declined, saying they had already looked at him but could find nothing criminal. The CIA agent then suggested the Germans contact Darkazanli and try to turn him into a double agent. The last the CIA agent in Hamburg heard, the BKA informed him they had made an overture to Darkazanli, but that he had rebuffed them.

Although the CIA has taken no official position, it has internally concluded that the BKA lied about their overture to Darkazanli, and that instead of failing, they did establish an informer relationship. Intercepted telephone conversations after September 11 have provided additional evidence of this relationship, claims a highly placed American intelligence source.

According to CIA officials, the Germans used Darkazanli as an informant who provided them with information about Islamic extremists in Germany. Understandably, the BKA decided to keep him to themselves as opposed to sharing their asset with the Americans. The Agency believes that Darkazanli delivered when he gave the Germans a tip that led to the arrest of five Algerians in December 2000, breaking up a plot to bomb a Christmas fair in the French city of Strasbourg.

The quid pro quo for Darkazanli, according to the CIA analysis, is that the BKA agreed to try to shield him from police and judicial inquiries, and also keep him free of the Americans.*

If the German authorities had aggressively investigated Darkazanli as the Americans had requested several times, that might well have led to surveillance on Atta and al-Shibh while the two were in the early planning stages for 9/11. "If that CIA report is right," a senior American intelligence officer says, "then it means that since the information we passed to the Germans didn't affect them directly, and it touched one of their assets, they didn't do a thing. And that's a shame, because Darkazanli could have led them in a daisy chain to the 9/11 cell."[27]

*German authorities refused to comment. Darkazanli also declined to comment.

CHAPTER 18

"WE COULD HAVE GOTTEN LUCKY"

While the Germans failed to pursue leads that might have exposed the 9/11 plotters, as investigators soon discovered, there was more than enough blame to assign inside the United States as numerous chances to have prevented the attacks were lost through a mixture of incompetence and bad judgment.

When Hani Hanjour, the pilot of the Pentagon plane, entered the country in December 2000, he arrived on an I-20 student visa. He became one of 550,000 overseas students who are part of an $11 billion annual industry. The government acknowledged as early as 1994 that the failure to track foreign students once they entered the country was a potential security problem. Back then, FBI director Louis Freeh had discussed what to do with Deputy Attorney General Jamie Gorelick. Although Gorelick ordered the INS to suggest a fix, the matter sat unattended for two years until Congress got involved and made changes as part of immigration reforms passed that year.

The INS formed a pilot program, CIPRIS (Coordinated Interagency Partnership Regulating International Students). It called for an electronic database that would require enough personal information from foreign applicants that it could then be cross-checked against other government databases to spot possible terrorists. The proposed system would also check the student's enrollment and planned study with the school, and then the Treasury Department's Financial Crimes Enforcement Network (FinCEN) would double-check that the student's tuition money was from legitimate sources, not terror-funded.

Every applicant approved for a student visa would receive an identity card with a photo, fingerprint, and a unique machine-readable code. Students would not only have to register for a school, but each school would then have to verify that they showed up. If they did not, or dropped out, the visa would automatically be revoked. If the student stayed in the country and was stopped for something as minor as a traffic ticket, an FBI system that carried information on anyone sought for a warrant would alert the local policeman. The student would then be detained and deported.

Certain problems endemic to the current foreign student visa program would be corrected. For instance, CIPRIS would check whether a new application was merely a duplicate of that of a student already enrolled in the U.S. The system would also be accessible by overseas consular offices, so if anything suspicious turned up, a visa could be denied at the source country. If the suspect student had already entered the U.S., an INS investigator would be assigned to that case immediately.

The pilot CIPRIS program was launched in Atlanta in April 1997, and twenty-one exchange program schools participated, including prestigious universities like Duke and Auburn, as well as language center schools popular with foreign students, and even a flight school in South Carolina, also a favorite destination for students coming to America. The pilot program ran eighteen months. The goal was to roll out CIPRIS nationwide on January 1, 2001.

But it was hobbled from the start by money problems. The full trial service would have cost $11 million a year. INS decided to only fund $4 million. That meant that some critical features, like the identification card, were discarded from the start. Many schools, even those participating in the trial, strongly opposed any rules that required them to police their own students, instead viewing it as the government's responsibility. CIPRIS was authorized to collect a fee from the students, up to $100, to help offset costs, but again the schools refused to collect the fee for the government.

In 1999, the Association of International Educators, a private group representing educational administrators involved with foreign students' programs, began a concerted campaign to kill CIPRIS. In October, CIPRIS's creator and director inside the INS, Maurice Berez, was reassigned to a different division. Four months after his removal, twenty-one senators signed a letter to the INS calling for an indefinite delay. CIPRIS was soon dismantled and rolled into a program called SEVIS, a passive database remarkably similar to the system that existed before the FBI director had raised his initial concerns in 1994.

Hani Hanjour—who had not attended a school with his student visa—would have been banned from reentering the U.S. under the CIPRIS program. And Mohamed Atta and Marwan al-Shehhi had both applied to change their status in the U.S. from tourist visas to student status, because they knew that student visas received the least amount of attention from U.S. authorities. No one checked to see if they had registered at a school or later attended one (they did not). And when Atta was pulled over on April 26, 2001, in Broward County, Florida, and given a traffic ticket, he would have been nabbed then, as his name would have been in the CIPRIS system for being in violation of not having registered at any accredited school nor having attended one.

The INS was so overwhelmed that, incredibly, six months after 9/11, it sent out routine notices informing a flight school that Atta and al-Shehhi—whose names had been front-page news for months as the pilots who crashed the planes into the World Trade Center—had been approved for student visas to study there.*

But the INS was not the only government agency that failed in the lead-up to 9/11. For anyone familiar with the history of the FBI in the war on terror, the mistakes made should not come as a surprise, but as a continuation of a series of blunders that started in the early 1990s.

In July 2001, the Phoenix field office sent a memo to the Bureau's Washington headquarters suggesting that the FBI should investigate

---

*The INS did not only make mistakes when it came to some of the nineteen hijackers involved in 9/11. On July 4, 2001, an Egyptian immigrant, Hesham Mohamed Hadayet, went on a shooting spree near the El Al counter at the Los Angeles International Airport, killing two and wounding three. The FBI concluded that Hadayet had acted on his own and could not determine his motivation. Only later did investigators discover that when Hadayet entered the country in 1992, he applied for political asylum and told the INS that he had been accused in Egypt of being a member of al-Gamaa al-Islamiya, a group classified by the State Department as a terrorist organization. The INS made no attempt during the two and a half years his asylum application was pending to investigate him. In 1995, however, his asylum application was denied. When he stayed in the country, the INS tried to deport him, but could not find him. The following year, he and his family won permanent legal status in a federal visa lottery, and no one at the INS noticed his earlier problems. After 9/11, the INS admitted that it could not account for 314,000 foreigners ordered deported, and had a backlog of over five million pending cases for legal residency.

whether Islamic fundamentalists were training at American flight schools.[1] FBI agent Kenneth Williams's interest was initially piqued when he had learned earlier that year that ten Middle Eastern men enrolled at local flight schools were not just interested in learning to fly, but also had shown ardent enthusiasm about airport construction and security and airplane engineering. In his follow-up investigation, Williams discovered that one of the students may have communicated through a middleman with al Qaeda leader Abu Zubaydah, and that several others had links to Al-Muhajiroun, a British-based radical group that is virulently anti-American, has vocally supported bin Laden, and urges the establishment of a global Muslim state.[2] (Unknown then to Williams, Hani Hanjour, who later flew American Airlines Flight 77 into the Pentagon, had learned to fly at a Phoenix area flight school only four months earlier.)

Williams's supervisor was Bill Kurtz, who had previously worked on the bin Laden unit at the Bureau's international terrorism division. He had been frustrated when earlier in the year, citing budget cutbacks, the FBI had disbanded the office's surveillance unit used by the terrorism squad.[3] Out of Phoenix's 230 agents, only 8 concentrated on international and domestic terrorism (versus 60 dedicated to drug cases). But now Kurtz had an intuition that Williams might have stumbled onto something big.

FBI headquarters asked the CIA to perform some background traces on some of the individuals listed in Williams's memo. But the Bureau only asked for name searches and did not share the contents of the memo with the Agency.[4] According to FBI officials, the Agency did not produce any definitive links between the students and terror organizations. The CIA, after 9/11, said, however, that their work had in fact confirmed that two of the names had links to al Qaeda and that one had communicated through another person to Zubaydah.

What is undeniable is that the Phoenix memo never made it above middle management at FBI headquarters. American flight schools are traditionally popular with thousands of international students, and many foreign airlines send their pilots to the schools for refresher courses.[5] The FBI considered the Phoenix idea too costly and time-consuming, and a few even expressed concerns that such a probe might be criticized in Congress as racial profiling.[6] Others found the memo "speculative and not particularly significant."[7]

The failure to take the Phoenix memo seriously at FBI headquarters is even more striking in light of a request Bush had made of Condoleezza Rice only five days earlier—to find out what might be happening domestically regarding al Qaeda. The president was privately concerned about the stream of terror alerts that came in during the summer.[8]

Beginning in the spring of 2001, terror alerts were frequently issued by various government agencies, with FAA warnings predominating. Here is a list from April to September 11:

April 18, 2001: FAA issues an advisory. "The FAA does not have any credible information regarding specific plans by terrorist groups to attack U.S. civil aviation interests. . . . Nonetheless some of the current active groups are known to plan and train for hijackings. . . . The FAA encourages U.S. carriers to demonstrate a high degree of alertness."

June 22, 2001: FAA issues an information circular to private air carriers. "Although we have no specific information that this threat is directed at civil aviation, the potential for terrorist operations, such as an airline hijacking to free terrorists incarcerated in the U.S., remains a concern."

June 26, 2001: State Department issues a worldwide caution to Americans traveling or living abroad.

July 2, 2001: As a result of a Counterterrorism Security Group meeting the day before about possible plots, the FBI releases a memo about threats overseas. In a message to law enforcement agencies, the FBI says there were threats to American interests overseas and that a domestic strike could not be ruled out.

July 2, 2001: FAA issues an internal communication that says a terrorist convicted in a plot to wreak havoc with the millennium celebrations had intended to use explosives in an airport terminal.

July 6, 2001: The Counterterrorism Security Group meets again and suspends nonessential travel of U.S. counterterrorism staff because of concern about potential attacks in Paris, Turkey, and Rome.

Mid-July 2001: Intelligence agencies warn of specific threats against President Bush at the G-8 summit in Genoa, Italy.

July 18, 2001: The FAA issues an internal communication suggesting a "high level of caution" on the part of the airlines. It refers entirely to concern about attacks in the Arabian Peninsula.

July 18, 2001: The FBI issues an advisory reiterating its July 2 message. "We're concerned about threats as a result of the millennium plot conviction," the advisory says, referring to the July 13 conviction of an Algerian accused of being part of a plot to detonate a suitcase bomb at Los Angeles International Airport.

July 31, 2001: The FAA issues an internal communication encouraging airlines to be on a high level of alert, saying terror groups are known to be planning and training for hijackings. Only three days earlier, Djamel Beghal, an al Qaeda operative, was arrested in Dubai and revealed plans to attack the U.S. embassy in Paris.

August 1, 2001: The FBI issues an advisory noting the third anniversary of the deadly bombings of two U.S. embassies in Kenya and Tanzania.

August 6, 2001: Bush receives a report that does not have warning information but does discuss Osama bin Laden's methods of operation. It also mentions a concern about a traditional hijacking.

August 16, 2001: The FAA issues a warning about disguised weapons. Officials cite reports that the terrorists have made breakthroughs in using cell phones, key chains, and pens as weapons.

August 28, 2001: The FAA issues an advisory about possible violence against U.S. carriers flying in and out of Israel.

Williams's memo about terrorists possibly using flight schools made such little impression at FBI headquarters that a few months later, when a separate case developed in the Minneapolis field office, it set off no alarms. An instructor from the Pan Am International Flight School near Minneapolis–St. Paul had first noticed a French-Moroccan student, Zacarias Moussaoui, after he had paid thousands in cash—pulling $6,800 in small bills out of a small satchel—for his lessons. Then he became suspicious when his new student was only interested in learning how to steer planes, not land them. At one point, Moussaoui asked "about how much fuel was on board a 747-400 and how much damage that could cause if it hit anything."[9] The instructor, a former military pilot who thought Moussaoui was alternately belligerent and evasive, reported his concerns to the FBI. The next day, August 16, Moussaoui was detained on an immigration violation, overstaying his visa.

The Minneapolis field office immediately sought the CIA's help. The Agency, which had nothing on him, in turn reached out to French and British intelligence. Although Moussaoui had lived in Britain for years, MI6 had nothing on him either. The French, however, had been wanting to question him since 1999 about a series of attacks in Paris.[10] The day after the CIA request, French intelligence relayed that Moussaoui had a "radical fundamentalist background" and that he had been a regular at a radical mosque in north London.[11] French records revealed that Moussaoui traveled between Kuwait, Turkey, and several European countries, all to recruit volunteers to fight jihad in Chechnya. And the French believed that Moussaoui had not only spent time in Afghanistan, but had visited Pakistan before arriving in the U.S. in February 2001.[12] That information so alarmed the CIA that it sent out an advisory to its intelligence stations worldwide that Moussaoui had been arrested after raising suspicion that he might be "a suspect airline suicide hijacker" who could be "involved in a larger plot to target airlines traveling from Europe to the U.S."[13]

A friend of Moussaoui's told the Minneapolis agents that he had expressed a desire to hurt America. Only two days after Moussaoui's detention, the field office applied, under the Foreign Intelligence Surveillance Act, for a warrant that would have allowed the agents to examine his notebook computer. FBI headquarters, however, blocked the application for the warrant, concluding that there was no evidence that Moussaoui was "acting on behalf of a foreign power." The Washington supervisors and lawyers considered that a prerequisite to granting the warrant. The field office kept asking for approval, but headquarters repeatedly resisted.[14]

After 9/11, the Senate Judiciary Committee issued a report concluding that counterterrorism specialists and lawyers at headquarters did not understand that they had ample evidence to grant the Moussaoui warrant. The law under which the Minneapolis office asked for the warrant actually set a standard of evidence lower than that for regular criminal warrants. Senator Arlen Specter, the author of the report, said it was "inexplicable" and "scandalous" that FBI supervisors were ignorant of the standards of evidence required in a terror investigation.

In the Minneapolis field office, the agents had played it strictly by the book, and were now the victims of a stifling bureaucracy at headquarters. If the Bureau had instead allowed an investigation to proceed, they would have quickly learned that Moussaoui had attended the same Norman, Oklahoma, flight school that an al Qaeda operative, Ihab Ali, had attended a few years earlier. On his computer, they would also have discovered he had downloaded a crop-dusting manual (Mohamed Atta had shown a similar interest in Florida)* and technical details about jumbo jets. In his personal belongings, he had Atta's telephone number.[16] Some of the other things that a search would have uncovered were knives, fighting gloves, shin guards, flight deck videos for different planes, a flight simulator program, an aviation radio, and a computer disk with information about the aerial dispersal of pesticides.[17]

Almost $19,000 had been wired to Moussaoui from Ramzi bin al-Shibh, the plot's paymaster in Germany (the entire 9/11 plot is estimated to have cost about $500,000). One of the four German telephone numbers Moussaoui had was al-Shibh's.[18] And a business card found at the site of the United Airlines flight that crashed in Pennsylvania, which had been in the possession of Ziad al-Jarrah, the terrorist at the controls in the final minutes, bore a telephone number that Moussaoui had also called in the weeks before the attacks.[19]

Some investigators believe that Moussaoui's arrest forced al Qaeda to speed up their hijacking plans lest they be compromised. The hijackers began buying their tickets, two by two, on August 25—only nine days after Moussaoui had been detained.

Coleen Rowley, a twenty-one-year veteran of the FBI and the general counsel in the Minneapolis field office, had been responsible for making the warrant request. She was furious that a supervisor at headquarters had "toned down" the information from French intelligence she had included in her search warrant application.[20] Then, when Washington blocked the warrant, she sought permission to interrogate the detained Moussaoui. That was also rejected. Instead, the Bureau reprimanded her

---

*Atta's interest went far beyond just downloading a manual from the Internet. In February 2001, Atta and two other men who appeared to be Middle Eastern visited a company that cleans and loads crop dusters at the Belle Glade Municipal Airport in Florida. Atta asked pointed questions about the amount of fuel and chemicals the planes could hold. Later that same month, Atta went to the U.S. Department of Agriculture's Farm Credit Service, near Miami, and inquired about borrowing money to buy a crop duster. Subsequently, he and some other men made repeated visits to the airport, watching crop dusters load, take off, and land, one time videotaping them. Investigators are still puzzled by precisely what type of attack the terrorists were considering with the crop dusters, although one involving chemicals or biological agents has received the most speculation.[15]

and others in the Minneapolis office for reaching out to the CIA for information without first clearing it through bureaucratic channels.

No one at FBI headquarters ever told Rowley or her fellow Minneapolis colleagues of the July Phoenix memo warning that al Qaeda agents could be training at U.S. flight schools. But Rowley was still not finished. On August 21, she sent another e-mail to headquarters saying it was "imperative" that the Secret Service be warned that unknown terrorists working with Moussaoui might try to hijack a plane and divert it to Washington. That was also ignored.[21]

On September 4, only a week before the attacks, the FBI finally informed the Federal Aviation Administration's liaison to the Bureau, Jack Salata, about Moussaoui's detention. The Bureau told him that Moussaoui might have intended to hijack a plane, but that there was no evidence he was part of a larger plot. Since he was already in custody, the FAA decided not to warn U.S. airlines to increase security. In part, the FAA was reticent to issue a new alert because it had issued several over the summer that terrorists might be training for hijackings. Since nothing had happened after those warnings, the FAA did not want to increase the level once again only to find there was no real threat.[22]

Warnings from FBI field agents in Phoenix and Minneapolis about possible hijackings should have caused greater concern at FBI headquarters given the Bureau's history on the matter. The FBI was familiar with Ramzi Yousef's aborted plans to blow up commercial jetliners over the Pacific, as well as a related plot for a kamikaze-style plane attack on CIA headquarters. The FBI knew that in 1994 four Algerian terrorists had hijacked a giant airbus in Algiers with the goal of either crashing it into the Eiffel Tower or blowing it up over Paris (French commandos stormed the plane when it refueled in Marseilles). In July 1998, the Bureau had received a report from the CIA that a Caribbean police official claimed an Islamic fundamentalist group had been hired by Libya to fly a plane packed with explosives into the World Trade Center. Although it was considered "very unlikely" at the time, it was still a signal that planes as weapons were on the Islamic terror agenda.[23] The Bureau knew also that the FAA, in 1998, had issued a warning to airlines to be on "a high degree of alertness" for possible hijackings by bin Laden followers.[24]

In 1999, the Bureau had investigated the crash of the EgyptAir jet off the Atlantic coast of the U.S. Although it was later deemed that the Muslim copilot had committed suicide, killing all 227 aboard, it first raised the specter that a fundamentalist at the controls of a jumbo airliner might use it on his own suicide mission. And in September 1999, a 131-page report prepared for the National Intelligence Council was prescient regarding the possible use of planes in upcoming terror operations.[25] It focused on bin Laden as the "prototype of a new breed of terrorist" and predicted "more destructive attacks of international terrorism in the United States." While it discussed the possibility of a suitcase nuclear bomb, it also said, "Suicide bomber(s) belonging to Al-Qaeda's Martyr-dom Battalion could crash-land an aircraft packed with high explosives (C-4 and Semtex) into the Pentagon, the headquarters of the Central Intelligence Agency, or the White House. Ramzi Yousef had planned to do this against the CIA headquarters."[26]

During the spring of 2001, Ahmed Ressam, who had been convicted for his aborted millennium bombing of Los Angeles International Airport, had finally begun talking to investigators. He told them, in reports sent to the CIA and FBI, that al Qaeda not only had plans to strike inside the U.S., but that airports were a prime target, since they were "sensitive politically and economically."[27]

And in October 2001, American intelligence had received information that fundamentalists had received training near Baghdad in hijacking techniques.[28] But none of this evidently prompted any further concern at FBI headquarters.[29]

In a press conference immediately following 9/11, FBI director Robert Mueller said categorically that the FBI had no knowledge of Arabs attending American flight schools. Since he had only taken office on September 4, it is certain that he was relying on what senior career officials had told him. But Rowley and her fellow agents in Minneapolis were so infuriated at what they considered headquarters' cover-up of their Moussaoui probe that she wrote a scorching thirteen-page letter to Mueller in which she detailed how her Washington superiors had consistently impeded the field office's probe. She told Mueller that even if the Bureau had given her colleagues the green light on Moussaoui, it was "doubtful" 9/11 could have been prevented, but as she noted, "we could have gotten lucky. . . . [Now] no one will ever know." Six months after the World Trade Center attack, as the Rowley letter was leaked to the press, Mueller backtracked. He told *The New York Times* that he had misspoken at the early news conference. "I cannot say for sure," he said, "that there wasn't a possibility we could have come across some lead that would have led us to the hijackers."[30]*

And the CIA was also not blame-free in the period running up to 9/11. Two of the hijackers, Khalid al-Midhar and Nawaf Alhazmi, were known to the CIA from an intercepted telephone conversation made from an al Qaeda safe house in Yemen in late December 1999. From that call, the CIA learned about an upcoming terror summit in Kuala Lumpur, and the caller named the two future hijackers as two of the participants.[31] At the urging of the CIA, Malaysian intelligence ran surveillance of that meeting in Malaysia in January. It showed that the two met with an al Qaeda terrorist—Tawfiq al-Atash—linked to the *Cole* attack. The Malaysians, who had been pressed by the CIA to monitor the meeting, only ran video surveillance without any audio. Without knowing what the men were saying, it was of limited intelligence use.[32] But suspicions were heightened when the pair rendezvoused with Yazi Sufaat, a former Malaysian army captain, whom Malaysian intelligence fingered as a leading Southeast Asian al Qaeda representative. Sufaat would meet a month later with Moussaoui during his visit to Malaysia, and pass $35,000 to Moussaoui, but by that time Malaysian security had dropped their surveillance.[33]

After 9/11, the CIA at first said that it did not know of al-Midhar's connections to al Qaeda or his entry in the United States until a month before 9/11, when chatter about terror threats forced them to review some terrorism files. But only months after the World Trade Center attack, the CIA provided a classified chronology to congressional investigators that revealed the Agency had been tracking al-Midhar and

*In May 2002, Attorney General John Ashcroft relaxed many restrictions on the FBI's ability to conduct domestic spying in counterterrorism investigations. The old guidelines had been in effect since the 1970s after outrage over public disclosure of COINTELPRO, a domestic surveillance program in which the FBI monitored the Reverend Martin Luther King, Jr., antiwar demonstrators, and others deemed possible subversives by then director J. Edgar Hoover. The changes instituted by Ashcroft also addressed many of the issues raised by Rowley in the Moussaoui case. Under the new guidelines, field offices no longer have to wait for headquarters to approve intelligence investigations. George Tenet also made changes at the CIA. Since 1995, case officers had to get the approval of supervisors and attorneys at headquarters before recruiting so-called dirty informers, people who had been involved in human rights abuses, criminal activities, or terrorism. "That pretty much meant we weren't going to penetrate al Qaeda," one retired Agency employee told me. Now, case officers have much greater latitude in using dirty informers.

Alhazmi and had known about their connections since January 2000. The CIA had known that al-Midhar had a multiple-entry visa to get into the U.S., but failed to put him on a State Department watch list so he would be barred from entry.[34] So when the pair flew from Kuala Lumpur to Bangkok, and then caught a connecting flight to Los Angeles, they breezed through Customs. (Only after 9/11 did the CIA finally provide the State Department with 1,500 reports containing terrorist names. After analyzing them, 150 suspected terrorists were identified, and 58 new names were added to the watch list.)[35]

The CIA not only failed to pass along any information about the pair's terror links to any other government department, but it also lost track of the men after they came into the U.S. (The CIA later claimed it did not know the two were in the country until the INS informed them on August 23, but some at the Agency familiar with the case say that is not true—instead the laws prohibiting the CIA from spying on people domestically prevented the Agency from tracking them.)[36]

When in July the CIA learned about FBI agent Williams's memo that bin Laden's followers might be studying at U.S. flight schools in preparation for terror attacks, that did not set off any alarms, as the Agency did not know that al-Midhar and Alhazmi had taken flight training.

The CIA's failure to share its information on al-Midhar and Alhazmi blinded other government agencies when they encountered the pair. When, for instance, al-Midhar was in Saudi Arabia in June, his visa expired. Since he was not on any watch list, the State Department's consular office in Saudi Arabia routinely issued a new one. When Alhazmi was pulled over for speeding in April 2001 by an Oklahoma state trooper, the policeman ran his driver's license through the database and checked the registration to make sure that there was no arrest warrant and that the car was not stolen. A listing by the FBI on their terror watch list would have ended Alhazmi's odyssey then, but without any sharing from the CIA, Alhazmi left with just two tickets totaling $138. (He had not paid them by September 11.)

Even more disturbing was that if the CIA had passed their names as risks to the Transportation Department, they would have been on a list that would have cross-checked them against all airline reservations. Both al-Midhar and Alhazmi used their own names when making reservations on American Airlines Flight 77, which was flown into the Pentagon.[37]

And the CIA's failure to focus on al-Midhar and Alhazmi was not due to the Agency's failure to realize that al Qaeda was planning new attacks. In July, at a briefing of senior administration officials, CIA analysts warned, "Based on a review of all-source reporting over the last five months, we believe that UBL (bin Laden) will launch a significant terrorist attack against U.S. and/or Israeli interests in the coming weeks. The attack will be spectacular and designed to inflict mass casualties against U.S. facilities or interests. Attack preparations have been made. Attack will occur with little or no warning."[38]

On August 6, after finishing his daily four-mile run, President Bush, who was on a working vacation at his Texas ranch, sat down for his daily intelligence briefing. The briefer that day was not the director, George Tenet, as was typical, but instead a low-level Agency officer who had moved to Texas for the president's vacation. The briefing was an analytic report on the recent history and methods of al Qaeda. Included were a couple of sentences mentioning that al Qaeda might hijack commercial airliners in the United States to secure the release of some prominent prisoners, most notably Sheikh Rahman. The information came from a fragment of intelligence based in a single British report from 1999.[39] The information was nonspecific and seemed dated enough that it did not raise immediate concerns with Bush or his top advisors. While it is not certain whether the analyst briefing the president that day knew about the Agency having lost al-Midhar and Alhazmi, he did not, in any case, mention it. And Tenet, who did know about the bungled surveillance operation, had not told the president in any earlier briefing.

On August 23, almost twenty months after al-Midhar and Alhazmi had entered the U.S., the CIA notified the INS that their names should be placed on the terrorist watch list. The INS ran the names through their computer database and then informed the CIA and the FBI that the men were already in the country. The CIA, of course, already knew this but said nothing.

The FBI, aware for the first time that two suspected terrorists were somewhere in the U.S., curiously never notified Clarke's Counterterrorism Security Group or the White House, either one of which could have mobilized much greater federal resources in hunting the two. Although the Bureau began a massive search, it obviously did not find them before

September 11. However, that was not because the two terrorists had so cleverly covered their tracks. The FBI traced them to Southern California, where they had flown in from Malaysia back in January 2000. Although the pair had traveled since coming back to America, San Diego was their American base. But no one in the Bureau evidently checked to see if the men were listed in the phone book. Alhazmi was in the San Diego white pages: "ALHAZMI, Nawaf M, 6401 Mount Ada Rd, 858-279-5919." Nor did the FBI check with local banks to see if the men had accounts there. Again, Alhazmi had an account at a local Bank of America branch. They also used their real names on driver's licenses, Social Security cards, and credit cards. A blue 1998 Toyota Corolla bought by al-Midhar for $3,000 in cash listed his real name and San Diego address. At the time the FBI had traced the pair to Southern California, both were still in San Diego, waiting for the 9/11 plan to get the green light.[40]

CHAPTER 19

THE INTERROGATION

Shortly after 2:00 A.M. on March 28, 2002, several planes arrived on the outskirts of Faisal Town, a suburb of Faisalabad, an industrial city in western Pakistan. On board were heavily armed military commando units—from Pakistan's Punjab Elite Force. Working with them were American Special Forces and FBI SWAT teams, some dressed as Pakistani policemen and military.* They were acting on NSA electronic intercepts of telephone calls from Afghanistan pinpointing the location of one of al Qaeda's top men, Abu Zubaydah. He had been on the run for years, but had gone even deeper underground after September 11.

Soon after the planes had landed, Special Forces used jamming equipment to knock out local communications towers, shutting down the police radio and all mobile phones.

---

*The Faisal Town raid was one of nine lightning strikes in Faisalabad that night, and another four were carried out simultaneously in Lahore and Karachi. The information about those raids, the capture of top al Qaeda operative Abu Zubaydah, and his subsequent transfer, interrogation, and the results of those questioning sessions comes from two government sources, both in a position to know the details of Zubaydah's capture and interrogation, as well as his admissions. Both sources separately provided information. Their accounts often overlapped and confirmed each other in important aspects. Without any possibility of independently verifying much of the information, I have had to make a judgment about the sources themselves. In this instance, I believe them to be credible, knowledgeable, and truthful about what transpired. Additionally, an intelligence report on the dispersal and capture of al Qaeda operatives has confirmed some of the interrogation techniques discussed in this chapter. And finally, a Defense Intelligence Agency employee has independently also acknowledged the accuracy of some of the interrogation methods.

The commando teams spread out silently around a two-story house owned by one of the leaders of Lashkar-e-Toiba, a militant Muslim group banned by Pakistan's president, General Pervez Musharraf, in January 2002. A team at CIA headquarters in Langley monitored the progress of the assault with live video images of the team and the surrounding compound. Once in place, military satellites under the auspices of the National Security Agency provided the CIA with infrared images inside the house's second floor. Those revealed that there were more than a dozen people inside the main room, but none seemed to be moving.

Two of the Special Forces soldiers quietly approached a front window. Using night vision goggles, they peered through the gaps in the blind that covered the glass from the inside. A slender man was sleeping on a cot near the rear of the room. Arrayed around him, on thin mats spread over the floor, were other men, also asleep. A computer screen provided some dim light. A fax machine against the back wall had a small flashing indicator showing that it was on.

Just before 4:00 A.M., the assault team got the go-ahead. Scores of FBI agents and Special Forces troops knocked down the front door, smashed the windows, and shouted as they swept in, throwing small concussion stun grenades. Some of the fighters inside reached for their weapons, but had no chance to get them. A few pulled knives and lunged at the Americans. One jumped from his cot and was making a dash for a back door. An FBI agent opened fire, striking the fleeing man in the stomach, groin, and thigh. He collapsed to the floor.

In less than twenty minutes, thirty-five Pakistanis and twenty-seven foreigners*—some were captured on the perimeter—were handcuffed and shoved aboard waiting custom-built vans. Four suspects were wounded inside the house (one, a Syrian, died later) and two FBI agents were also wounded.

As each suspect was taken to the prison vans, the American assault team checked the faces against a set of pictures they had brought. None matched Zubaydah. Then two soldiers went to each of the wounded sus-

---

*The nationalities of the suspects arrested show the diverse nature of al Qaeda recruits in the Muslim world. They included thirteen Yemenis, three Palestinians, three Libyans, three Saudis, two Syrians, one Russian, one Moroccan, and one Sudanese.

pects, shone a flashlight in their faces, and checked them against the photographs. One looked like a match. He was the one who had been wounded three times trying to escape. A Pakistani intelligence agent, who was along on the mission because he had personally met Zubaydah, picked up the man's head by grabbing a handful of his hair. He nodded to the Americans. "It's him."

A medical unit with the assault team set up immediately around the man, who was groaning on the floor.

"Stabilize him so we can move him," one officer said to one of the incoming medics. "Just don't lose him."

Special Forces support teams had taken up positions around the complex ensuring that no al Qaeda units could try a rescue before they left the area with their target. Within twenty minutes, the medical unit gave the signal. It was safe to move the prisoner.

He was placed on a stretcher, an IV running into his arm, and a towel was thrown over his face. Two soldiers ran him down the stairs and in a minute he was placed into the rear of an armored transport vehicle and was on his way to a waiting plane.

Zayn al-Abidin Mohamed Husayn, aka Abu Zubaydah, was long considered to be a key member of al Qaeda's inner circle. Zubaydah was born in Saudi Arabia in 1971, but grew up in the Palestinian refugee camps in the Gaza Strip. After early involvement with Hamas, he was recruited by al-Zawahiri's Islamic Jihad, and when al-Zawahiri fused his group with bin Laden's al Qaeda in 1996, the twenty-five-year-old Zubaydah was appointed chief of operations. He was in charge of the eastern Afghan camps responsible for training thousands of Muslim radicals (the estimates by Western governments range wildly between 10,000 and 110,000 who passed through those camps). Like the Taliban chieftain, Mullah Omar, Zubaydah also lost an eye fighting the Soviets.

Bin Laden trusted Zubaydah, and he was put in charge of the millennium plot to bomb the Radisson Hotel in Jordan and Los Angeles International Airport on New Year's Day, 2000. He also served as the field commander for the USS Cole attack.

After 9/11, Zubaydah was a loyalist who continued to work on new terror plans for al Qaeda. His satellite phone number was found on a mobile phone of a man charged with trying to blow up the U.S. embassy in Sarajevo. And Djamel Beghal, who helped recruit volunteers for al

Qaeda, said he had received his instructions to attack the U.S. embassy in Paris from Zubaydah. He is also thought to have briefed Richard Reid, the would-be shoe bomber who was thwarted by the crew and passengers on board a Paris-to-Miami flight in December 2001.

Zubaydah, who is known to have used thirty-seven different aliases, had slipped over the remote, mountainous frontier between Afghanistan and Pakistan in October 2001 when the heavy American bombing campaign against the Taliban was under way. Pakistan had become his new base of operations.

Since 1998, Pakistan had received several requests from U.S. intelligence to track him down. Pakistan's agency, ISI, had claimed to have made several failed attempts, but few in the U.S. believe they did more before September 11 than file away the request and possibly at times even warn Zubaydah of the Americans' interest.

CIA operatives were in the truck that transported the injured Zubaydah from the safe house. They were not interested in his condition, which doctors assured them was serious but not life-threatening, but in getting him to say some words, anything at all. They asked him for his name. He didn't answer. They said they knew who he was. He finally responded, telling them they had the wrong person, that he didn't know what they were talking about. He talked some more, mostly denials of knowing anything, before the pain kicked in and he stopped. But the agents had what they wanted: a few dozen words on a digital recorder. Before the truck stopped with its human cargo, those agents had prepared to transfer the recording they had made through an encrypted satellite uplink back to CIA headquarters. There, several speech forensics experts were waiting to compare the voiceprint of the wounded man in Pakistan with dozens of electronic intercepts gathered over the years of Zubaydah.

Shortly before dawn in Pakistan, the CIA team in Langley had a preliminary confirmation. The electronic voiceprints indicated they had the right man.

For the next two days, medical teams worked to stabilize Zubaydah, who was now in a protected American safe house outside Islamabad, 170 miles from where he was captured. They planned to move him out of the country as quickly as possible.

What the CIA wanted to learn as quickly as possible was whether Zubaydah knew about any imminent attack. The more extensive questioning would begin once he was stronger, but some took place during his early medical treatment. Those in charge had to balance the questioning so that his mind would not be so clouded by pain or drugs, or hobbled by sleep deprivation, that he would have trouble recalling important details. But his questioners also knew that a person under extreme physical duress might be quite willing to talk just to stop the agony.

A consensus was reached quickly that since Zubaydah would not even admit his identity, the best chance of finding out if he knew something of pending importance that might save lives was a four- to seven-day application of techniques intended to play off the pain he already had from his gunshot wounds. Once the doctors tending to him were certain that his wounds were not life-threatening (unless he developed complications such as an infection), they administered a narcotic infusion through an IV drip. The unidentified short-acting narcotic was to alleviate Zubaydah's pain. When the drip was activated, it had what doctors call a "quick on," taking less than a minute for Zubaydah to feel relief from his wounds (the groin injury was particularly painful). But the narcotic infusion used also had a "quick off," so that when the drip was turned off, in five to ten minutes the pain returned.* He was lucid when the narcotic alleviated his pain.

While the narcotic infusion was administered, doctors constantly monitored Zubaydah's vital signs to ensure the drip would not slow his respiratory system to the point where he could lapse into a coma. They also watched for any associative side effects like psychosis. For nearly forty-eight hours, around the clock, Zubaydah's condition went from complete relief when the drip was on to utter agony when it was off. Within twenty-four hours, with round-the-clock crews making sure that he had virtually no sleep, Zubaydah had finally confirmed his identity. When he began to cooperate, even though it was only a little, the

---

*Morphine and Demerol are drugs similar to the one used in the Zubaydah case. Morphine, however, has a much longer life than the narcotic used on Zubaydah, and Demerol, while benefiting from a "quick on," has a slower "off" mechanism, sometimes taking thirty minutes before the pain returns. Those holding Zubaydah wanted the switch between pain and comfort to be more frequent. It was a chemical form of a tried-and-true multistep interrogation technique dubbed reward and punishment. By turning the pain off through the narcotics, they offered Zubaydah a way out of the despair and isolation they were otherwise creating for him.

narcotic drip was administered for a longer time, giving him more relief. The administering of the drip was accomplishing its purpose—since Zubaydah realized that the longer he talked, the longer he would be pain-free, he slowly started saying a bit more.

Three days after his capture, on March 31, at 5:00 A.M., Zubaydah was taken in an armored convoy to Lahore Airport and flown out of Pakistan on board a U.S. military transport. Although there had been some discussion about taking him aboard a military ship, or even to a remote base of a friendly country such as Britain's Diego Garcia in the Indian Ocean, because he was still in the recovery stage from serious wounds it was decided to bring him to the Special Forces compound outside Kandahar, a complex that also had an extensive medical facility.

One of the ways American authorities have gotten around restrictions on the employment of torture by U.S. personnel is to turn a suspect over to a friendly third country, like Egypt or Jordan, where torture is a routine part of interrogation. In those instances, the Americans act as observers and become the beneficiaries of any information that is forthcoming.*

In the case of Zubaydah, officials had planned for a variation of this tactic, what the CIA refers to as a "false flag" operation, using fake decor and disguises to deceive a prisoner into believing he is in a country with a reputation for brutality. For Zubaydah, the CIA had set a room up at the Afghan complex that was meant to appear as though it was a medical room in a Saudi jail. Considerable effort went into duplicating every possible detail about what Zubaydah might expect if he had been handed over to the Saudis. Two Arab-Americans, now with Special Forces, would play the role of his new inquisitors.

Because bin Laden and the al Qaeda hierarchy were officially wanted by Saudi authorities for their roles in terror inside the Kingdom, the Americans thought that Zubaydah would fear that once the Saudis finished their questioning, they would execute him. Since he now knew

---

*Once Ari Fleischer, the White House spokesman, confirmed the capture of Zubaydah, Egyptian authorities began intense behind-the-scenes lobbying for him to be brought to Egypt for a hard interrogation. But U.S. officials were reluctant in part because Zubaydah had been al-Zawahiri's protégé in the Egyptian Islamic Jihad, and American officials were concerned that Egyptian inquisitors might concentrate too much on ferreting out information about fundamentalist cells in their own country and not enough on matters affecting the U.S.

that his American captors were at least willing to treat his pain, the thinking was that if he was sufficiently frightened of being handed over to the Saudis, he might be eager to be returned to the Americans. To stay away from the Saudis, he might even be willing to talk some more.

On the short flight to Afghanistan, Zubaydah was sedated so he would not have a clear idea of how long the trip took. His head was covered with a hood. Once on the ground, the hood was kept over him until he was inside the darkened room. He was left there initially alone, isolated, with the intent of disorienting him about his location and the time of day. There were no windows. The bed he was placed on had a thin mattress over a steel frame. It was intended to be uncomfortable. He was also hooked up to what appeared to be medical sensors, but in fact, when he was asked questions to which interrogators knew the answers, those sensors—which measured perspiration, voice stress, and heart rate—helped investigators gauge his truthfulness. The temperature in the room was very warm. The heat helped the sweat sensors work more accurately.

Within half an hour, medical personnel again attended to Zubaydah, monitoring his vital signs and inserting IVs for continued antibiotics and to ward off any dehydration. In addition, a new IV was now added. This one contained thiopental sodium. Known better by its Abbott Laboratories trademarked name, Sodium Pentothal, and often mistakenly referred to as "truth serum," thiopental sodium is in fact an ultra-short-term anesthetic. In regular doses, this barbiturate induces unconsciousness in less than a minute and is often used in surgery. In light doses it reduces inhibitions. It is possible to lie while under its influence, but it is also likely that someone will be more talkative while medicated.

Most of the time, when thiopental sodium is administered to a prisoner, that person is aware of the injection and the natural tendency is to fight the drug, countering its effectiveness. The benefit with Zubaydah was that since he was already on a number of IV drips for recovery from his gunshots, it was possible to give him the thiopental sodium without his knowledge. That made it more likely, the thinking went, for him to talk freely without realizing that part of the reason for doing so was drug-induced.*

---

*Although Zubaydah was the highest-ranking al Qaeda operative captured in the first six months following 9/11, and was also evidently the first to be given thiopen-

Again, as with the narcotic infusion administered during the first forty-eight hours, doctors had to closely monitor Zubaydah's vital signs to ensure that the drug did not unduly lower his heart rate or blood pressure and cause complications.

On the night of March 31, some fifteen hours after Zubaydah was flown into Afghanistan, his two "Saudi" interrogators made their appearance. The doctors were ordered out, although they continued to monitor their patient from an adjoining room. The interrogators wore tiny earpieces, so CIA personnel observing through a video camera could suggest questions.

What transpired in the next hour took the American investigators completely by surprise. When Zubaydah was confronted with men passing themselves off as Saudi security officers, his reaction was not fear, but instead relief. The prisoner, who had been reluctant even to confirm his identity to his American captors, suddenly started talking animatedly. He was happy to see them, he said, because he feared the Americans would torture and then kill him. Zubaydah asked his interrogators to call a senior member of the ruling Saudi royal family. He then provided a private home number and a cell phone number from memory. "He will tell you what to do," Zubaydah promised them.

The man named was Prince Ahmed bin Salman bin Abdul-Aziz, a nephew of King Fahd's and the chairman and majority owner of a Saudi publishing empire, the Research and Marketing Group (and to sports fans, the owner of Kentucky Derby winner War Emblem).*

American intelligence officials were immediately skeptical. The name thrown out by Zubaydah could be nothing more than a deception to buy time. The urbane Prince Ahmed, a Westernized member of the royal

---

tal sodium, a decision had been made shortly after 9/11 that allowed the use of "truth serum" on prisoners by FBI and CIA interrogators. Since the initial questioning was about imminent terror plots, the Bush administration believes that the Supreme Court has implicitly approved the use of such drugs in matters where public safety is at risk. A 1963 Supreme Court opinion by Justice Arthur Goldberg is cited frequently: "While the Constitution protects against invasions of individual rights, it is not a suicide pact."

*Prince Ahmed founded the Thoroughbred Corporation in 1994. Over the next eight years, he built Thoroughbred into one of the world's preeminent racing stables. Thoroughbred had won four Triple Crown races in the past five years through 2002.

family with little apparent involvement in the byzantine political jockeying for power inside Riyadh, was a well-known figure in London, where he had considerable businesses, and in the United States. The instant American reaction was that the University of California at Irvine graduate was more likely to be in the winner's circle waving his trademark striped green and white silks than maintaining a clandestine relationship with the number three man in al Qaeda.

Senior officials had to decide how next to proceed. Hours later, through which Zubaydah was maintained on bare minimum pain medication and regularly interrupted in sleep with bright lights maintained around the clock in his room, his two Saudi interrogators returned. The goal during the time he was free of questions was to create fatigue and a sense of disorientation that might make it easier to get information.

The thiopental sodium drip had been started again shortly before they arrived. The two harshly told him that Prince Ahmed had credibly denied any knowledge of Zubaydah and that the numbers he had provided them were wrong. He would be executed for disparaging the reputation of a member of the royal family. His ruse to cause a disturbance among the royals had been foiled, one of the interrogators told him.

It was at that point that some of the secrets behind 9/11 came rushing out of Zubaydah's mouth. He raised his voice, as much as he could in his weakened condition. In a short monologue, which one investigator refers to as the Rosetta stone of 9/11, Zubaydah laid out the details for his unbelieving interrogators of what he claimed was his "work" for senior Saudi and Pakistani officials. "He was essentially trying to play his Get Out of Jail Free card," said one of the agents involved in the post-capture treatment of Zubaydah. "He spoke to them as if they were the ones in trouble if they didn't take him seriously. And he was anxious to have his information confirmed before we [the Americans] returned."

According to Zubaydah, he was present in 1996, in Pakistan, when bin Laden struck a deal with Mushaf Ali Mir, a highly placed military officer with close ties to some of the most pro-Islamist elements in ISI. It was a relationship that was still active and provided bin Laden and al Qaeda protection, arms, and supplies. And that military deal with al Qaeda was blessed by the Saudis, claimed Zubaydah. Bin Laden had personally told him of the early (1991) meeting he had with Saudi intelligence chief Prince Turki, and again, Zubaydah claimed he was personally present several times when Turki and bin Laden met in Afghanistan and Pakistan during the 1990s. According to the now freely talking Zubaydah, he was the al Qaeda representative in Kandahar in the summer of 1998, when Prince Turki, and Taliban officials, struck a deal in which Turki gave assurances that more Saudi aid would flow to the Taliban and that the Saudis would never ask for bin Laden's extradition, so long as al Qaeda kept its long-standing promise of directing fundamentalism away from the Kingdom.

Zubaydah insisted that the Saudis not only sent money regularly to al Qaeda, but that he personally dealt through a series of intermediaries with several members of the royal family besides Prince Ahmed. He then gave the startled investigators private telephone numbers, again from memory, for a businessman and former military pilot, Prince Sultan bin Faisal bin Turki al-Saud, another nephew of King Fahd's and a friend of Prince Fahd's, and also for a contemporary to his own age, another distant relative of King Fahd's, twenty-five-year-old Prince Fahd bin Turki bin Saud al-Kabir.

The two "Saudi" interrogators called Zubaydah a liar. He gave them more details of meetings and names of intermediaries he said could confirm his friendship with the royal Saudis. Whatever he claimed was certainly changed by the attack of September 11 on the World Trade Center and the Pentagon, challenged the interrogators. "You have no friends after that," one told him.

To the surprise of the CIA team watching the event unfold live on video, Zubaydah said that 9/11 changed nothing because both Prince Ahmed and Mir knew beforehand that an attack was scheduled for American soil for that day. They just didn't know what it would be, nor did they want to know more than that. The information had been passed to them, said Zubaydah, because bin Laden knew they could not stop it without knowing the specifics, but later they would be hard-pressed to turn on him if he could disclose their foreknowledge. Zubaydah did not know, of course, whether the Saudis or Pakistanis had passed along a general warning to any American authorities to be on heightened alert for an attack in America on September 11. But the CIA personnel listening to what he said knew that if it were true, there had been no warnings of any kind from either ally.

Were these the boastful claims of someone who had heard rumors and wanted to make himself seem more important, or had the Americans stumbled onto a Zelig-type figure who was present at key moments in al Qaeda's collaboration with two Middle Eastern countries that were supposed to be U.S. allies?*

Zubaydah was moved within another two weeks to an undisclosed location described as "overseas." He was so distressed when he discovered that the "Saudis" questioning him were in fact Americans that he tried to use a bed tie to strangle himself, but was stopped. Even under renewed intense questioning by FBI and military interrogators, Zubaydah was again a noncooperating prisoner. He seemed resigned to his fate once he realized he was still in American custody, and while he did speak, it was often to taunt his CIA and FBI questioners. He boasted of his continued fealty to al Qaeda.

Zubaydah began providing false information intended to misdirect his captors. He caused the New York police to deploy massive manpower to guard the Brooklyn Bridge at the end of May, after he told his interrogators that al Qaeda had a plan to destroy "the bridge in the Godzilla movie." But U.S. intelligence matched and cross-checked tidbits of information they could glean from his diatribes against data collected inside Afghanistan, as well as what they were learning from other al Qaeda captives. They also fed Zubaydah false information about the status of other al Qaeda members, at one point even showing him an Arabic newspaper that had been created to make it appear that al-Zawahiri had been killed in a raid.

Eventually, investigators used the little they gleaned from Zubaydah to fill in parts missing from other puzzles. They learned more about Khalid Shaikh Mohammed, who was eventually run to ground a year later. They also used a few pieces of information to fit with other intelligence to locate and arrest Omar al-Faruq, one of the leading al Qaeda operatives in Southeast Asia. And finally, when they filtered through some of Zubaydah's statements, they were able to break up a possible dirty bomb plot. Part of that investigation led to the May arrest of an

---

*After 9/11, Egypt's Hosni Mubarak claimed that his country's security services had learned that al Qaeda was in the final stages of executing a significant attack on a domestic American target and that Egyptian intelligence officers had warned U.S. officials about a week before the attack. The disclosure made front-page headlines. But it turned out not to be quite as dramatic as portrayed by Mubarak. In fact, between March and May, Egyptian intelligence had told the CIA station chief in Cairo that al Qaeda might be gearing up for a major attack against U.S. or Egyptian interests. It was deemed too nonspecific to be useful, and certainly is different than the specific pre-knowledge Zubaydah claimed that the Saudis and Pakistanis had.

American, Jose Padilla, at the Chicago airport as he stepped off a flight from Switzerland. Padilla has yet to be tried.

When Zubaydah was confronted with what he had told the "Saudi" security forces, he denied it all, claiming it was merely a wild tale he had concocted to intimidate his interrogators and forestall his torture.

Understandably, senior CIA officials were directed to conduct an extensive probe to determine whether there was any truth to Zubaydah's claims. Within a month the Agency had a preliminary report. They had found nothing that could definitively prove Zubaydah a liar. And they had uncovered some minor corroborating evidence about the times and places of the meetings he had mentioned, which meant he could be telling the truth. Again, with a green light from the administration, the CIA delicately passed along some of its suspicions to counterparts in Pakistani and Saudi intelligence. The Agency was as interested in monitoring the behind-the-scenes responses of its two allies as in what they officially replied on the record. U.S. officials were already frustrated with the lack of Saudi assistance on the hijackers, fifteen of whom were citizens of the Kingdom. Saudi authorities had released almost no information about them. And that all of them evaded detection by Saudi internal security forces, who maintain massive domestic files, had puzzled American officials.

In less than a week, both countries returned with remarkably similar answers. They assured the U.S. that they had thoroughly investigated the claims, and they were false and malicious. If anyone in either country had known that a terror group like al Qaeda intended to strike the U.S., they would certainly have warned their American friends. Not everyone at Langley was convinced by the strong denials. But without concrete proof, creating an international incident and straining relations with those regional allies, when they were critical to the war in Afghanistan and the buildup for possible war with Iraq, was out of the question.

Subsequent events, however, have only raised further suspicions in Washington about who knew what, and when, in Pakistan and Saudi Arabia about the 9/11 plot.

On July 22, 2002, less than four months after Zubaydah's drug-induced revelations, the Saudis announced the unexpected death of Prince Ahmed. He was forty-three. The cause of death was a heart attack, said the official Saudi news agency. The following day, the second man named by Zubaydah in March, forty-one-year-old Prince Sultan bin Faisal bin Turki al-Saud, was killed in a car accident as he was driving from the resort of Jeddah to Riyadh for the funeral of his cousin, Prince Ahmed. According to the Saudi police, speed was the likely cause of the accident, which did not involve another car. The two cousins were buried side by side at Oudh Cemetery.

One week later, the third person named by Zubaydah, twenty-five-year-old Prince Fahd bin Turki bin Saud al-Kabir, was also found dead. He died while on a trip in the province of Remaah, fifty-five miles east of Riyadh. The Saudi Royal Court announced the death, saying the prince, who was traveling during the height of the Saudi summer heat, had "died of thirst."

As for Prince Turki, he had been dismissed from his post as head of Saudi intelligence only ten days before the September 11 attacks. He had run the Saudi spy agency for twenty-five years. He is still alive, having been confirmed in 2002 as the Saudi ambassador to Great Britain.*

Meanwhile, in Pakistan, seven months after the cluster of Saudi deaths, on February 20, 2003, Pakistani air force chief Air Marshal Mushaf Ali Mir, his wife, and fifteen others, including senior officers, were killed when their Fokker aircraft crashed near Kohat, in the unruly Northwest Frontier Province.

The victims included a Who's Who of Mir's closest confidants, including Air Vice Marshal Abdul Razzaq, Air Vice Marshal Saleem A. Nawaz, Air Commodore Syed Javaid Sabir, Air Commodore Rizwanullah Khan, Group Captain Aftab Cheema, and Wing Commander Syed Tabbassum Abbas.

The Fokker, from the Pakistan air force's VIP squadron, had recently passed a fitness and maintenance inspection. It took off from Islamabad at 8:00 A.M. The weather was good. After twenty-five minutes, the plane lost contact with the Kohat air base traffic control tower.

The Pakistanis have established a high-level board of inquiry to investigate the crash. The acting chief of the air staff, Air Marshal Syed Qaisar Hussain, has ruled out bad weather as a cause and promised that his

---

*Whatever relationship bin Laden may have maintained with senior Saudi officials, it seems to have fractured completely after a series of coordinated al Qaeda terror attacks in Saudi Arabia in May 2003. Triple bombings on May 12, 2003, at compounds housing foreigners killed 34 and wounded 194.

investigators will probe all other possibilities, including sabotage. Asked by reporters, he refused to estimate how long the investigation might take, saying that it could be more than a year. "We don't need any foreign assistance, however," he concluded.

"It's interesting that we can't talk to most of the people that Zubaydah named because they all died after he told us about them," one CIA official familiar with the Zubaydah disclosures told me. "And Turki wouldn't give us the time of day on this. But it does make a lot of us wonder what these people might have known about 9/11 and failed to tell us."

ACKNOWLEDGMENTS

This book would not have been possible without the assistance and help of many people who provided critical information still classified in the files of several governments. I am deeply indebted to those who at considerable risk in some instances to their own careers and safety supplied hidden details about what really led up to the 9/11 attacks. They know who they are, and how heartfelt my gratitude is for their selfless cooperation.

Beyond those who must remain anonymous, there are others who assisted me on less sensitive matters, but whose contribution was in some cases no less important. Daniel Pipes, director of the Middle East Forum, and author Steve Emerson were extremely generous in sharing some of their own voluminous research into Islamic terror. Ex–CIA director James Woolsey and former CIA official Duane Clarridge helped me gain an intimate perspective of events from inside the intelligence community. Author Laurie Mylroie was always supportive and ready with suggestions for new interviews. Journalist Peter Benjaminson helped me obtain documents that proved important and would have otherwise remained secret. Gus Jacob, a former Lebanese military commander, was instrumental in helping me decipher the byzantine political alliances that shift constantly in Middle Eastern and Gulf State politics. Saj Kuriakos, a wonderful reporter, was incredibly patient in constructing the ten-year timeline of all events connected to this sprawling story. The History Channel's Steven Jack endured my frequent requests, usually at inconvenient hours and on short notice, for some arcane piece of information that only he could find.

After publishing my last five books at Random House, with each project I feel like I am returning to a group of dear friends who make the process as painless as possible. Robert Loomis, my editor, is indispensable in keeping the story tight and focused. He understands how to get the best work from me, and his effort greatly polished the first draft of this book. Frederick Chase was a conscientious copyeditor who fine-tuned the manuscript, and I greatly appreciated the meticulous eye of the proofreader, Susannah Ryan. Beth Pearson, who oversaw the editorial production, again spent many hours beyond what was required in ensuring that the book was the best it could be. Laura Goldin's legal review was comprehensive yet painless. And designer Carole Lowenstein and editorial assistant Dominique Troiano gave extra effort to ensure that this book was finished under an incredibly tight deadline.

I am fortunate to be represented by Andrew Wylie and Jeffrey Posternak. Their constant enthusiasm and encouragement were always appreciated. They have an intimate understanding of the publishing business, and I am lucky to have their solid advice.

Finally, although only my name is on the front of this book, anyone who knows me realizes that anything I do that is worthwhile in life is a result of the amazing relationship I have with my wife, Trisha. An author in her own right, Trisha is a research maven, and I never cease to be amazed by her persistence and the information she uncovers. But much more than that, she is my muse, not only the person who inspires me, but also the reason for any success I have. She is my eternal partner.

NOTES

CHAPTER 1: THE TAKEOVER

1. Eric Lichtblau and William Glaberson, "Millions Raised for Qaeda in Brooklyn, U.S. Says," *The New York Times,* March 5, 2003, p. A1.

2. The most popular Western spellings of Arabic names, as they have appeared in most books and periodicals, are used in this book. For instance, Koran is used rather than Qu'ran. It should be noted, however, that there are many different codes of transliteration for Arabic words. Omar Abdel Rahman is a case in point. A more precise translation would result in Umar Abd-al-Rahman. Others spell the Abdel as Abdul. Osama bin Laden, for instance, the spelling used in this book and most other publications, is considered sloppy by many translators, who would prefer Ussamah bin Ladin.

3. Rohan Gunaratna, *Inside Al Qaeda: Global Network of Terror* (New York: Columbia University Press, 2002), p. 101.

CHAPTER 2: THE INTELLIGENCE WAR

1. Author interview, April 2, 2002.
2. Ibid.
3. Ibid.
4. Ibid.
5. Ibid.
6. Ibid.
7. Ibid.
8. Mark Riebling, *Wedge: The Secret War Between the FBI and CIA* (New York: Knopf, 1994), has a comprehensive history of the long animosity between the CIA and FBI that frequently hindered operations and intelligence gathering. The

two agencies had had a troubled relationship since J. Edgar Hoover—convinced that he was the only one capable of fighting communism—had fought the very notion of establishing a CIA after World War II. Once established, the two agencies seldom agreed on how to handle intelligence gathered by the CIA, particularly on the sensitive subject of Soviet defectors. The FBI usually wanted to prosecute espionage cases, while the CIA preferred trying to turn the defector into a double agent to use against the Soviets.

Throughout the 1950s, the FBI and CIA tried to maintain a veneer of cooperation through liaison officers who were supposed to coordinate the sharing of information. But any moves toward reconciliation were usually blunted by FBI efforts to probe the CIA for Soviet moles, often interfering with the CIA's own Office of Security, which had the same brief. Out of public view, each agency traded accusations that the other was either riddled with communist spies or homosexuals who could be compromised by the Soviets and therefore were security risks.

CIA spymaster James Jesus Angleton recalled that from the 1950s through the mid-1970s, Hoover met only three or four times with CIA directors, and that was usually when they ran into each other at National Security meetings. And Hoover, during his long tenure, often exacerbated the strains by placing stories with his media friends, such as columnist Walter Winchell, that embarrassed the CIA.

During the 1960s, the Bureau and Agency had a further falling out over the CIA's secret collaboration with the Mafia to kill Castro. When the FBI discovered the plots in early 1963, the CIA promised to stop. The Agency lied, however, and kept trying to kill Castro for the rest of the year.

The formal break in CIA and FBI relations came not, however, over finger pointing after JFK's assassination, but rather because of an acrimonious fight fueled by mutual distrust concerning possible Soviet moles during the 1960s and 1970s. The bickering between the two agencies was so visible at times that the White House was compelled to intervene. On June 5, 1970, for example, Richard Nixon called the FBI's J. Edgar Hoover and CIA's Richard Helms into the Oval Office. An angry Nixon cross-examined the country's leading intelligence chiefs and ordered them to work together.

But Nixon's pep talk had little effect. He failed in his ambition to create an Interagency Committee on Intelligence to coordinate foreign and domestic intelligence—the early effort was hobbled by a lack of cooperation from both agencies, and especially Hoover's intransigence. Throughout the 1970s the relationship between the FBI and CIA deteriorated.

In early 1975, a newly appointed presidential commission, headed by Vice President Nelson Rockefeller, tried tackling the Agency-Bureau feud. Although the commission presented President Gerald Ford with a report suggesting many improvements, none were ever instituted. The commission's recommendations had no force of law, and no new jurisdictional-liaison agreement between the two competitors was developed.

This failure to improve relations was one of the reasons that when the Senate Select Committee on Intelligence released its report in 1976, it was so harshly critical of both the Agency and the Bureau. Senator Church was uncharacteristically blunt: "These agencies are fiefdoms. CIA does not want the FBI to know what particular things it may be up to and vice versa."

In 1978, Jimmy Carter was briefed early on about the problems in getting his two top intelligence-gathering agencies to work together. He decided to personally interview all the candidates for the FBI director's spot, and ultimately chose federal appellate court judge William Webster. Webster was a good friend of then CIA director Stansfield Turner—the two having met in 1941 while undergraduates at Amherst—and Carter believed that such a long friendship would lead to a much improved relationship between the Bureau and Agency. Carter's choice initially seemed a good one. The two directors, with a small number of their top staff members, had lunch every eight weeks as a way of demonstrating their personal commitment to a harmonious relationship.

But the thaw ended the following year as the FBI increased its efforts to find and deport Soviet spies, while the Agency counseled caution, fearing retaliation from the Russians toward their own agents in the Soviet Union. Carter sided repeatedly with the Bureau, much to Turner's and the CIA's resentment.

In October 1978, Congress went even further and passed the Foreign Intelligence Surveillance Act (FISA), requiring both the Bureau and CIA to obtain warrants before conducting any surveillance of an American abroad, even if that person was "reasonably believed to be acting on behalf of a foreign power." There were stiff penalties for violating FISA. The covert operators, especially in the CIA, complained bitterly that the new restrictions greatly hampered their work, since they often needed some preliminary surveillance in order to uncover sufficient evidence to convince a judge there was probable cause.

By the summer of 1980, the necessity for improved relations between the CIA and FBI was a constant theme in almost every overhaul proposal in Washington. Few former officials of either agency thought that better cooperation could be legislated, but there was increasing talk that legislation might be the only alternative after so many previous efforts had failed. To forestall Congress's meddling, Turner and Webster attempted to force their agencies to work together on an important issue, the recruitment of Soviet intelligence personnel in Washington, D.C. But Turner proved too weak in the CIA to force the program through. After a series of international embarrassments, CIA morale was low, and most of Turner's deputies blamed his timid stewardship. Some, according to senior officials who served at the time, bordered on mutiny.

When Ronald Reagan won the presidential election in 1980, Turner was finished. The new CIA-FBI partnership to recruit Soviet spies was dead in the water.

William Casey, Reagan's choice for the CIA, reminded many veterans of the Agency's first chief, "Wild Bill" Donovan. There is widespread consensus that during the 1980s Casey infused vitality into the Agency, greatly expanding its covert operations in an aggressive Cold War against the Soviets. Morale boomed. But Casey was not in any mood to limit his agency's power by cooperating with the FBI. Like Donovan before him, Casey distrusted the FBI, did not think the Bureau was capable of keeping secrets in sensitive operations, and felt it was too antiquated to assist the Agency in its work. And many at the FBI were irritated by Casey's focus on relaxing restraints on the CIA's domestic work, turf that the FBI jealously guarded as its own.

Early in the Reagan administration, some prominent voices, such as Kenneth deGraffenreid, the senior director of intelligence programs for the National Security Council, argued strenuously that the lack of seamless cooperation between the FBI and the CIA could only be resolved by the creation of a super-agency that would oversee all counterintelligence work at home and abroad. But fears that such an agency could infringe on Americans' civil liberties prevented the idea from getting off the ground.

9. Author interview, April 2, 2002.

10. Robert Baer, *See No Evil: The True Story of a Ground Soldier in the CIA's War on Terrorism* (New York: Crown, 2002), pp. 86–92.

11. *U.S. News & World Report*, October 31, 1988.

12. Federal News Service, August 7, 1989, and July 13, 1993.

13. Author interview, January 2002.

14. Duane Clarridge, *A Spy for All Seasons: My Life in the CIA* (New York: Scribner, 1997), p. 384.

15. Author interview, April 2, 2002; Clarridge, *A Spy for All Seasons*, p. 370.

16. *Los Angeles Times*, November 27, 1988.

17. Author interview, November 12, 2002.

18. Author interview with Duane Clarridge, April 2, 2002.

19. Clarridge, *A Spy for All Seasons*, p. 371.

20. Riebling, *Wedge*, p. 388.

21. Tom Polgar, "Has Webster's No-Risk CIA Lost Its Punch?," *The Washington Post*, June 5, 1988, p. C1.

22. Conversation with CIA source, November 11, 2002.

23. Riebling, *Wedge*, p. 402; *The Washington Post*, May 11, 1989.

24. *Los Angeles Times*, May 12, 1989; *Sunday Telegraph*, April 2, 1989; Riebling, *Wedge*, p. 402.

25. Author interview with CIA employee, as background only, May 28, 2002.

26. Interview by ABC News with Vincent Cannistraro, March 18, 1993.

27. Riebling, *Wedge*, pp. 434–35.

CHAPTER 3: BIRTH OF A TERRORIST

1. Jane Corbin, *Al-Qaeda: In Search of the Terror Network That Threatens the World* (New York: Thunder's Mouth Press/Nation Books, 2002), p. 4.

2. Ibid., p. 7.

3. Ibid., p. 13.

4. Sam Tanenhaus, "The C.I.A.'s Blind Ambition," *Vanity Fair,* January 2002, p. 140.

5. Milt Beardon, CIA station chief in Pakistan, late 1980s, quoted in ibid., p. 140.

6. Corbin, *Al-Qaeda*, p. 17.

7. Yossef Bodansky, *Bin Laden: The Man Who Declared War on America* (New York: Forum, 1999), p. 13.

8. Corbin, *Al-Qaeda*, p. 18.

9. Gunaratna, *Inside Al Qaeda*, p. 20.

10. Douglas Jehl, "Holy War Lured Saudis as Rulers Looked Away," *The New York Times*, December 27, 2001, p. B5.

11. Author interview with retired CIA officer; see also, Bodansky, *Bin Laden*, p. 17.

12. Author interviews with retired CIA analyst.

13. Al-Naggar quoted in Susan Sachs, "An Investigation in Egypt Illustrates Al-Qaeda's Web," *The New York Times*, November 21, 2001, p. B5.

14. Gunaratna, *Inside Al Qaeda*, p. 26.

15. Gul quoted Christopher Hitchens, "On the Frontier of Apocalypse," *Vanity Fair,* January 2002, p. 86.

16. See generally, Ed Blanche, "The Egyptians Around Bin Laden," *Jane's Intelligence Review,* December 2001, p. 20.

CHAPTER 4: THE FIRST SHOT

1. "Guerilla Group Offers to Pay for Nosair's Defense," Reuters wire service, *Newsday*, December 8, 1990, p. 4.

2. "Error in List in Kahane Case," *The New York Times*, December 13, 1990, p. B6.

3. See Peter Waldman and Gerald F. Seib, Jerry Markon, and Christopher Cooper, "Ali Mohamed Served in the U.S. Army—And bin Laden's Circle," *The Wall Street Journal*, November 26, 2001, p. A1.

4. John Kifner, "Kahane Suspect Is a Muslim with a Series of Addresses," *The New York Times*, November 7, 1990, p. A1.

5. For documents relating to Nosair's false employment application to become a city worker: Memorandum, New York Department of Investigation, From Joseph Ferraro, Assistant Inspector General, DGS, to File, Subject:

Interview of Mohsen Mahmoud, January 23, 1991; Memorandum, New York Department of Investigation, From Bob Brackman, Deputy Commissioner, to Susan E. Shepard, Commissioner, July 23, 1991; Memorandum, From Sam Amorese, First Deputy Inspector General, to John Stagnari, Inspector General, Re: Status Report—High Pressure Plant Tenders (DOI #8900618), July 5, 1991; Memorandum, New York Department of Investigation, From Joseph Ferraro, Assistant Inspector General, DGS, to File, Re: Telephone Conversation with Louis Barricelli, January 10, 1991.

6. John Miller with Michael Stone and Chris Mitchell, *The Cell: Inside the 9/11 Plot, and Why the FBI and CIA Failed to Stop It* (New York: Hyperion, 2002).

7. Conversation of Norris and Borelli re-created in ibid., p. 44; see also, Kifner, "Kahane Suspect Is a Muslim with a Series of Addresses," p. A1.

8. John Kifner, "Police Think Kahane Slaying Suspect Acted Alone," *The New York Times*, November 8, 1990, p. B17.

9. Chris Hedges, "F.B.I. Investigates Groups of Zealots Who Praise Kahane Slaying," *The New York Times*, November 13, 1990, p. B1.

10. Ibid.

11. Neil Herman quoted in Miller with Stone and Mitchell, *The Cell*, p. 56.

12. Selwyn Raab, "Suspect Acquitted of Major Charges in Kahane Slaying," *The New York Times*, December 22, 1991, p. A1.

13. Selwyn Raab, "Jury Selection Seen as Critical to Verdict," *The New York Times*, December 23, 1991.

CHAPTER 5: THE SECRET DEAL

1. Corbin, *Al-Qaeda*, p. 28.

2. Author interview with retired CIA officer who had served in Saudi Arabia during the 1990s. This story of Prince Turki is related from a conversation between the CIA agent and a colleague in Saudi intelligence.

CHAPTER 6: ALLIES AT WAR

1. Author interview with CIA employee, as background only, November 19, 2002.

2. Senator Boren, quoted in the Federal News Service, February 5, 1992.

3. See generally, *The Washington Post*, July 22, 1992; *The New York Times*, August 4, 1992.

4. See generally, the comments of U.S. Representative Henry Gonzalez, Congressional Record, *Statement Regarding Banco Nazionale del Lavoro* (BNL).

CHAPTER 7: SHELTER IN SUDAN

1. Bodansky, *Bin Laden*, p. 42.

2. Daniel Benjamin with Steven Simon, *The Age of Sacred Terror* (New York: Random House, 2002), pp. 112–13.

3. Gunaratna, *Inside Al Qaeda*, p. 26.

4. Ali Mohamed quoted in Stephen Engelberg with additional reporting by Craig Pyes and Judith Miller, "One Man and a Global Web of Violence," *The New York Times*, Part 1 of 3, January 14, 2001, p. A1.

5. Corbin, *Al-Qaeda*, p. 42.

6. Bodansky, *Bin Laden*, p. 74.

7. Ibid., p. 77.

8. Corbin, *Al-Qaeda*, pp. 43–44.

9. Bin Laden quoted in ibid., pp. 43–44.

10. Robert Risk, *Independent*, March 1997, quoted in Bodansky, *Bin Laden*, p. 89.

CHAPTER 8: "WHO THE HELL IS SEEING HIM?"

1. James Rowe quoted in "Iraqgate: The Making of an Investigation," *Harper's*, January 1993, p. 59.

2. Author interview with James Woolsey, January 15, 2002.

3. Ibid.

4. Reconstruction of telephone conversation between Warren Christopher and James Woolsey based on author interview with Woolsey, January 15, 2002.

5. Author interview with James Woolsey, January 15, 2002.

6. Thomas Friedman, "Clinton Backs Raid but Muses About a New Start," *The New York Times*, January 14, 1993, p. A1.

7. Robert O'Harrow, Jr., "Kansi's Shadowy Stay in the U.S. Leaves a Hazy Portrait," *The Washington Post*, March 3, 1993, p. A1.

8. See also Miller with Stone and Mitchell, *The Cell*, pp. 84–91.

9. Simon Reeve, *The New Jackals: Ramzi Yousef, Osama Bin Laden and the Future of Terrorism* (Boston: Northeastern University Press, 1999), pp. 27–31. Actually, investigators had located the secondary VIN, a portion of the seventeen-digit number that is stamped on every dashboard.

10. Ibid., p. 32.

11. Author interview with James Woolsey, January 15, 2002.

12. Reeve, *The New Jackals*, p. 55.

13. Report of the Inspector General, Justice Department, 1997; see also, speech of Madeleine Albright to the United Nations, June 27, 1993.

14. Neil Herman quoted in Miller with Stone and Mitchell, *The Cell*, p. 125.

15. Gil Childers quoted in ibid., pp. 125–26.

16. U.S. House of Representatives, Republican Research Committee, September 13, 1993; see also, Peter L. Bergen, *Holy War, Inc.: Inside the Secret World of Osama bin Laden* (New York: Free Press, 2001).

17. Reeve, *The New Jackals*, p. 57.

18. Author interview with James Woolsey, January 15, 2002.

19. Jim Fox quoted in Laurie Mylroie, *The War Against America: Saddam Hussein and the World Trade Center Attacks* (New York: Regan, 2001), pp. 213–14.

20. Author interview with James Woolsey, January 15, 2002.

21. Ibid.

22. Ibid.

23. Ibid.

24. Ibid.

25. Ibid.

26. Ibid.

27. Ibid.

28. Ibid.

29. Charles Fenyvesi, "Ames Fallout Further Strains FBI-CIA Relations," *U.S. News & World Report*, March 21, 1994, p. 27.

30. Riebling, *Wedge*, p. 447.

31. R. Jeffrey Smith and Pierre Thomas, "Plan Shifts CIA Tasks to FBI Staff; Changes Intended to Speed Detection of Foreign Spies," *The Washington Post*, April 26, 1994, p. A1.

32. Author interview with James Woolsey, January 15, 2002.

33. Ibid.

34. Federal News Service, April 22, 1994.

35. Federal News Service, May 3, 1994.

36. Reconstruction of conversation between Woolsey and Gore based on author interview with Woolsey, January 15, 2002.

37. Jerry Seper, "Bin Laden Among Suspects," *The Washington Times*, October 15, 2000, p. C1. Also, while the best evidence is that Khalifa is married to one of bin Laden's daughters, a number of published sources say he is married to a bin Laden sister, while a few even list him as one of bin Laden's many brothers.

38. Author interview with James Woolsey, January 15, 2002.

CHAPTER 9: JIHAD IN AMERICA

1. Steven Emerson, *American Jihad: The Terrorists Living Among Us* (New York, Free Press, 2002), p. 6.

2. Ibid.

3. Walter Pinkus, "FBI Wary of Investigating Extremist Muslim Leaders," *The Washington Post*, October 29, 2001, p. A4.

4. Mylroie, *The War Against America*, p. 7.

5. Engelberg with Pyes and Miller, "One Man and a Global Web of Violence," *The New York Times*, January 14, 2001, p. A1.

6. Steve Emerson quoted in ibid., p. A1.

7. Statement of Ambassador L. Paul Bremer III, Chairman, National Commission on Terrorism, before the Senate Committee on the Judiciary, Subcommittee on Terrorism, Technology and Government Information, June 28, 2000.

8. Emerson, *American Jihad*, p. 7.

9. Michael Fechter, "Ties to Terrorists," *The Tampa Tribune*, May 28, 1995, p. 1; author interview with Oliver "Buck" Revell, February 2002.

10. Author interview with Oliver "Buck" Revell, February 2002.

11. Josh Devon and Evan Kohlmann, "Terrorist State: Florida's Shadow of Terrorism," *National Review Online*, June 26, 2002.

12. Ibid.

13. Transcript, *Jihad in America*, November 1994, PBS.

14. Tim Collie and Michael Fechter, "Program Links USF Professor to Terrorism," *The Tampa Tribune*, November 23, 1994, p. 1.

15. Ibid.

16. See generally, David Tell, "Al-Arian Nation," *The Weekly Standard*, March 10, 2003, Vol. 8; No. 25.

CHAPTER 10: RUSH TO JUDGMENT

1. Author review of portion of multi-agency file relating to Murrah bombing, November 1996.

2. Ibid.

3. Author review of Murrah investigation FBI 302 files, November–December, 1996.

4. CNBC News transcripts, quoting Emerson on *Rivera Live*, April 19, 1995.

5. Steve Emerson, quoted on *CBS This Morning*, April 20, 1995.

6. Author interview with retired Dallas field office analyst, September 2002.

7. Engelberg with Pyes and Miller, "One Man and a Global Web of Violence," p. A1.

8. Reuel Gerecht quoted in ibid., p. A1.

CHAPTER 11: SAFE HAVEN IN AFGHANISTAN

1. Bodansky, *Bin Laden*, p. 139.

2. Joshua Teitelbaum, *Holier Than Thou: Saudi Arabia's Islamic Opposition*

(Washington, D.C.: Washington Institute for Near East Policy, November 2000), pp. 73, 77.

3. Bodansky, *Bin Laden*, p. 164.

4. David S. Cloud, "Caught Off-Guard by Terror, the CIA Fights to Catch Up," *The Wall Street Journal*, April 15, 2002, p. A15.

5. Miller with Stone and Mitchell, *The Cell*, pp. 150–51.

6. Bill Gertz, *Breakdown: How America's Intelligence Failures Led to September 11* (Washington, D.C.: Regnery, 2002), p. 13.

7. CIA officer quoted in Reuel Gerecht, "The Counterterrorist Myth," *Atlantic Monthly*, 2001.

8. Author interview with James Woolsey, April 2002.

9. Peterson quoted by David Rose, "The Osama Files," *Vanity Fair*, January 2002, p. 68.

10. Author interview with retired CIA officer.

11. Barton Gellman, "U.S. Was Foiled Multiple Times in Efforts to Capture Bin Laden or Have Him Killed: Sudan's Offer to Arrest Militant Fell Through After Saudis Said No," *The Washington Post*, October 3, 2001, p. A1.

12. Jehl, "Holy War Lured Saudis as Rulers Looked Away," p. A1.

13. Susan Rice interviewed on CNN, *Late Edition with Wolf Blitzer*, December 2, 2001.

14. Gertz, *Breakdown*, pp. 28–29.

15. Jen McCaffery, "Ijaz Tried to Bridge Gap Between U.S. and Sudan," *The Roanoke Times & World News*, April 28, 2002, p. A7.

16. Carney quoted in Rose, "The Osama Files," p. 67.

17. Morrison quoted on AllAfrica.com, December 7, 2001, "Did US Ignore Khartoum Offer to Help Stop Bin Laden?"

18. Jen McCaffery, "Did Clinton Miss Shot at Bin Laden?" *The Roanoke Times & World News*, December 9, 2001, p. A1.

19. Berger quoted in Gellman, "U.S. Was Foiled Multiple Times," p. A1.

20. "U.S. Missed Three Chances to Seize Bin Laden," *Sunday Times of London*, An Insight Team Investigation, January 6, 2002, p. 1.

21. See generally, Gellman, "U.S. Was Foiled Multiple Times," p. A1.

22. Erwa quoted in ibid., p. A1.

23. See ibid.

24. Clinton quoted in "U.S. Missed Three Chances to Seize Bin Laden," p. 1.

25. Rose, "The Osama Files," p. 72.

26. Author interview with retired CIA counterterrorist agent, based on that agent's personal knowledge from review of Agency files regarding bin Laden.

27. Bodansky, *Bin Laden*, p. 157.

28. Author interview with CIA source, June 2002.

29. Author interview with CIA source, May 2002.

30. "Top Secret UMBRA," CIA analysis memorandum, July 1, 1996, in Gertz, *Breakdown*, p. 10.

31. David Johnston and Don Van Natta, Jr., "Wary of Risk, Slow to Adapt, F.B.I. Stumbles in Terror War," *The New York Times*, June 2, 2002, p. A30.

32. Benjamin and Simon, *The Age of Sacred Terror*, pp. 224–25.

33. See generally, Elsa Walsh, "Louis Freeh's Last Case," *The New Yorker*, May 14, 2001; see also, Louis J. Freeh, "American Justice for Our Khobar Heroes," *The Wall Street Journal*, May 20, 2003.

34. Morris quoted in Byron York, "Clinton Has No Clothes: What 9/11 Revealed About the Ex-President," *National Review*, December 17, 2001.

35. Judith Miller, Jeff Gerth, and Don Van Natta, Jr. "Planning for Terror but Failing to Act," *The New York Times*, December 30, 2001, p. B5.

36. Morris quoted in York, "Clinton Has No Clothes."

37. Dick Morris, "While Clinton Fiddled," *The Wall Street Journal*, February 5, 2002.

38. Leon Panetta quoted in Miller, Gerth, and Van Natta, Jr., "Planning for Terror but Failing to Act," p. B4.

39. See generally, ibid., p. A1.

40. Morris, "While Clinton Fiddled."

41. Author interview with CIA source, June 2002.

42. See generally, Bodansky, *Bin Laden*, pp. 178–80.

43. Ibid., p. 180; however, investigators doubted the legitimacy of most of those claims simply because they did not believe that those taking credit had the sophistication to have developed an explosive device of such complexity and planted it on board the plane.

44. Morris quoted in York, "Clinton Has No Clothes."

45. Author interview with Dick Morris, December 2001.

46. Author interview with FBI official.

47. Herman quoted in Miller with Stone and Mitchell, *The Cell*, p. 173.

48. Lawrence Wright, "The Counter-Terrorist," *The New Yorker*, January 14, 2002, p. 55.

49. "Middle-East Connected Terror Attacks on Americans," compiled by Caroline Taillandier, MERIA, 2002.

50. Author interview with retired FBI supervisor in charge, June 2002.

CHAPTER 12: THE MONEY TRAIL

1. Technically, the new legislation is a series of amendments to the Bank Secrecy Act of 1970. Under the old law, a bank had to file a Suspicious Activity Report (SAR) only if it was party to a transaction of more than $5,000 and the bank had reason to suspect that the funds might be from illegal activities or that

the transaction itself might be out of the ordinary for that particular customer. The October 2001 amendments extended the rules on SARs far beyond banks. Now investment and insurance companies; currency exchanges; dealers in precious metals, stones, or jewels; loan and finance firms; pawnbrokers; auto, airplane, and boat dealers; and real estate agents also have to provide SARs. Also, under the old law, only Treasury or IRS agents could inspect a bank's SARs without a subpoena, and without the customer's knowledge. Under the new amendments, the CIA, FBI, and NSA can also get unlimited access to SARs. (See generally, Peter Carbonara, "Dirty Money," *Money,* January 2002, pp. 91–95.)

2. Daniel Pipes, *Militant Islam Reaches America* (New York: Norton, 2002), p. 199.

3. See generally, Federal affidavit filed July 20, 2000, U.S. District Court, Charlotte, North Carolina, eighty-five pages, and Affidavit in Support of Warrants for Arrests, Searches, and Seizures, unsealed July 21, 2000, U.S. District Court, Western District of North Carolina. See also, Pipes, *Militant Islam Reaches America,* p. 194.

4. Gordon Fairclough, "Alleged Donors to Hezbollah Facing Trial," *The Wall Street Journal,* December 3, 2001, p. B1.

5. Federal affidavit, p. 35.

6. Ibid., p. 33; Pipes, *Militant Islam Reaches America,* p. 196.

7. Pipes, *Militant Islam Reaches America,* p. 194.

8. Kurt Eichenwald, "Terror Money Hard to Block, Officials Find," *The New York Times,* December 10, 2001, p. A1.

9. Author interview with CIA source.

10. Bodansky, *Bin Laden,* p. 43.

11. Eichenwald, "Terror Money Hard to Block, Officials Find," p. A1.

12. Douglas Farah, "Report Says Africans Harbored Al-Qaeda; Terror Assets Hidden in Gem-Buying Spree," *The Washington Post,* December 29, 2002, p. A1.

13. Ibid.; U.S. Congressional Hearings before Financial Services and Consumer Credit Subcommittee, hearings on "Recovering Dictators' Plunder," May 9, 2002.

14. Davan Maharaj, "Gem Tied to Terror Loses Sparkle," *Los Angeles Times,* March 20, 2002, p. A1.

15. Conversation with retired CIA analyst, based on his review of German intelligence briefings supplied to the CIA after September 11, 2001. According to this analyst, federal prosecutors in Germany had investigated, in 1998 and 1999, possible links between an Internet child pornography ring that sold and swapped contraband videotapes, and the Caliphate, a radical Muslim organization that was banned by German authorities in December 2001. Under anti-terrorist laws passed in the wake of 9/11, the German authorities cited "domestic security" concerns as being behind the closure of Caliphate. There

had been earlier suspicions that some Muslims associated with Caliphate had acted as facilitators on the Internet child porn sites, earning money that was funneled out of Germany, but the prosecutors were unable to make a case they could bring to trial. (For more on Caliphate, see also, Steven Erlanger, "Germany, Under New Antiterrorist Law, Bans a Radical Muslim Group," *The New York Times*, December 13, 2001, p. A35.)

The failure of German authorities to make a case against the Islamic fundamentalist pornography venture may have been more costly than merely allowing the funding of terror networks. Less than a month after 9/11, British authorities announced they had blocked a French-based terrorist cell from opening an Internet café in London to provide cover for their communications network. The idea was that the heavy volume of online activity at such a business would bury any suspicious e-mail traffic and make it virtually impossible to monitor. As part of the investigation, the British investigators discovered that a favored means of communicating between different al Qaeda cells was to encrypt maps, strategy messages, and details about money in pornographic sites and hard-core photographs. The belief was that if discovered on their own computers, the pornography would not raise security concerns. (See generally, Charlotte Edwardes and Chris Hastings, "London Cyber Café Was to Be Terrorists' E-Mail Hotline," *The Sunday Telegraph*, October 7, 2001, p. 12.)

16. See generally, "Terrorist Financing: Report of an Independent Task Force," sponsored by the Council on Foreign Relations, November 2002, pp. 1, 6.

17. Ibid., p. 1. For instance, in February 2001, British police raided the London home of a Jordanian cleric, Abu Qatada, and discovered $255,000 in British pounds, Spanish pesetas, and German marks. Although British authorities suspected Qatada of being involved in terrorism, they could not make a case before 9/11, and Qatada claimed the funds were donations he had collected from his local mosque. After 9/11, a Spanish judge investigating an al Qaeda cell in Madrid dubbed Qatada "the spiritual leader of the mujahedeen in Europe." Qatada, according to Spanish investigators, had personally distributed the cash he received to terrorists. (Even more aggravating to British authorities was the discovery that Qatada and his wife and five children had lived on public assistance since arriving in the U.K. in 1993.)

18. Kurt Eichenwald, "U.S. Help Sought to Monitor Aid Groups," *The New York Times*, December 15, 2001, p. B6.

19. Glenn R. Simpson, "Al-Qaeda List Points to Saudi Elite," *The Wall Street Journal*, March 18, 2003, p. A7.

20. See generally, Michael Isikoff and Evan Thomas, "The Saudi Money Trail," *Newsweek*, December 2, 2002, pp. 28–33.

21. "Terrorist Financing: Report of an Independent Task Force," p. 1. The issue of Saudi financing of terrorism is not a new one to U.S. officials. In the early

1980s, the Reagan State Department asked the Saudis to stop sending financial support to Islamic militants in Algeria. The official Saudi response was that it could not tell its citizens where to spend their money. (Jeff Gerth and Judith Miller, "Saudi Arabia Is Called Slow in Helping Stem the Flow of Cash to Militants," *The New York Times*, December 1, 2002, p. A32.)

22. Glenn R. Simpson, "Tracing the Money, Terror Investigators Run into Mr. Qadi," *The Wall Street Journal*, November 26, 2002, p. A1.

23. So-called facilitators assume many different roles, and may not do anything illegal in facilitating the movement of money. One prime example that came to light after 9/11 is Yassin Qadi, the son of a wealthy Saudi merchant family, who has excellent connections and friendships with senior Saudi government officials. His diverse business interests range from investments in medical equipment suppliers to South African diamond companies to travel companies that organize pilgrimages to Saudi holy sites. He also owns a lucrative consulting firm that advises devout, wealthy Muslims how to invest profitably in business while adhering to rules set forth in the Koran. Qadi has investments and real estate crisscrossing from Jeddah to Europe to the U.S. to Malaysia. Tall and bearded, he alternates between traditional Muslim garb and Western suits, and had a reputation as a quiet and religious man who was a clever and reliable business tycoon. But a month after the September 11 attacks, the U.S. Treasury named the forty-seven-year-old Qadi as a "specially designated terrorist" and froze his American and European assets. U.S. investigators had become convinced that Qadi was moving money from many different Saudi sources through many international businesses and charities, and that some of it was deliberately ending up with terror groups. Qadi, who has denied the charges through his attorneys, has not been charged with any crime.

Qadi headed the Muwafaq Foundation, a Saudi charity that had long been suspected by American officials as being a conduit for terror funds. The same month that the U.S. blocked Qadi's personal funds, it also froze Muwafaq's assets and identified it as an al Qaeda front.

Although the government's action against Qadi seemed very fast after September 11, it was based on an investigation that had begun in the late 1990s in the U.S. Attorney's Office in Chicago. For two years, Qadi had lived on Chicago's upscale Lake Shore Drive while apprenticing at a local architecture firm. The federal probe—called Operation Vulgar Betrayal—resulted in no indictments, but its purpose was to unmask the financial backers of terror groups.

What originally had U.S. authorities focus on Qadi was a 1991 transaction. He used a Swiss bank account to transfer $820,000 through one of his companies—Qadi International—to a suburban Chicago charity, the Quranic Literacy Institute, a group that disseminates Muslim texts. Qadi has claimed the money was an interest-free loan. Shortly after the money arrived, the Quranic Institute used the funds to buy some property in another Chicago suburb, Woodridge. Most of the income generated from the Woodridge property—about $110,000—ended up in the pocket of a Quranic employee, Mohammad Salah. Also, Qadi sent Salah $27,000 on his own. None of that might have been cause for concern if it were not for Salah's arrest in Israel in 1993. He had large amounts of cash on him when the Israelis arrested him, and also had notes on meeting with Hamas terror cells. Salah pleaded guilty in an Israeli court to raising funds for Hamas.

And in 1998, seven years after the Woodridge purchase, the U.S. government, relying on anti-terrorism and money-laundering statutes, seized the Quranic Institute's assets.

In another incident, a Saudi-sponsored charity based in Virginia invested more than $2 million in a real estate company, of which Qadi was formerly an investor. The real estate company shared offices with another of Qadi's firms, and though the money disappeared, prosecutors are convinced that it went to foreign terrorists. (See generally, Simpson, "Tracing the Money, Terror Investigators Run into Mr. Qadi," p. A1; Gerth and Miller, "Saudi Arabia Is Called Slow in Helping Stem the Flow of Cash to Militants," p. A32.)

24. Gerth and Miller, "Saudi Arabia Is Called Slow in Helping Stem the Flow of Cash to Militants," p. A32.

25. Eichenwald, "Terror Money Hard to Block, Officials Find," p. A1.

26. Ibid.

27. Stuart Eizenstat quoted in Gerth and Miller, "Saudi Arabia Is Called Slow in Helping Stem the Flow of Cash to Militants," p. A32.

28. Philip Shenon, "F.B.I. Raids 2 of the Biggest Muslim Charities; Assets of One are Seized," *The New York Times*, December 15, 2001, p. B6. Significant foreign charities publicly identified by the U.S. government after 9/11 as supplying funds to terrorists included the Pakistan-based Al Rashid Trust and Wafa Humanitarian Organization, the Afghanistan-based Afghan Support Committee, the Kuwait-based Revival of Islamic Heritage, and the Saudi-based al-Haramain Organization.

29. Judith Miller, "U.S. to Block Assets It Says Help Finance Hamas Killers," *The New York Times*, December 4, 2001, p. A9.

30. Shenon, "F.B.I. Raids 2 of the Biggest Muslim Charities; Assets of One are Seized," p. B6. A few days after the raid on the Illinois charities, the nation's second largest public charity, Fidelity Investments' Charitable Gift Fund, as well as similar funds run by Charles Schwab and the Vanguard Group, blocked any donations to Islamic relief groups in the United States. (Philip Shenon and Neil A. Lewis, "Big Charity Blocks Money to Several Islamic Groups," *The New York Times*, December 7, 2001, p. B8.)

31. Firestone, David, "After a Long, Slow Climb to Respectability, a Muslim

Charity Experiences a Rapid Fall," *The New York Times*, December 10, 2001, p. A18.

32. Author interview, March 2002.

33. FBI Report on the Holy Land Foundation, confidential, forty-nine pages, dated November 5, 2001, made available to author.

34. Glenn R. Simpson, "Hesitant Agents: Why the FBI Took Nine Years to Shut Group It Tied to Terror," *The Wall Street Journal*, February 27, 2002, p. A6.

35. FBI Report on the Holy Land Foundation.

36. Informant, quoted in ibid.

37. See generally, David Firestone, "F.B.I. Traces Hamas's Plan to Finance Attacks to '93," *The New York Times*, December 6, 2001, p. A16.

38. Matt Levitt quoted in Simpson, "Hesitant Agents: Why the FBI Took Nine Years to Shut Group It Tied to Terror," p. A6.

39. Author interview, March 2002.

40. Simpson, "Hesitant Agents: Why the FBI Took Nine Years to Shut Group It Tied to Terror," p. A1.

41. Review of internal Israeli Justice Department file regarding 1995 raid, Jerusalem.

42. FBI Report on the Holy Land Foundation.

43. Simpson, "Hesitant Agents: Why the FBI Took Nine Years to Shut Group It Tied to Terror," p. A1.

44. Internal Central Intelligence Agency summary review, September 30, 2002; still classified. In January 2002, the Treasury Department acted to freeze the assets of two purportedly humanitarian groups—the Afghan Support Committee and the Revival of Islamic Heritage Society—for transferring funds to al Qaeda. See also, Eichenwald, "U.S. Freezes Assets of 2 Groups, Saying They Diverted Gifts to Al-Qaeda," *The New York Times*, January 10, 2002, p. A13.

CHAPTER 13: CAMPAIGN OF TERROR

1. Bodansky, *Bin Laden*, p. 199.

2. Ibid., p. 189.

3. Ibid., p. 198.

4. Ibid., p. 206.

5. Ibid., p. 208.

6. Waldman, Seib, Markon, and Cooper, "Ali Mohamed Served in the U.S. Army—and bin Laden's Circle," p. A6.

7. Gertz, *Breakdown*, p. 19.

8. Bodansky, *Bin Laden*, p. 248.

9. Author interviews with CIA source, June 2002; see also, Bodansky, *Bin Laden*, p. 283.

10. Bodansky, *Bin Laden*, p. 252.

11. Rose, "The Osama Files," p. 71.

12. Bodansky, *Bin Laden*, p. 287.

13. Benjamin and Simon, *The Age of Sacred Terror*, p. 261.

14. Daniel Benjamin, "The Failure of Intelligence," *The New York Review of Books*, December 20, 2001.

15. Miller, Gerth, and Van Natta, Jr., "Planning for Terror but Failing to Act," p. B5.

16. Ibid.

17. See generally, Tanenhaus, "The C.I.A.'s Blind Ambition," p. 96.

18. See generally, E. Thomas Ricks and Dana Priest, "Security Duties in Dispute; Defense Department Points to Embassy, State Department Points Back," *The Washington Post*, October 14, 2000, p. A18.

19. Benjamin and Simon, *The Age of Sacred Terror*, p. 283.

20. Ibid., p. 294.

CHAPTER 14: "WE GOT IT COVERED"

1. Benjamin and Simon, *The Age of Sacred Terror*, pp. 306–7.

2. Johnston and Van Natta, Jr., "Wary of Risk, Slow to Adapt, F.B.I. Stumbles in Terror War," p. A30.

3. Ibid.; see also, James Risen, "C.I.A.'s Inquiry on Qaeda Aide Seen as Flawed," *The New York Times*, September 23, 2002, p. A15.

4. Benjamin and Simon, *The Age of Sacred Terror*, p. 289.

5. Author interview with Gary Hart, December 2001.

6. See generally, Miller, Gerth, and Van Natta, Jr., "Planning for Terror but Failing to Act," p. B5.

7. Benjamin and Simon, *The Age of Sacred Terror*, p. 317.

CHAPTER 15: ENTER THE HIJACKERS

1. Kate Zernike and James Risen, "Tracing a 16-Month Infusion of Men and Money, Culminating in the Horror of Sept. 11," *The New York Times*, December 12, 2001, p. B7.

2. Ibid.

CHAPTER 16: "NONE OF THIS IS EVER GOING TO HAPPEN"

1. Barton Gellman, "A Strategy's Cautious Evolution; Before September 11, the Bush Anti-Terror Effort Was Mostly Ambition," *The Washington Post*, January 20, 2002, p. A1.

2. Author interview with Armitage, December 2001; see also, ibid.

3. Condoleezza Rice recounting her conversation with President Bush in Gellman, "A Strategy's Cautious Evolution; Before September 11, the Bush Anti-Terror Effort Was Mostly Ambition," p. A1.

4. See generally, Benjamin and Simon, *The Age of Sacred Terror,* p. 341.

5. Tanenhaus, "The C.I.A.'s Blind Ambition," p. 96.

6. Michael Elliott, "They Had a Plan," *Time,* August 12, 2002, p. 27.

CHAPTER 17: THE GERMAN CONNECTION

1. Testimony of Shadi Abdullah, in the trial of Mounir el-Motassadeq, Federal Republic of Germany, October 2002.

2. Author's review of Abdullah's testimony, as well as some summary transcriptions of intercepted telephone conversations and police interrogations involving Abdullah, available as exhibits, and also background prosecution preparatory information attendant to his witness appearance in the trial of Mounir el-Motassadeq, Federal Republic of Germany, October 2002; see also, Desmond Butler, "Yemeni's Role in Attacks on Sept. 11 Is Stressed," *The New York Times,* February 10, 2003, p. A11; and Desmond Butler with Don Van Natta, Jr., "A Qaeda Informer Helps Investigators Trace Group's Trail," *The New York Times,* February 17, 2003, p. A1.

3. Butler, "Yemeni's Role in Attacks on Sept. 11 Is Stressed," p. A11.

4. Author interview with FBI counterintelligence agent, August 2002.

5. See David Johnston and Don Van Natta, Jr., "9/11 Inquiry Eyes Possible 5th Pilot," *The New York Times,* October 11, 2002, p. A1.

6. *Inside 9-11: What Really Happened,* by the reporters, writers, and editors of *Der Spiegel* (New York: St. Martin's, 2002), p. 178.

7. Testimony of Shadi Abdullah, in the trial of Mounir el-Motassadeq. See also Johnston and Van Natta, Jr., "9/11 Inquiry Eyes Possible 5th Pilot," p. A1.

8. *Inside 9-11: What Really Happened,* p. 197.

9. For public sources, see generally, Terrorism News, "Germans Continue Probe of Businessman with Ties to Al-Qaeda," Bulletin Broadfaxing Network, the Bulletin's *Frontrunner,* June 20, 2002: "German officials say they still do not have enough hard evidence to put the Syrian-born Mr. Darkazanli in jail, much to the annoyance of some American officials, who contend that he has been a major link in the financing of Qaeda operations." See also James Dorsey, "Syrian May Provide a Link to Bin Laden," *The Wall Street Journal,* October 8, 2001, p. A14: "German authorities believe that Mahmoun Darkazanli, Syrian exile living in Hamburg, may have funneled money from Osama bin Laden's Al-Qaeda network to September 11 hijackers, whom he knew through a Hamburg mosque."

10. *Inside 9-11: What Really Happened*, p. 192.

11. Reporting of correspondent Deborah Feyerick, CNN, *The Point with Greta Van Susteren*, October 15, 2001, Transcript #101500CN.V68. Darkazanli's import-export business was one of twenty-seven initially frozen by the Bush administration in the immediate aftermath of the 9/11 attack.

12. Ibid.

13. Steven Erlanger, "Germans Press Investigation of Qaeda-tied Business-man," *The New York Times*, June 20, 2002, p. A20.

14. *Inside 9-11: What Really Happened*, p. 198.

15. Steven Erlanger, "Germans Say Figure Linked to Sept. 11 is in Syria Jail," *The New York Times*, June 19, 2002, p. A8; see also, Daniel Wakin, "Tempers Flare After U.S. Sends a Canadian Citizen Back to Syria on Terror Suspicions," *The New York Times*, November 11, 2001, p. A9.

16. Tim Golden and Judith Miller, "Threats and Responses: The Saudi Connection," *The New York Times*, September 21, 2002, p. A10.

17. *United States of America v. Usama bin Laden et al.*, S (9) 98 Cr. 1023, Southern District of New York, pp. 11–12, 34; see also, *Hunting bin Laden: Who Is bin Laden?*, PBS *Frontline* (1999); Larry Neumeister, "5 More Indicted in Embassy Bombings," Associated Press, December 21, 2000; Joe Lauria, "A Wide Plot to Kill Americans Alleged in Embassy Bomb Trial," *The Boston Globe*, February 6, 2001, p. A11; see generally, Yonah Alexander and Michael S. Swetnam, *Usama Bin Laden's al-Qaida: Profile of a Terrorist Network* (Ardsley, New York: Trans-national, 2001).

18. Rose, "The Osama Files," p. 64.

19. Reporting of correspondent Deborah Feyerick, CNN, *The Point with Greta Van Susteren*.

20. This information was introduced in evidence during the embassy bombing trial in New York. See also reporting of correspondent Deborah Feyerick, CNN, *The Point with Greta Van Susteren*.

21. Author interview with retired CIA agent, April 2002.

22. Douglas Frantz and Desmond Butler, "The 9/11 Inquest: Now Americans Say Germans Bungled," *The New York Times*, July 11, 2002, p. A9.

23. Ibid.

24. Although most reports list Zammar as the best man at the wedding, some published sources claim that Darkazanli himself was the best man at the wed-ding (see generally, Todd Richissin, "German Openness Gave Cover to Plotters," Baltimore *Sun*, September 8, 2002, p. A1). Darkazanli refused an interview, so it was not possible to even confirm this otherwise small fact.

25. *Inside 9-11: What Really Happened*, p. 178.

26. Author interview with CIA source, June 2002.

27. Author interview with CIA source, January 12, 2003.

CHAPTER 18: "WE COULD HAVE GOTTEN LUCKY"

1. Eric Lichtblau and Josh Meyer, "Terrorist Ties Cited in Memo," *Los Angeles Times*, May 23, 2002, p. A1.

2. Author interview with Steve Emerson, June 2002.

3. Jim Yardley with Jo Thomas, "For Agent in Phoenix, the Cause of Many Frustrations Extended to His Own Office," *The New York Times*, June 19, 2002, p. A18.

4. Neil A. Lewis, "F.B.I. Chief Admits 9/11 Might Have Been Detectable," *The New York Times*, May 30, 2002, p. A1.

5. David Firestone and Matthew L. Wald, "Flight Schools See Downside to Crackdown," *The New York Times*, May 27, 2002, p. A1.

6. Johnston and Van Natta, Jr., "Wary of Risk, Slow to Adapt, F.B.I. Stumbles in Terror War," p. A1.

7. James Risen, "F.B.I. Agent Was Tracking Radical Linked to Hijacker," *The New York Times*, September 25, 2002, p. A14.

8. Michael Hirsh and Michael Isikoff, "What Went Wrong," *Newsweek*, May 27, 2002, p. 27.

9. Jim Yardley, "E-Mail Sent to Flight School Gave Terror Suspect's 'Goal,' " *The New York Times*, February 8, 2002, p. A10.

10. *Inside 9-11: What Really Happened*, p. 194.

11. Gary Fields and David S. Cloud, "France Described Moussaoui as Radical in Cables to FBI," *The Wall Street Journal*, May 28, 2002, p. A6.

12. Romesh Ratnesar and Michael Weisskopf, "How the FBI Blew the Case," *Time*, June 3, 2002, p. 23.

13. Philip Shenon, "Early Warnings on Moussaoui Are Detailed," *The New York Times*, October 18, 2002, p. A13.

14. Neil A. Lewis with David Johnston and Don Van Natta, Jr., "F.B.I. Inaction Blurred Picture Before Sept. 11," *The New York Times*, May 27, 2002, p. A1.

15. See John J. Fialka, Tom Hamburger, and Gary Fields, "Hijackers' Interest in Crop Dusters Puzzles Investigators," *The Wall Street Journal*, November 19, 2001, p. A22.

16. Mark Hosenball and Michael Isikoff, "Are the Feds at Sea?", *Newsweek*, June 3, 2002, p. 22.

17. Gunaratna, *Inside Al Qaeda*, p. 109.

18. *Inside 9-11: What Really Happened*, p. 194.

19. Philip Shenon, "Prosecutors Say Business Card Ties Suspect to Flight 93 Pilot," *The New York Times*, September 25, 2002, p. A14.

20. Lewis with Johnston and Van Natta, Jr., "F.B.I. Inaction Blurred Picture Before Sept. 11," p. A1.

21. Shenon, "Early Warnings on Moussaoui Are Detailed," p. A13.

22. Stephen Power, David S. Cloud, and Gary Fields, "FAA Chose Not to Warn Airlines on Pivotal Arrest Before Sept. 11," *The Wall Street Journal*, May 20, 2002, p. A1.

23. James Risen, "Intelligence Officials Discount '98 Report from Caribbean of Plot to Hit Trade Center," *The New York Times*, September 20, 2002, p. A14.

24. Jonathan D. Salant, "FAA Warned Airlines in 1998 That bin Laden Might Hijack an Airplane," *San Francisco Chronicle*, May 26, 2002.

25. *The Sociology and Psychology of Terrorism: Who Becomes a Terrorist and Why?*, prepared for the National Intelligence Council by the Library of Congress's Federal Research Division, September 1999; available online at http://www.loc .gov/rr/frd/Sociology-Psychology%20of%20Terrorism.htm.

26. Ibid.

27. Hirsh and Isikoff, "What Went Wrong," p. 32.

28. Tanenhaus, "The C.I.A.'s Blind Ambition," p. 98.

29. Philip Shenon and David Johnston, "2 Agencies Say Silence Prevented Pair's Tracking," *The New York Times*, October 2, 2002, p. A17.

30. Mueller quoted in David Johnston, "Self-Criticism and Its Risks," *The New York Times*, May 30, 2002, p. A1; see also, Lewis, "F.B.I. Chief Admits 9/11 Might Have Been Detectable," p. A1.

31. Michael Isikoff and Daniel Klaidman, "The Hijackers We Let Escape," *Newsweek*, June 10, 2002, p. 25.

32. Wright, "The Counter-Terrorist," p. 59.

33. Gertz, *Breakdown*, pp. 45–46.

34. Risen, "C.I.A.'s Inquiry on Qaeda Aide Seen as Flawed," p. A15.

35. Shenon and Johnston, "2 Agencies Say Silence Prevented Pair's Tracking," p. A17.

36. David Johnston and Elizabeth Becker, "C.I.A. Was Tracking Hijacker Months Earlier Than It Had Said," *The New York Times*, June 3, 2002, p. A1.

37. Shenon and Johnston, "2 Agencies Say Silence Prevented Pair's Tracking," p. A17.

38. Dana Priest and Dan Eggen, "9/11 Probers Say Agencies Failed to Heed Attack Signs," *The Washington Post*, September 19, 2002, p. A1.

39. Lewis with Johnston and Van Natta, Jr., "F.B.I. Inaction Blurred Picture Before Sept. 11," p. A1.

40. Hirsh and Isikoff, "What Went Wrong," p. 32; see also, Isikoff and Klaidman, "The Hijackers We Let Escape," p. 19.

BIBLIOGRAPHY

BOOKS

AbuKhalil, As'ad. *Bin Laden, Islam and America's New 'War on Terrorism.' "* New York: Seven Stories, 2002.

Alexander, Yonah, and Michael S. Swetnam. *Usama bin Laden's al-Qaida: Profile of a Terrorist Network.* Ardsley, New York: Transnational, 2001.

The al-Qaeda Documents, Vol. 1. Alexandria: Tempest, 2002.

Baer, Robert. *See No Evil: The True Story of a Ground Soldier in the CIA's War on Terrorism.* New York: Crown, 2002.

Benjamin, Daniel, with Steven Simon. *The Age of Sacred Terror.* New York: Random House, 2002.

Bergen, Peter L. *Holy War, Inc.: Inside the Secret World of Osama bin Laden.* New York: Free Press, 2001.

Bodansky, Yossef. *Bin Laden: The Man Who Declared War on America.* New York: Forum, 1999.

Clarridge, Duane R. *A Spy for All Seasons: My Life in the CIA.* New York: Scribner, 1997.

Cooley, John K. *Unholy Wars: Afghanistan, America and International Terrorism.* London: Pluto, 1999.

Corbin, Jane. *Al-Qaeda: In Search of the Terror Network That Threatens the World.* New York: Thunder's Mouth Press/Nation Books, 2002.

Emerson, Steven. *American Jihad: The Terrorists Living Among Us.* New York: Free Press, 2002.

Gertz, Bill. *Breakdown: How America's Intelligence Failures Led to September 11.* Washington, D.C.: Regnery, 2002.

Gunaratna, Rohan. *Inside Al Qaeda: Global Network of Terror.* New York: Columbia University Press, 2002.

Herda, D. J. *The Afghan Rebels: The War in Afghanistan.* Danbury, Connecticut: Franklin Watts, 1990.

How Did This Happen? Terrorism and the New War. Edited by James F. Hoge, Jr., and Gideon Rose. New York: Public Affairs, 2001.

Inside 9-11: What Really Happened. By the reporters, writers, and editors of *Der Spiegel.* New York: St. Martin's, 2001.

Landau, Elaine. *Osama bin Laden: A War Against the West.* Brookfield, Connecticut: Twenty-First Century, 2002.

Miller, John, with Michael Stone and Chris Mitchell. *The Cell: Inside the 9/11 Plot, and Why the FBI and CIA Failed to Stop It.* New York: Hyperion, 2002.

Mohaddessin, Mohammad. *Islamic Fundamentalism: The New Global Threat.* Washington, D.C.: Seven Locks, 1993.

Mylroie, Laurie. *The War Against America: Saddam Hussein and the World Trade Center Attacks.* New York: Regan, 2001; published in hard cover as *Study of Revenge* (Washington, D.C.: American Enterprise Institute, 2000).

Oates, Robert M. *Permanent Peace: How to Stop Terrorism and War—Now and Forever.* Fairfield, Iowa: Institute of Science, Technology and Public Policy, 2002.

O'Balance, Edgar. *Islamic Fundamentalist Terrorism, 1979–95: The Iranian Connection.* London: Macmillan, 1997.

Pillar, Paul R. *Terrorism and U.S. Foreign Policy.* Washington, D.C.: Brookings Institution, 2001.

Pipes, Daniel. *Militant Islam Reaches America.* New York: Norton, 2002.

Rashid, Ahmed. *Taliban: Militant Islam, Oil and Fundamentalism in Central Asia.* New Haven: Yale University Press, 2001.

Reeve, Simon. *The New Jackals: Ramzi Yousef, Osama bin Laden and the Future of Terrorism.* Boston: Northeastern University Press, 1999.

Riebling, Mark. *Wedge: The Secret War Between the FBI and CIA.* New York: Knopf, 1994.

Sharma, Rajeev. *Pak Proxy War: A Story of ISI, bin Laden and Kargil.* New Delhi, India: Kaveri, 2002.

Teitelbaum, Joshua. *Holier Than Thou: Saudi Arabia's Islamic Opposition.* Washington, D.C.: Washington Institute for Near East Policy, November 2000.

Tibi, Bassam. *The Challenge of Fundamentalism, Political Islam and the New World Disorder.* Berkeley: University of California Press, 1998.

Wilkinson, Paul, and Brian Jenkins. *Aviation Terrorism and Security.* London: Frank Cass, 1999.

Williams, Paul L. *Al Qaeda: Brotherhood of Terror.* Alpha, 2002.

Wright, Robin. *Sacred Rage: The Wrath of Militant Islam.* New York: Touchstone, 1985.

SELECTED ARTICLES AND PERIODICALS

Anti-Defamation League. "Special Background Report: Hamas, Islamic Jihad, and the Muslim Brotherhood—Islamic Extremists and the Terrorist Threat to America." Anti-Defamation League, New York, 1993.

Butler, Desmond. "Yemeni's Role in Attacks on Sept. 11 Is Stressed." *The New York Times,* February 10, 2003, p. A11.

———, with Don Van Natta, Jr. "A Qaeda Informer Helps Investigators Trace Group's Trail." *The New York Times,* February 17, 2003, p. A1.

Carbonara, Peter. "Dirty Money." *Money,* January 2002, p. 91.

Cloud, David S. "Caught Off-Guard by Terror, the CIA Fights to Catch Up." *The Wall Street Journal,* April 15, 2002, p. A15.

Eichenwald, Kurt. "U.S. Freezes Assets of 2 Groups, Saying They Diverted Gifts to Al-Qaeda." *The New York Times,* January 10, 2002, p. A13.

Elliott, Michael. "They Had a Plan." *Time,* August 12, 2002, p. 27.

Emerson, Steven. "A Terrorist Network in America?" *The New York Times,* April 7, 1993.

———, with Richard Rothschild. "Taking on Terrorists." *U.S. News & World Report,* September 12, 1988.

Erlanger, Steven. "Germans Press Investigation of Qaeda-tied Businessman." *The New York Times,* June 20, 2002, p. A20.

Fairclough, Gordon. "Alleged Donors to Hezbollah Facing Trial." *The Wall Street Journal,* December 3, 2001, p. B1.

Fialka, John J., Tom Hamburger, and Gary Fields. "Hijackers' Interest in Crop Dusters Puzzles Investigators." *The Wall Street Journal,* November 19, 2001, p. A22.

Fields, Gary, and David S. Cloud. "France Described Moussaoui as Radical in Cables to FBI." *The Wall Street Journal,* May 28, 2002, p. A6.

Firestone, David. "After a Long, Slow Climb to Respectability, a Muslim Charity Experiences a Rapid Fall." *The New York Times*, December 10, 2001, p. A18.

————. "F.B.I. Traces Hamas's Plan to Finance Attacks to '93." *The New York Times*, December 6, 2001, p. A16.

————, and Matthew L. Wald. "Flight Schools See Downside to Crackdown." *The New York Times*, May 27, 2002, p. A1.

Frantz, Douglas, and Desmond Butler. "The 9/11 Inquest: Now Americans Say Germans Bungled." *The New York Times*, July 11, 2002, p. A9.

Gerecht, Reuel. "Afghanistan: Two Visits to the North—The Terrorists' Encyclopedia." *Middle East Quarterly*, Summer 2001, Vol. 8, No. 3.

————. "The Counterterrorist Myth." *Atlantic Monthly*, July/August, 2001, pp. 38–42.

Gerth, Jeff, and Judith Miller. "Saudi Arabia Is Called Slow in Helping Stem the Flow of Cash to Militants." *The New York Times*, December 1, 2002, p. A32.

Gertz, Bill. "Senator's Plan Calls for 'Intelligence Czar.' " *The Washington Times*, February 5, 1992.

Hirsh, Michael, and Michael Isikoff. "What Went Wrong." *Newsweek*, May 27, 2002, p. 27.

Hitchens, Christopher. "On the Frontier of Apocalypse." *Vanity Fair*, January 2002, p. 84.

Hosenball, Mark, and Michael Isikoff. "Are the Feds at Sea?" *Newsweek*, June 3, 2002, p. 22.

Isikoff, Michael, and Daniel Klaidman. "The Hijackers We Let Escape." *Newsweek*, June 10, 2002, p. 19.

————, and Evan Thomas. "The Saudi Money Trail." *Newsweek*, December 2, 2002, p. 28.

Jehl, Douglas. "Holy War Lured Saudis as Rulers Looked Away." *The New York Times*, December 27, 2001, p. A1.

Johnston, David. "Self-Criticism and Its Risks." *The New York Times*, May 30, 2002, p. A1.

————, and Elizabeth Becker. "C.I.A. Was Tracking Hijacker Months Earlier Than It Had Said." *The New York Times*, June 3, 2002, p. A1.

————, and Don Van Natta, Jr. "Wary of Risk, Slow to Adapt, F.B.I. Stumbles in Terror War." *The New York Times*, June 2, 2002, p. A1.

————, and Don Van Natta, Jr. "9/11 Inquiry Eyes Possible 5th Pilot." *The New York Times*, October 11, 2002, p. A1.

Kilian, Michael. "Spy Case Puts Spotlight on CIA-FBI Turf Battle." *Chicago Tribune,* April 30, 1994.

Lewis, Neil A. "F.B.I. Chief Admits 9/11 Might Have Been Detectable." *The New York Times,* May 30, 2002, p. A1.

———, with David Johnston and Don Van Natta, Jr. "F.B.I. Inaction Blurred Picture Before Sept. 11." *The New York Times,* May 27, 2002, p. A1.

McDermott, Terry, Josh Meyer, and Patrick J. McDonnell. "The Plots and Designs of Al Qaeda's Engineer." *Los Angeles Times,* December 22, 2002, p. A1.

Miller, Judith, Jeff Gerth, and Don Van Natta, Jr. "Planning for Terror but Failing to Act." *The New York Times,* December 30, 2001, p. A1.

Pinkus, Walter. "FBI Wary of Investigating Extremist Muslim Leaders." *The Washington Post,* October 29, 2001, p. A4.

Power, Stephen, David S. Cloud, and Gary Fields. "FAA Chose Not to Warn Airlines on Pivotal Arrest Before Sept. 11." *The Wall Street Journal,* May 20, 2002, p. A1.

Ratnesar, Romesh, and Michael Weisskopf. "How the FBI Blew the Case." *Time,* June 3, 2002, p. 23.

Risen, James. "C.I.A.'s Inquiry on Qaeda Aide Seen as Flawed." *The New York Times,* September 23, 2002, p. A1.

———. "F.B.I. Agent Was Tracking Radical Linked to Hijacker." *The New York Times,* September 25, 2002, p. A14.

———. "Intelligence Officials Discount '98 Report from Caribbean of Plot to Hit Trade Center." *The New York Times,* September 20, 2002, p. A14.

Rose, David. "The Osama Files." *Vanity Fair,* January 2002, p. 64.

Sachs, Susan. "An Investigation in Egypt Illustrates Al-Qaeda's Web." *The New York Times,* November 21, 2001, p. B5.

Sciolino, Elaine. "Egypt Warned U.S. of Terror, Mubarak Says." *The New York Times,* April 5, 1993, p. A1.

Shenon, Philip. "Early Warnings on Moussaoui Are Detailed." *The New York Times,* October 18, 2002, p. A13.

———. "Prosecutors Say Business Card Ties Suspect to Flight 93 Pilot." *The New York Times,* September 25, 2002, p. A14.

———, and David Johnston. "2 Agencies Say Silence Prevented Pair's Tracking." *The New York Times,* October 2, 2002, p. A17.

Simpson, Glenn R. "Hesitant Agents: Why the FBI Took Nine Years to Shut Group It Tied to Terror." *The Wall Street Journal,* February 27, 2002, p. 1.

Tanenhaus, Sam. "The C.I.A.'s Blind Ambition." *Vanity Fair,* January 2002, p. 96.

Van Natta, Jr., Don. "Government Will Ease Limits on Domestic Spying by F.B.I." *The New York Times,* May 30, 2002, p. A1.

Waldman, Peter, and Gerald F. Seib, Jerry Markon, and Christopher Cooper. "Ali Mohamed Served in the U.S. Army—and bin Laden's Circle." *The Wall Street Journal,* November 26, 2001, p. A1.

Wright, Lawrence. "The Counter-Terrorist." *The New Yorker,* January 14, 2002, p. 50.

———. "The Man Behind Bin Laden." *The New Yorker,* September 16, 2002, p. 56.

Yardley, Jim. "E-Mail Sent to Flight School Gave Terror Suspect's 'Goal.' " *The New York Times,* February 8, 2002, p. A10.

———, with Jo Thomas. "For Agent in Phoenix, the Cause of Many Frustrations Extended to His Own Office." *The New York Times,* June 19, 2002, p. A18.

Zernike, Kate, and James Risen. "Tracing a 16-Month Infusion of Men and Money, Culminating in the Horror of Sept. 11." *The New York Times,* December 12, 2001, p. B7.

GOVERNMENT PUBLICATIONS

Countering the Changing Threat of International Terrorism. Report of the National Commission on Terrorism, June 6, 2000.

Counterterrorism Intelligence Capabilities and Performance Prior to 9-11. A Report to the Speaker of the House, Subcommittee on Terrorism and Homeland Security, House Permanent Select Committee on Intelligence, July 2002.

Department of Defense. *Terror 2000: The Future Face of Terrorism.* Washington, D.C.: U.S. Department of Defense, 1994.

"Effective Immigration Controls to Deter Terrorism." Statement of Mary A. Ryan, Assistant Secretary for Consular Affairs, United States Department of State, before the Judiciary Committee, Subcommittee on Immigration, United States Senate, October 17, 2001.

Federal Bureau of Investigation. *Terrorism in the United States,* 1993 and 1994 summaries. Washington, D.C.: U.S. Department of Justice.

Reports of the Advisory Panel to Assess Domestic Response Capabilities for

Terrorism Involving Weapons of Mass Destruction. December 15, 1999, December 15, 2000, December 15, 2001.

Terrorism in the United States. 1996 Counterterrorism Threat Assessment and Warning Unit, National Security Division, FBI, Washington, D.C.

Terrorism: Threat Assessment, Countermeasure and Policy. U.S. Foreign Policy Agency, electronic journal of the U.S. State Department, Vol. 6, No. 3, November 2001.

Testimony of Steven Emerson at a hearing on H.R. 2121, the Secret Evidence Repeal Act of 1999, before the Committee on the Judiciary, U.S. House of Representatives, May 23, 2000.

The Sociology and Psychology of Terrorism: Who Becomes a Terrorist and Why?, prepared for the National Intelligence Council by the Library of Congress's Federal Research Division, September 1999; available online at http://www.loc .gov/rr/frd/Sociology-Psychology%20of%20Terrorism.htm.

United States Congress, House Committee on the Judiciary. *Terrorism: Oversight Hearing Before the Subcommittee on Civil and Constitutional Rights.* 99th Congress, 1st and 2nd Sessions. Washington, D.C.: Government Printing Office, 1987.

United States Congress, Senate Select Committee on Intelligence. *Meeting the Espionage Challenge: A Review of United States Counterintelligence and Security Programs.* 99th Congress, 2nd Session. Washington, D.C.: Government Printing Office, 1986.

TRIAL TRANSCRIPTS

The following five trial records comprise nearly fifty thousand pages of testimony, often from Muslims involved directly with terror strikes on the U.S. and with al Qaeda, as well as from American law enforcement who worked on counterterrorism. The material in the trial transcripts, and attached voluminous exhibits, may be the most important public repository of information on the pre-9/11 history of terror and the U.S. Two former Clinton administration officials, Steven Simon and Daniel Benjamin, who were involved in counterterrorism for the National Security Council, said of these five cases in preparing their own book, *The Age of Sacred Terror*, that "these records are a treasure trove. . . . In many instances, we discovered information so crucial that we were amazed that the relevant agencies did not inform us while we were at NSC." Having personally reviewed all the trial materials listed below, I can vouch that their view is not an overstatement.

United States of America v. Eyad Ismoil, S1293 Cr. 180 (KTD).

United States of America v. Mohammed A. Salameh et al., S593 Cr. 180 (KTD).

United States of America v. Omar Ahmad Ali Abdel Rahman et al., S593 Cr. 181 (MBM).

United States of America v. Ramzi Ahmed Yousef, Abdul Hakim Murad, Wali Khan Amin Shah, S1293 Cr. 180 (KTD).

United States of America v. Usama bin Laden et al., S(9)98 Cr. 1023, Southern District of New York.

Other useful trial materials include:

Complaint, *United States of America v. Abu Doha,* U.S. Magistrate Judge, Southern District of New York, Q1MAG1242, July 2, 2001.

Complaint, *United States of America v. Osama Awadallah,* U.S. Magistrate Judge, Southern District of New York, Q1MAG1833, October 12, 2001.

Indictment, *United States of America v. Zacarias Moussaoui,* U.S. District Court, Eastern District of Virginia, Alexandria Division, December 2001 Term.

Memorandum and Order on Issue of Probable Cause and on Government's Motion for Detention, *United States of America v. Richard C. Reid,* Magistrate No. 01-M-1124-JGD, December 28, 2001.

INDEX

Egypt Air Flight 990, 139, 175–76
Egyptian intelligence, 51*n*, 60, 131,
    156, 191*n*
Eizenstat, Stuart, 125
El Al, 12, 169*n*
el-Gawli, Ibraham, 35
Elashi, Ghassan, 127, 128*n*
elections: of 1992, 46; of 1996, 109–10,
    109–10*n*, 113–14; of 2000, 149, 151
embassy, British, in Riyadh, 97
embassy, Israeli, 56, 70, 132–33
embassy, U.S.: in Eritrea, 98*n*; in Kenya,
    132–33; in Lebanon, 13–14;in Paris,
    172; in Riyadh, 97; in Sarajevo, 183;
    terror warnings issued for, 155. *See
    also* embassy, U.S., bombing of East
    Africa
embassy, U.S., bombing of East Africa:
    alerts on anniversaries of, 172; bin
    Laden/al Qaeda linked to, 129–30,
    134–35, 142; casualties in, 8; and
    CIA, 135, 136; Clinton administra-
    tion's reaction to, 122, 125; convic-
    tions in, 8, 103*n*, 130*n*; damage in,
    134; and FBI, 136, 144; and German
    connection, 163, 163*n*, 164; and
    Ijaz-Sudan-bin Laden proposal,
    102; media coverage of, 135*n*; and
    Mohamed, 133*n*; plots to capitalize
    on, 139–40; and rule/restrictions on
    FBI, 143; and Saudi Arabia, 125; sus-
    pects in, 76*n*, 144*n*, 163, 163*n*, 164;
    whisper campaign after, 138–39
Emerson, Steve: and Alkifah Refugee
    Center records, 16–17; and bin
    Laden-World Trade Center bombing
    (1993) link, 74; and hate crimes
    against Muslims, 92; mosque visits
    of, 72*n*; and Murrah bombing, 88,
    93; and Muslim conferences in U.S.,
    71–72, 74; PBS documentary of, 75,
    76, 77; and Rahman trial, 93, 94
Emilio, Sal, 141
Empire State Building, 116
Eritrea, 49, 98*n*
Erwa, Elfatih, 99–100, 100*n*, 103
evidence, standards of, in terrorist inves-
    tigations, 173. *See also specific case*
Executive Order 11905 (Ford), 12

Fadl, Jamal al-, 98*n*
Fahd bin Turki bin Saud al-Kabir (Saudi
    prince), 190, 193
Fahd (Saudi king), 28
Fahd (Saudi prince), 190
Faisal, Haifa bint (Saudi princess), 124*n*
Faisal ibn Musaid (Saudi prince), 26
Faisal (Saudi king), 26
false information, in interrogations, 191

Faruq, Omar al-, 191
fatwas, 6–7, 10, 133
Fawwaz, Khalid al-, 76*n*
Federal Aviation Administration (FAA),
    57*n*, 171, 175
Federal Building (New York City), plot to
    attack, 51*n*
federal buildings, as terrorist targets,
    51*n*, 82–83
Federal Bureau of Investigation (FBI):
    and Alkifah Refugee Center records,
    116; and attempted assassination of
    Bush (George H.W.), 61; and Baz-
    Hasidics incident, 75*n*; bin Laden/al
    Qaeda investigation by, 98, 99, 103,
    103*n*, 104–5, 108, 129–30, 146*n*,
    158; and bomb factory in Brooklyn
    apartment, 116; and Bremer Com-
    mission, 154; budget and personnel
    at, 62–63, 62*n*, 157*n*; and Bush
    (George W.) administration, 158; and
    chances to have prevented attacks
    on September 11, 169–77, 177*n*,
    179–80; and charities as terrorist
    fronts, 111; and CISPES, 129; coun-
    terspy work in foreign countries of,
    21; and CSG, 91*n*; and CTC, 16;
    defensiveness of, 143–44; and flight
    schools in U.S., 79*n*; and funding
    for terrorism, 126, 127–29, 128*n*,
    129–30; and German connections,
    164–65; interrogations by, 188*n*; lack
    of coordination between INS and, 35;
    and millenium, 140; and Muslim
    conferences in U.S., 72, 74–75; plot
    to blow up New York City headquar-
    ters of, 72; and plot to bomb New
    York City landmarks, 51, 51*n*; and
    Restricted Interagency Group for
    Terrorism, 14; rules/restrictions
    governing, 143, 177*n*; and September
    11 investigation, 160; Sessions as
    head of, 21; subcontracting of back-
    ground investigations by, 62–63;
    and Sudanese expulsion of bin Laden,
    103, 104–5; and Sudan's offer to
    extradite al Qaeda members, 135; and
    suicide plane missions, 79*n*; terror
    watch list of, 178; terrorism as low
    priority for, 115; and "Terrorism for
    Dummies" conference, 144; terrorist
    warnings issued by, 156; underesti-
    mation of threat posed by Islamic ter-
    rorists by, 59*n*; and visa problems,
    168, 169. *See also* Central Intelligence
    Agency–Federal Bureau of Inves-
    tigation (CIA-FBI) relations; Joint
    Terrorism Task Force; *specific person
    or case*

Hoover, J. Edgar, 177*n*
Hotis, John, 19, 21
House of Representatives, U.S. *See specific person or committee*
Hubbell, Webb, 54
Huffman Aviation (Venice, Florida), 148
Husayn, Zayn al-Abidin Mohamed. *See* Zubaydah, Abu
Hussain, Syed Qaisar, 193–94
Hussein, Saddam, 15, 55–56*n*, 56, 61*n*, 84. *See also* Iraq

identity theft, 120
Ijaz, Mansour, 101–2, 101*n*, 104
Immigration and Nationality Act, 17, 23
Immigration and Naturalization Service (INS): bookkeeping at, 121; and chances to have prevented attacks on 9/11, 167–69, 169*n*, 178, 179–80; databases of, 167–69; flight school notification sent by, 169; and Hammoud investigation, 120; and hijackers' entry into U.S., 150, 167–69; ineffectiveness of, 145, 169; and JTTF, 57*n*; and Khalifa detainment, 70; lack of coordination between FBI and, 35; and Mammoud investigation, 121; reform of, 167; sexual activities of officers with, 148; and student visas, 167–69; and World Trade Center bombing (1993), 59–60
India, 105*n*, 145–46
InfoCom, 130
Intelligence Committee (U.S. Senate), 68–69
Intelligence Division (FBI), 62*n*
interrogation: false information from, 191; of Shibh, 162*n*; and torture, 186; truth serum in, 187–88, 187–88*n*, 189; of Zubaydah, 181*n*, 184–94, 185*n*, 187–88*n*
Iran: al-Qaeda connections with, 163; and CIA, 112; and Clinton administration, 108, 109*n*, 110–11; and downing of Iranian airbus, 22; and Israeli intelligence, 112; and Khobar bombing, 108–9, 157; Khomeini comes to power in, 27; and Murrah bombing, 82; and Pan Am Flight 103, 111; and Somalia, 50*n*; and terrorist conferences, 12, 49*n*, 51, 82, 106–7, 111, 132; U.S. sale of missiles to, 17; U.S. sanctions against, 110–11, 112. *See also* Iran-Contra; Iranian intelligence
Iran-Contra, 17–18, 19, 20, 21, 44, 71
Iranian intelligence, 24, 49*n*, 111, 112, 132
Iraq: and attempted assassination of

Bush (George H.W.), 61, 61*n*; and BCCI, 44; and BNL, 45–46; and CIA-FBI relations, 45–46; and Clinton administration, 55–56*n*, 61*n*, 63–64; Kuwaiti invasion by, 40; and Murrah bombing, 90*n*; no-fly zone in, 101; and NSC, 63; nuclear weapons program in, 45–46; and Operation Babylon, 45; and Soviet Union, 15; training in hijackings in, 176; U.N. sanctions against, 55*n*, 84; U.S. missile attack on, 61*n*; U.S. war in, 192; and World Trade Center bombing (1993), 63–64, 63–64*n*, 73; and Yousef, 63, 64*n*. *See also* Gulf War; Hussein, Saddam; Iraqi intelligence
Iraq-Gate, 46
Iraqi intelligence, 43, 61, 61*n*, 64*n*
Iraqis, in U.S., 43
Irish Noraid, 128–29
ISI. *See* Pakistani intelligence
Islamic Army of Aden, 70
Islamic Association for Palestine, 72
Islamic Change Movement, 97, 112, 113
Islamic Committee for Palestine (ICP), 75, 76
Islamic Front, formation of, 134
Islamic fundamentalists: funding for, 7; and madrassas, 105*n*; and Murrah bombing, 81, 83–90, 90*n*, 93; and Rahman's blueprint for radical Muslim anger at U.S., 95; surge in, 3; and TWA 747 accident, 113; in U.S., 93–94. *See also specific person or organization*
Islamic Jihad: al Qaeda merged with, 49, 96, 183; and Azzam's murder, 31*n*; and Buckley kidnapping, 14; and domestic Islamic militancy, 75, 76; funding for, 118; and ICP, 75; and Murrah bombing, 84; Shallah takes command of, 75; and terrorist summits, 106; and TWA Flight 847, 15; Zawahiri as leader of, 30; and Zubaydah, 183, 186*n*. *See also* Zawahiri, Ayman al-
Ismoil, Eyad, 73
Israel: Arab relations with, 5, 7; bombings in, 77*n*; and Brooklyn's Muslim community, 5, 8; embassies of, 56, 70, 132–33; and Holy Land Foundation, 129; and Munich Olympics (1972), 13; Palestinian relations with, 101, 111, 116, 142, 142*n*; and Somalia, 50*n*; U.S. carriers flying in and out of, 172; U.S. relations with, 5, 8, 13, 50*n*. *See also* Israeli intelligence
Israeli intelligence, 22, 26*n*, 45, 112

Seattle, Washington, 140, 141
Secret Service, U.S., 57n, 100n, 175
seditious conspiracy statute, 93
Senate, U.S., 23, 112, 168, 173. *See also specific person or committee*
September 11, 2001: Brooklyn's Muslim community reaction to, 5; and Caribbean officials alert to CIA, 175; chances to have prevented attacks on, 167–80; funding for, 160, 161, 165, 174; and funding for terrorism investigation, 125; and German connection, 159–66, 159n; and hijackers' entry into U.S., 147–50; and Israeli-U.S. relations, 5; Massoud assassination as prelude to, 158n; people killed on, 115; planning for, 80n, 142, 159–61, 160n, 161n; rewards for participants in, 96; role models for participants in, 3; Rosetta stone of, 189; suspects in, 16n; and Zubaydah interrogation, 184–94. *See also specific person*
Serbian Liberation Front, 58n
Sessions, William, 21, 46, 57, 62–63, 62n
SEVIS program, 169
Shabib, Muin Kamel Mohammed, 127n
Shalabi, Emir Mustafa, 7–8, 9–10, 9n, 32, 35, 103n
Shallah, Ramadan Abdullah, 75, 75n, 106
Sharon, Ariel, 5
Sheehan, Michael, 152
Shehhi, Marwan al-, 148, 149, 162n, 169
Shelton, Henry, 136, 152
Shelton, Hugh, 142
Shibh, Ramzi bin al-, 159–61, 161n, 162, 162n, 165, 166, 174
Shiite muslims, 163
Shikaki, Khalil, 75
Shinn, David, 99–100
shoe bomber (Richard Reid), 184
Siddiqy, Anis, 85
Siddiqy, Asad R., 85
Simmelman, Jacques, 34n
Simon, Steven, 103
Simpson, O. J., 94–95
Six Day War (1967), 27
Siyam, Sheikh Muhammed, 128
Snider, David, 87
Social Security numbers, fake, 120
Somalia, 50–52, 50n, 55, 65–66, 103, 134
Sorbi Fly Club (San Diego, California), 148
Soviet Union/Russians: and Afghanistan, 7, 8, 24, 27, 29, 105n,

183; as al Qaeda recruits, 182n; and Iraq, 15
Space Needle (Seattle, Washington), plot to blow up, 141
Spain, 161, 163
Special Forces, U.S., 138, 181–83, 186
Specter, Arlen, 173
Sphinx (check-cashing company), 33n
Starr, Kenneth, 109n
State Department, U.S.: and bin Laden, 99, 102, 103, 134; and CSG, 91n; and JTTF, 57n; and Khalifa case, 70; and Murrah bombing, 83; and Simpson trial, 95; terrorist sponsorship list of, 102, 104, 141, 169n, 178; travel alerts issued by, 155, 171; and Yousef hunt, 62
Statue of Liberty, 92
Stephanopoulos, George, 54–55, 56n, 65, 66, 111
Stern, Chuck, 81–82n
Strasbourg, France, plot to bomb fair in, 166
Sudan: al Qaeda members offered to U.S. by, 135, 136; and al Qaeda recruits, 182n; bin laden, 104–5; as bin Laden base, 9n, 42, 48–52, 99n, 122, 132, 134, 163; bin Laden's expulsion from, 99–105, 99n, 100n; commitment to terror by, 102; and Ijaz-bin Laden proposal, 101–2, 101n, 104; Iranian-al Qaeda meetings in, 163; and Lake assassination threat, 100n; National Islamic Front in, 42; Rahman in, 24; Rashid in, 15; state sponsorship of terrorism by, 99n, 104, 105; U.S. relations with, 100; U.S. strike in, 135–37; and World Trade Center bombing (1993), 94. *See also* Sudanese intelligence
Sudanese intelligence, 62, 100, 101, 101n, 104
Sufaat, Yazi, 177
suicide bombers, 77n, 82, 129, 176
suicide planes, 79, 79n, 80n, 156, 173, 175, 176. *See also specific airline flight or person*
The Sullivans, USS, 140, 141
Sultan bin Faisal bin Turki al-Saud (Saudi prince), 190, 193
Sunni Muslims, 106
Supreme Council for Intelligence Affairs (Iran), 106
Supreme Court, U.S., 188n
Syria, 16, 16n, 49n, 82, 182n

Taba Investments, 48
Taha, Ali Othman, 103–4
Talha, Abu, 50

ABOUT THE AUTHOR

GERALD POSNER, a former Wall Street lawyer, is an award-winning author of eight books on subjects ranging from Nazi war criminals, to assassinations, to the careers of politicians. A regular panelist on the History Channel's *HistoryCENTER*, he has also written for many national publications, including *The New York Times, The New Yorker, Time, Newsweek, The Wall Street Journal,* and *U.S. News & World Report.* He lives in Miami and New York City with his wife, the author Trisha Posner. More information is available at www.posner.com

ABOUT THE TYPE

This book was set in Photina, a typeface designed by José Mendoza in 1971. It is a very elegant design with high legibility, and its close character fit has made it a popular choice for use in quality magazines and art gallery publications.

DATE DUE

NO 18 '03			
DE 05 '03			
JE 11 '03			
DE 22 '03			
JA 20 '04			
FE 28 '04			
MR 16 '04			
AP 08 '04			
MY 05 '04			
JE 14 '04			
JE 12 '06			
JA 09 '09			
AP 20 '10			
MR 28 '12			
MY 13 '13			
GAYLORD			PRINTED IN U.S.A.